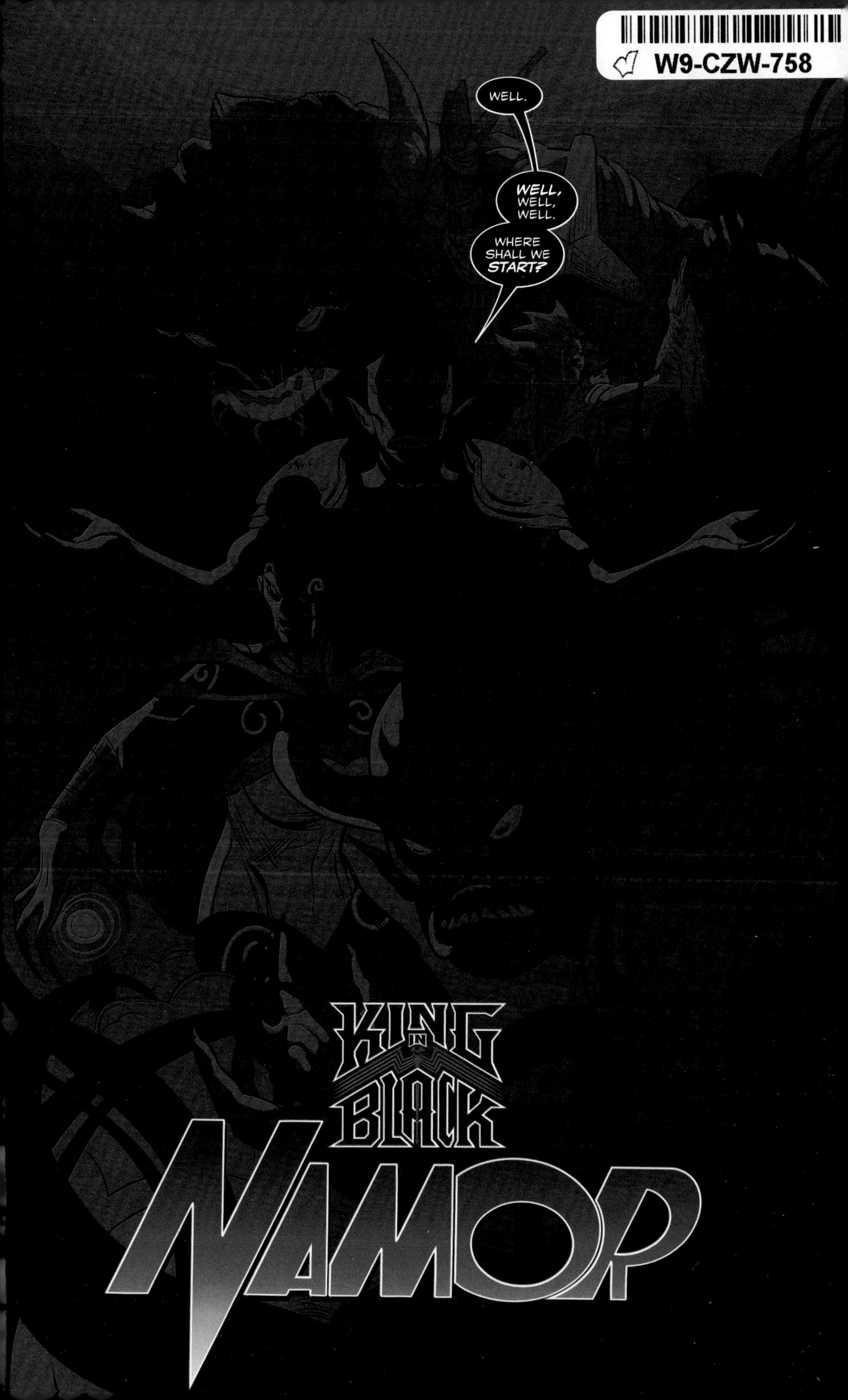
WELL.
WELL, WELL, WELL.
WHERE SHALL WE START?
KING IN BLACK
NAMOR

RECENTLY, A DARKNESS BEGAN TO STIR IN THE SYMBIOTIC ANTIHERO CALLED VENOM —
SOMETHING ANCIENT, PRIMORDIAL AND FULL OF MALICE, REACHING OUT FROM
THE CREATURE'S HOMEWORLD: KNULL, THE CREATOR AND GOD OF THE SYMBIOTES.

OLDER THAN MEMORY AND IMPRISONED AT THE EDGE OF THE GALAXY FOR MILLENNIA,
THE GOD-KING OF THE SYMBIOTES HAS BEEN FREED, LEADING A HORDE OF
MORE THAN ONE HUNDRED THOUSAND DRAGONS ACROSS THE COSMOS
WITH A TRAIL OF DESTRUCTION AND DEATH IN THEIR WAKE.

NOW VENOM'S NIGHTMARES HAVE BEEN MADE MANIFEST AS THE LORD OF THE ABYSS, THE
BEGINNING AND END OF THE SYMBIOTES, THE KING IN BLACK, HAS ARRIVED ON EARTH.

BUT THE FIGHT TO STOP THE KING IN BLACK DOES NOT ONLY HAPPEN TODAY. IT
REACHES FAR INTO THE PAST, INTO NAMOR'S YOUTH. A MORE INNOCENT TIME,
A MORE HOPEFUL TIME...OR SO HE THOUGHT. WHO ARE THE SWIFT TIDE
— AND WHAT ROLE WILL THEY PLAY IN THE BATTLE?

KING IN BLACK: NAMOR. Contains material originally published in magazine form as KING IN BLACK: NAMOR (2020) #1-5. First printing 2021. ISBN 978-1-302-92813-1. Published by MARVEL WORLDWIDE, INC.,
a subsidiary of MARVEL ENTERTAINMENT, LLC. OFFICE OF PUBLICATION: 1290 Avenue of the Americas, New York, NY 10104. © 2021 MARVEL. No similarity between any of the names, characters, persons, and/or
institutions in this magazine with those of any living or dead person or institution is intended, and any such similarity which may exist is purely coincidental. Printed in Canada. KEVIN FEIGE, Chief Creative Officer;
DAN BUCKLEY, President, Marvel Entertainment; JOE QUESADA, EVP & Creative Director; DAVID BOGART, Associate Publisher & SVP of Talent Affairs; TOM BREVOORT, VP, Executive Editor; NICK LOWE, Executive
Editor, VP of Content, Digital Publishing; DAVID GABRIEL, VP of Print & Digital Publishing; JEFF YOUNGQUIST, VP of Production & Special Projects; ALEX MORALES, Director of Publishing Operations; DAN EDINGTON,
Managing Editor; RICKEY PURDIN, Director of Talent Relations; JENNIFER GRÜNWALD, Senior Editor, Special Projects; SUSAN CRESPI, Production Manager; STAN LEE, Chairman Emeritus. For information regarding
advertising in Marvel Comics or on Marvel.com, please contact Vit DeBellis, Custom Solutions & Integrated Advertising Manager, at vdebellis@marvel.com. For Marvel subscription inquiries, please call 888-511-
5480. Manufactured between 5/28/2021 and 6/29/2021 by SOLISCO PRINTERS, SCOTT, QC, CANADA.

10 9 8 7 6 5 4 3 2 1

NAMOR, THE SUB-MARINER — SON OF AN ATLANTEAN PRINCESS FROM THE DEPTHS OF THE OCEAN AND A HUMAN SAILOR. BORN A MUTANT, WITH THE POWERS OF FLIGHT, INCREDIBLE STRENGTH AND DURABILITY. NOW THE RULER OF THE UNDERWATER EMPIRE OF ATLANTIS, HE HAS BEEN BOTH FRIEND AND FOE TO HUMANITY.

KING IN BLACK
NAMOR

KURT BUSIEK WRITER
BENJAMIN DEWEY ARTIST
JONAS SCHARF ARTIST, PRESENT DAY SEQUENCES
TRÍONA FARRELL COLOR ARTIST

VC's JOE CARAMAGNA LETTERER
LEINIL FRANCIS YU AND **SUNNY GHO** COVER ART

MARTIN BIRO ASSISTANT EDITOR
ALANNA SMITH ASSOCIATE EDITOR
TOM BREVOORT EDITOR

JENNIFER GRÜNWALD COLLECTION EDITOR
DANIEL KIRCHHOFFER ASSISTANT EDITOR
MAIA LOY ASSISTANT MANAGING EDITOR
LISA MONTALBANO ASSISTANT MANAGING EDITOR
JEFF YOUNGQUIST VP PRODUCTION & SPECIAL PROJECTS
SARAH SPADACCINI WITH **ANTHONY GAMBINO**
& **JAY BOWEN** BOOK DESIGNERS
DAVID GABRIEL SVP PRINT, SALES & MARKETING
C.B. CEBULSKI EDITOR IN CHIEF

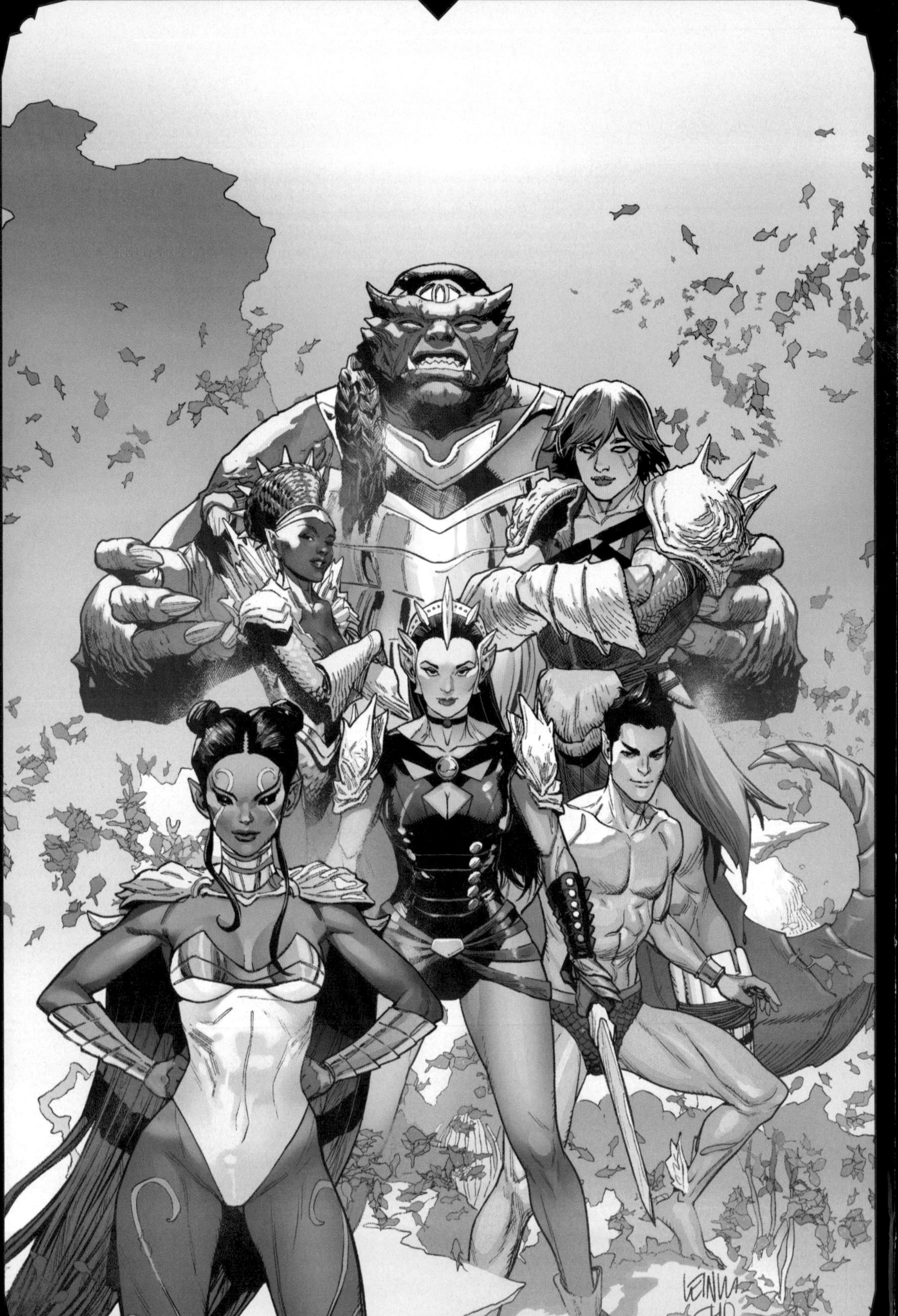

IN THE DEPTHS

1

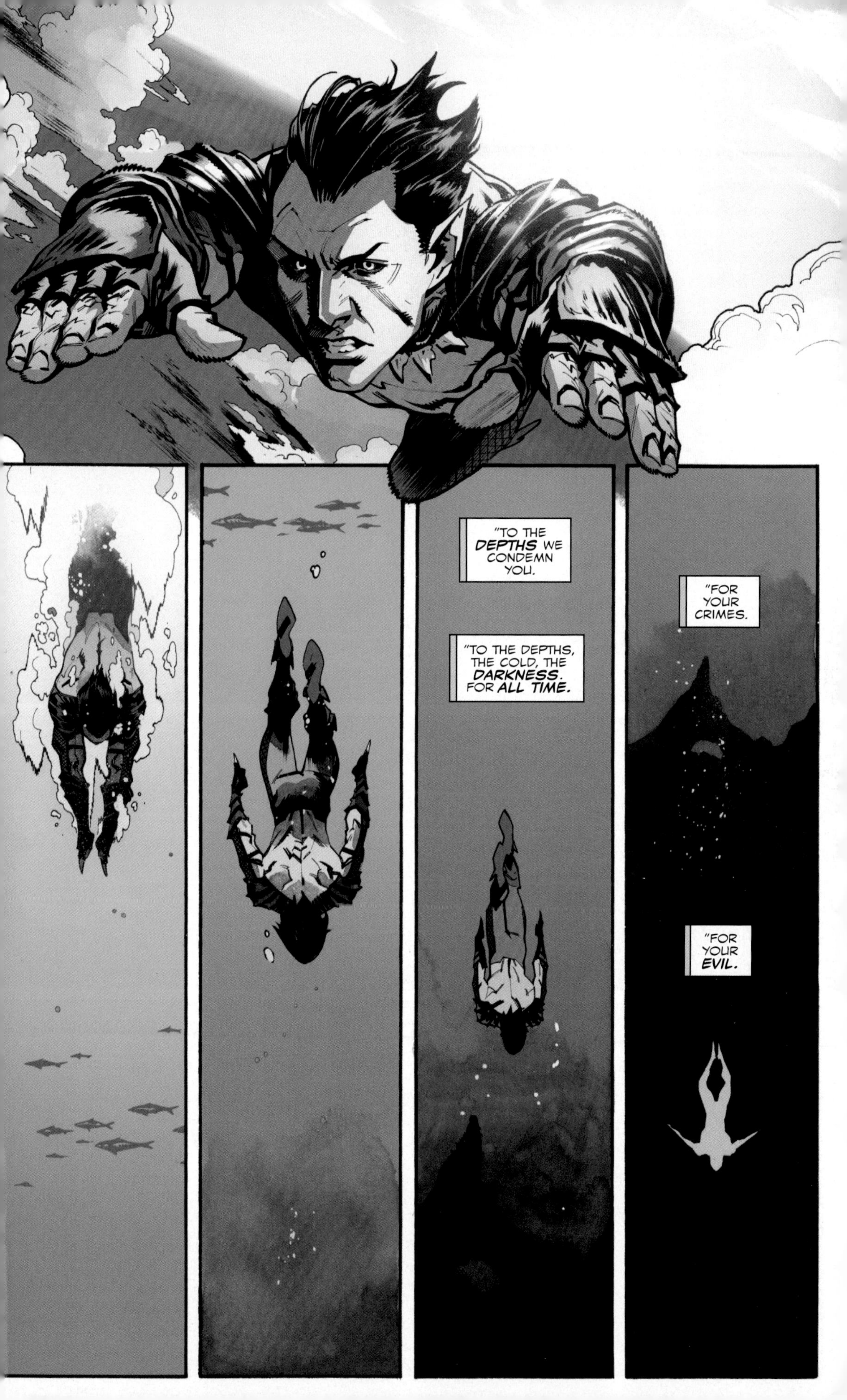
"TO THE DEPTHS WE CONDEMN YOU.
"TO THE DEPTHS, THE COLD, THE DARKNESS. FOR ALL TIME.
"FOR YOUR CRIMES.
"FOR YOUR EVIL.

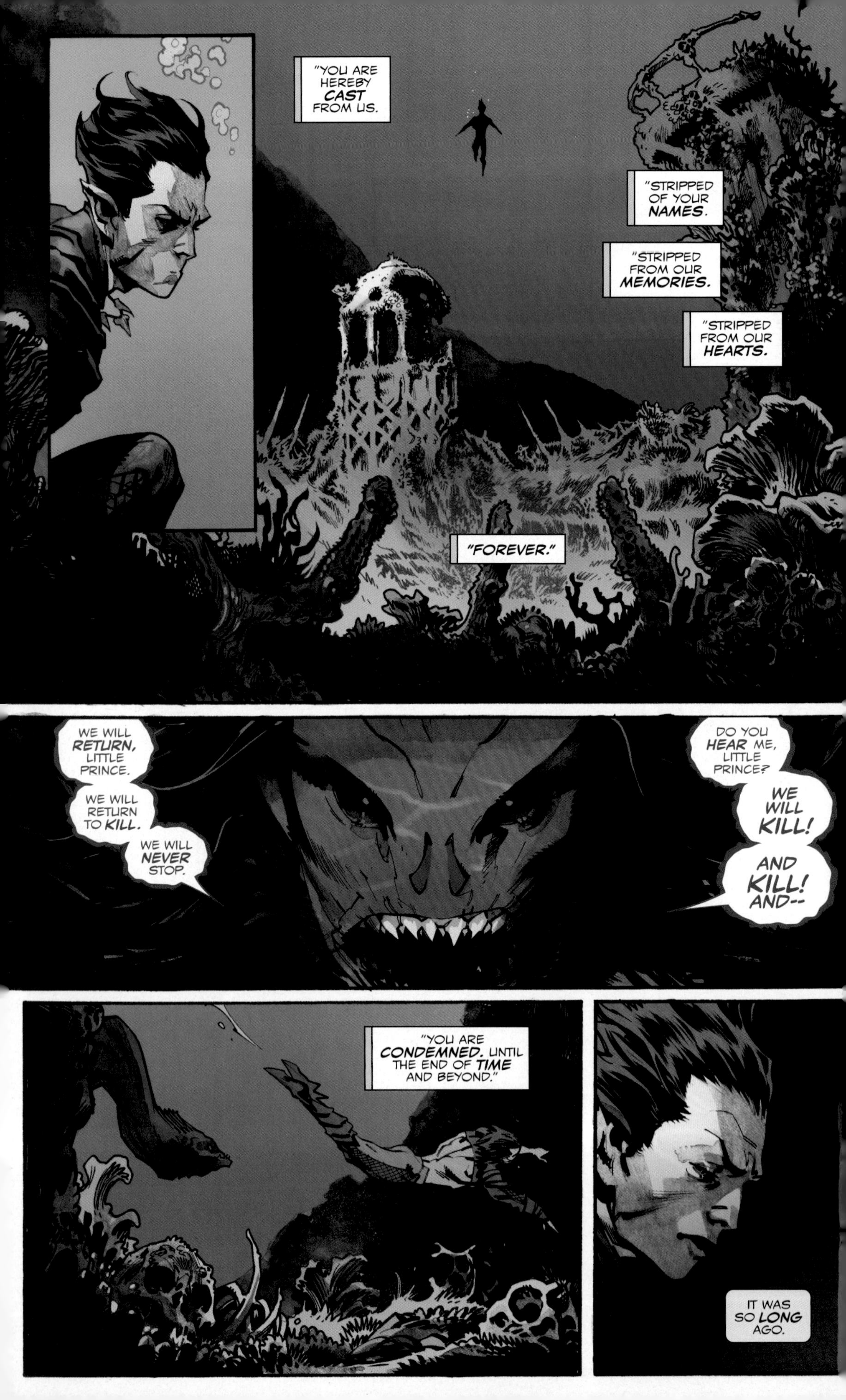
"YOU ARE HEREBY CAST FROM US.
"STRIPPED OF YOUR NAMES.
"STRIPPED FROM OUR MEMORIES.
"STRIPPED FROM OUR HEARTS.
"FOREVER."
WE WILL RETURN, LITTLE PRINCE.
WE WILL RETURN TO KILL.
WE WILL NEVER STOP.
DO YOU HEAR ME, LITTLE PRINCE?
WE WILL KILL!
AND KILL! AND--
"YOU ARE CONDEMNED. UNTIL THE END OF TIME AND BEYOND."
IT WAS SO LONG AGO.

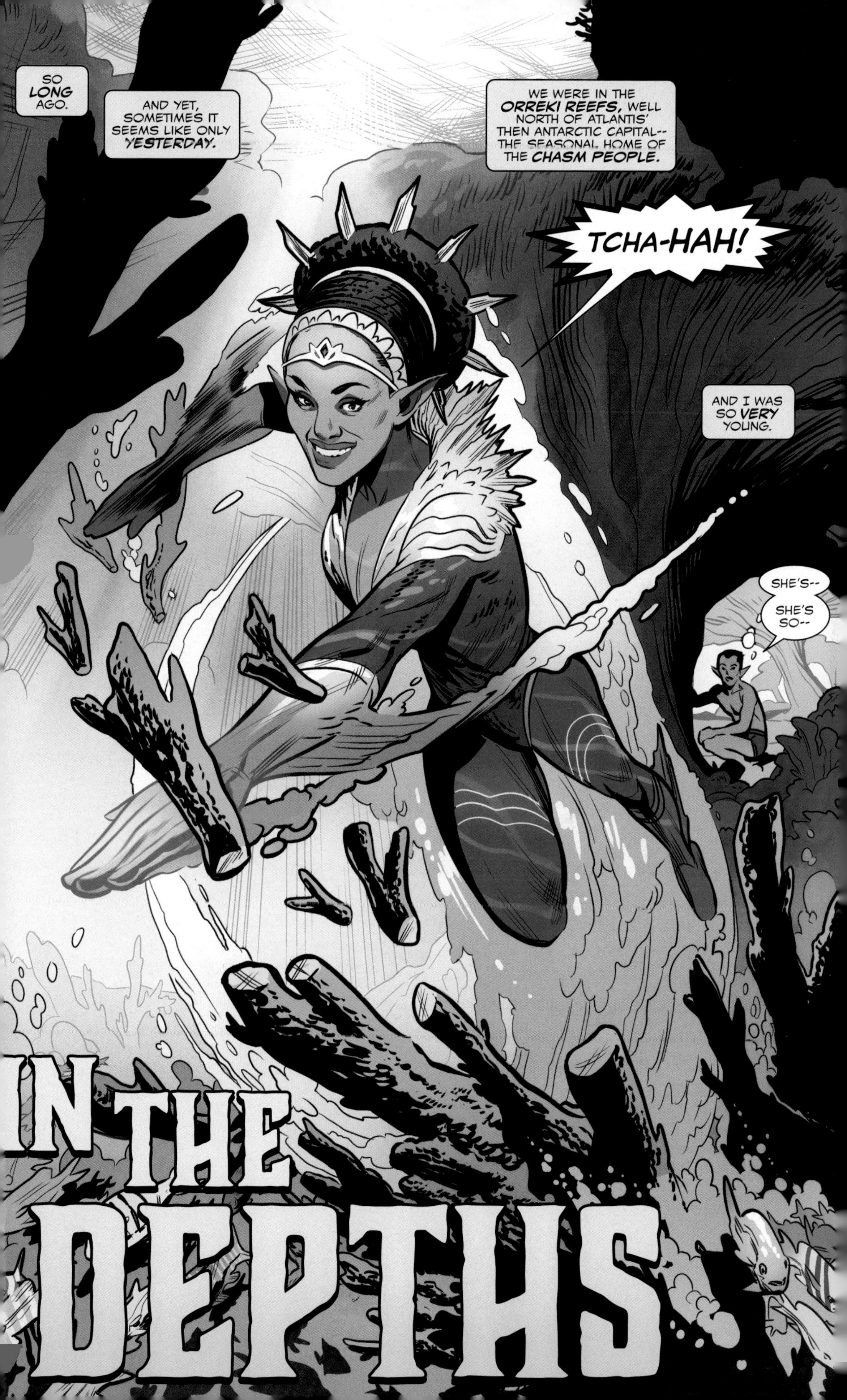

SO LONG AGO.
AND YET, SOMETIMES IT SEEMS LIKE ONLY YESTERDAY.
WE WERE IN THE ORREKI REEFS, WELL NORTH OF ATLANTIS' THEN ANTARCTIC CAPITAL-- THE SEASONAL HOME OF THE CHASM PEOPLE.
TCHA-HAH!
AND I WAS SO VERY YOUNG.
SHE'S--
SHE'S SO--
IN THE DEPTHS

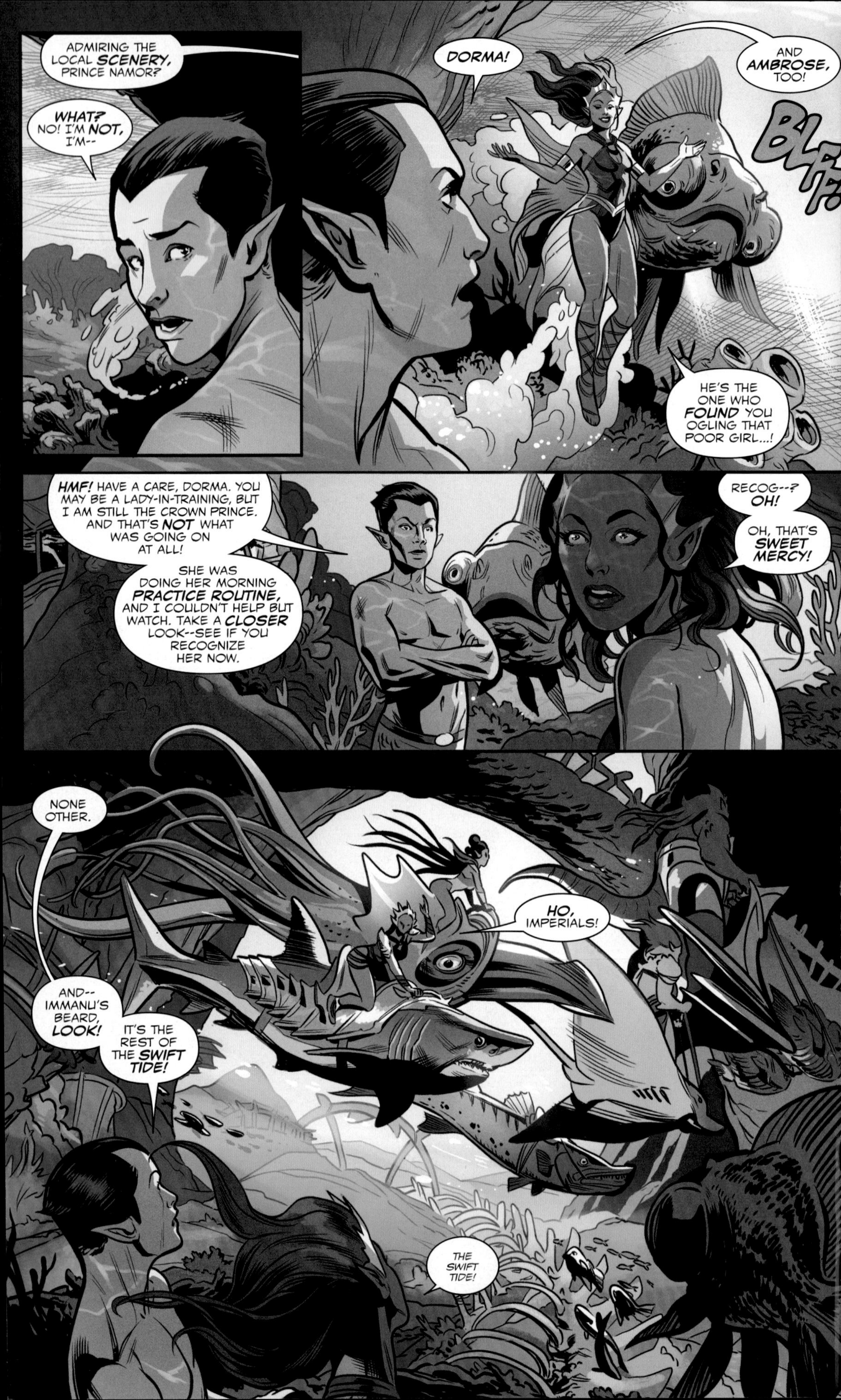

ADMIRING THE LOCAL SCENERY, PRINCE NAMOR?
WHAT? NO! I'M NOT, I'M--
DORMA!
AND AMBROSE, TOO!
BLFF
HE'S THE ONE WHO FOUND YOU OGLING THAT POOR GIRL...!
HMF! HAVE A CARE, DORMA. YOU MAY BE A LADY-IN-TRAINING, BUT I AM STILL THE CROWN PRINCE. AND THAT'S NOT WHAT WAS GOING ON AT ALL!
SHE WAS DOING HER MORNING PRACTICE ROUTINE, AND I COULDN'T HELP BUT WATCH. TAKE A CLOSER LOOK--SEE IF YOU RECOGNIZE HER NOW.
RECOG--? OH!
OH, THAT'S SWEET MERCY!
NONE OTHER.
HO, IMPERIALS!
AND-- IMMANU'S BEARD, LOOK!
IT'S THE REST OF THE SWIFT TIDE!
THE SWIFT TIDE!

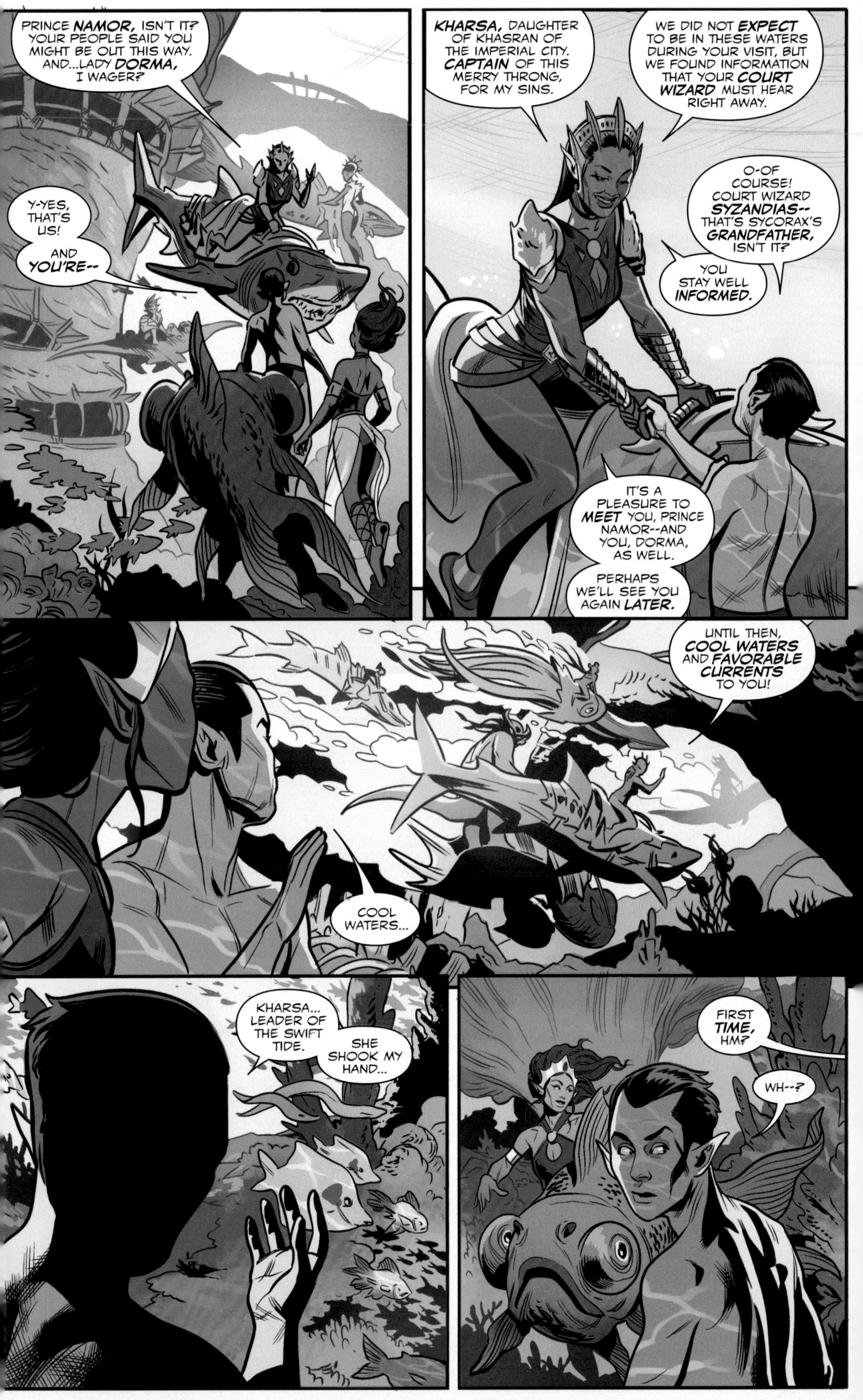
PRINCE NAMOR, ISN'T IT? YOUR PEOPLE SAID YOU MIGHT BE OUT THIS WAY. AND...LADY DORMA, I WAGER?
Y-YES, THAT'S US!
AND YOU'RE--
KHARSA, DAUGHTER OF KHASRAN OF THE IMPERIAL CITY. CAPTAIN OF THIS MERRY THRONG, FOR MY SINS.
WE DID NOT EXPECT TO BE IN THESE WATERS DURING YOUR VISIT, BUT WE FOUND INFORMATION THAT YOUR COURT WIZARD MUST HEAR RIGHT AWAY.
O-OF COURSE! COURT WIZARD SYZANDIAS-- THAT'S SYCORAX'S GRANDFATHER, ISN'T IT?
YOU STAY WELL INFORMED.
IT'S A PLEASURE TO MEET YOU, PRINCE NAMOR--AND YOU, DORMA, AS WELL.
PERHAPS WE'LL SEE YOU AGAIN LATER.
UNTIL THEN, COOL WATERS AND FAVORABLE CURRENTS TO YOU!
COOL WATERS...
KHARSA... LEADER OF THE SWIFT TIDE.
SHE SHOOK MY HAND...
FIRST TIME, HM?
WH--?

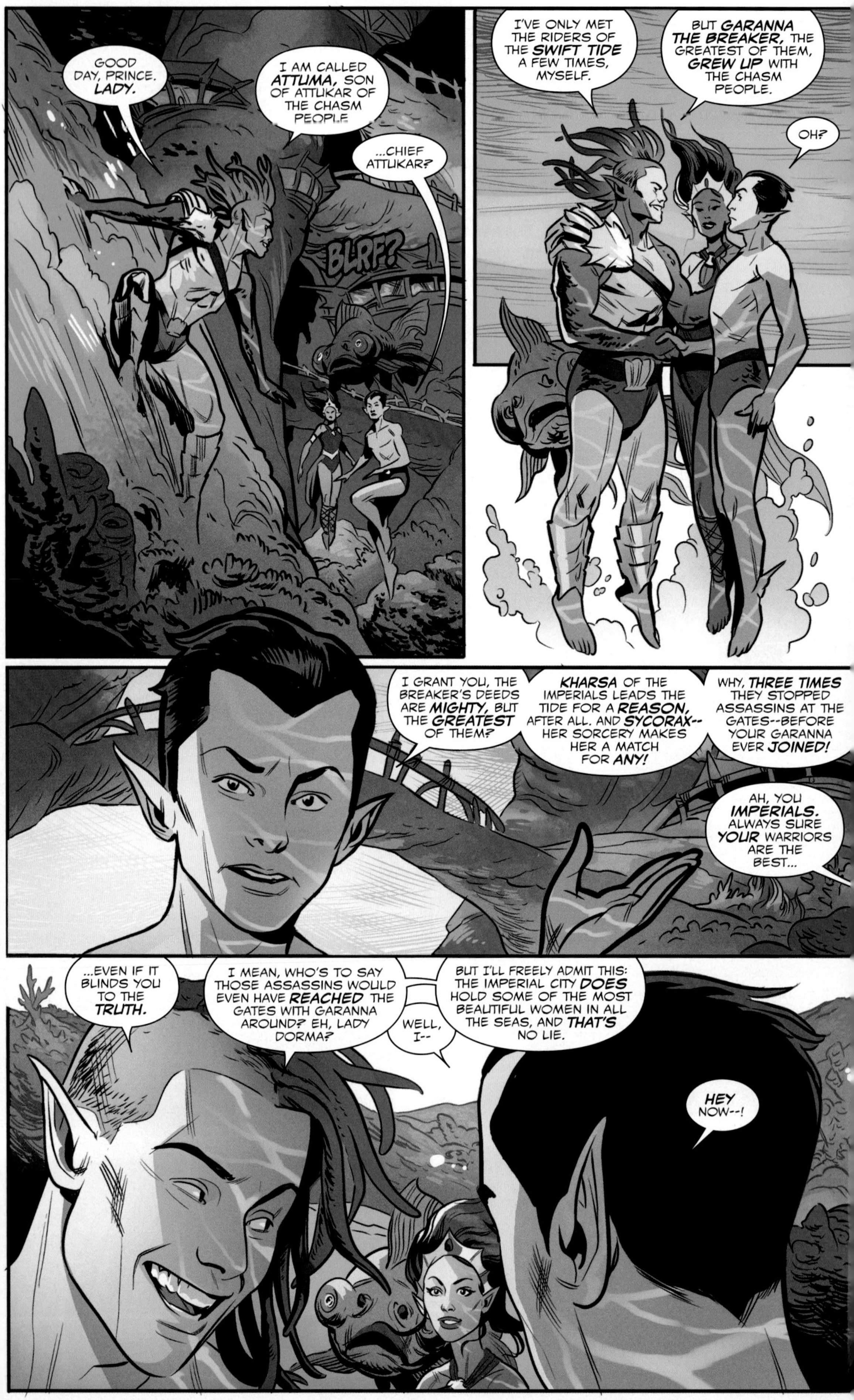
GOOD DAY, PRINCE. LADY.
I AM CALLED ATTUMA, SON OF ATTUKAR OF THE CHASM PEOPLE.
...CHIEF ATTUKAR?
BLRF?
I'VE ONLY MET THE RIDERS OF THE SWIFT TIDE A FEW TIMES, MYSELF.
BUT GARANNA THE BREAKER, THE GREATEST OF THEM, GREW UP WITH THE CHASM PEOPLE.
OH?
I GRANT YOU, THE BREAKER'S DEEDS ARE MIGHTY, BUT THE GREATEST OF THEM?
KHARSA OF THE IMPERIALS LEADS THE TIDE FOR A REASON, AFTER ALL. AND SYCORAX-- HER SORCERY MAKES HER A MATCH FOR ANY!
WHY, THREE TIMES THEY STOPPED ASSASSINS AT THE GATES--BEFORE YOUR GARANNA EVER JOINED!
AH, YOU IMPERIALS. ALWAYS SURE YOUR WARRIORS ARE THE BEST...
...EVEN IF IT BLINDS YOU TO THE TRUTH.
I MEAN, WHO'S TO SAY THOSE ASSASSINS WOULD EVEN HAVE REACHED THE GATES WITH GARANNA AROUND? EH, LADY DORMA?
WELL, I--
BUT I'LL FREELY ADMIT THIS: THE IMPERIAL CITY DOES HOLD SOME OF THE MOST BEAUTIFUL WOMEN IN ALL THE SEAS, AND THAT'S NO LIE.
HEY NOW--!

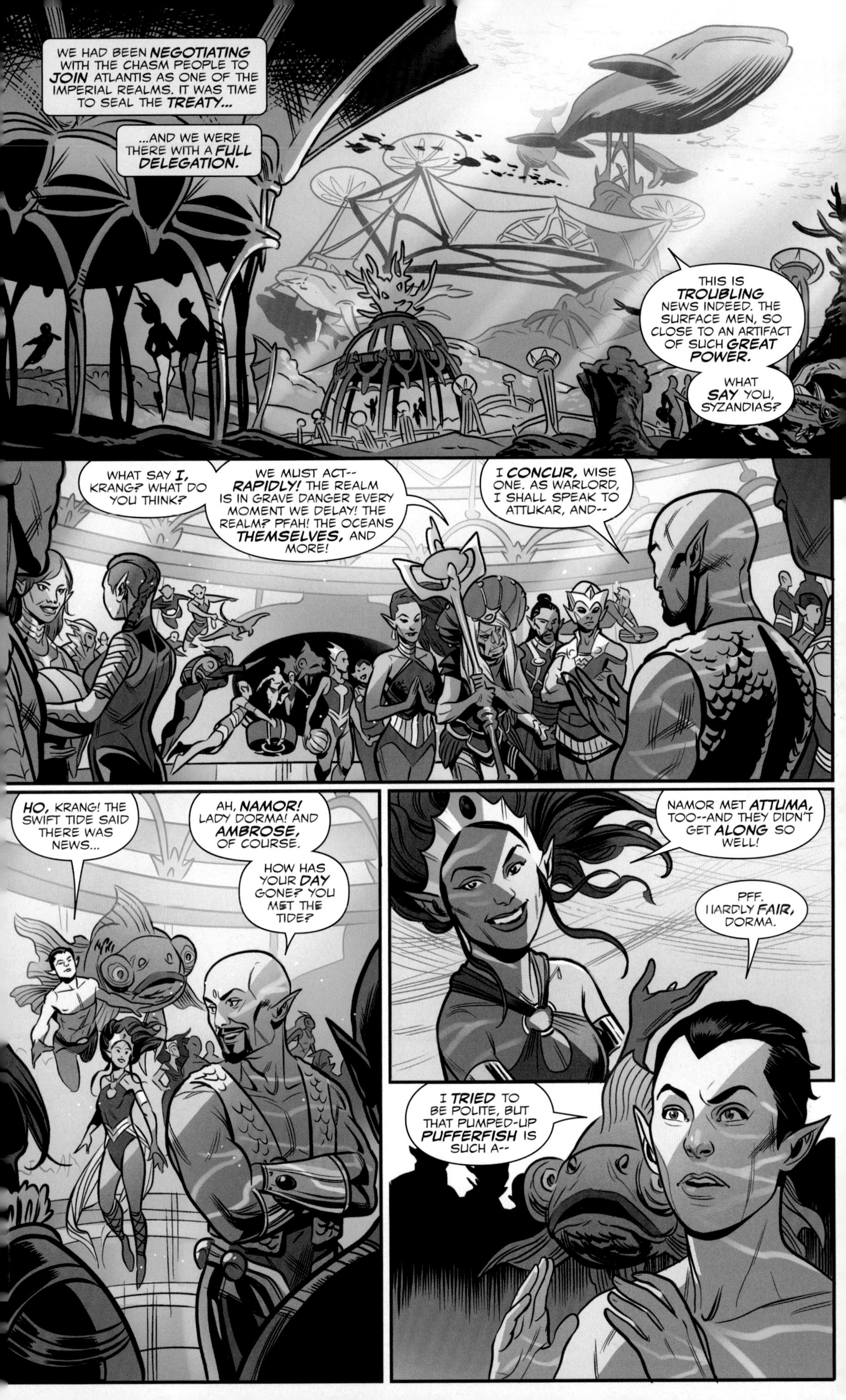

WE HAD BEEN NEGOTIATING WITH THE CHASM PEOPLE TO JOIN ATLANTIS AS ONE OF THE IMPERIAL REALMS. IT WAS TIME TO SEAL THE TREATY...
...AND WE WERE THERE WITH A FULL DELEGATION.
THIS IS TROUBLING NEWS INDEED. THE SURFACE MEN, SO CLOSE TO AN ARTIFACT OF SUCH GREAT POWER.
WHAT SAY YOU, SYZANDIAS?
WHAT SAY I, KRANG? WHAT DO YOU THINK?
WE MUST ACT--RAPIDLY! THE REALM IS IN GRAVE DANGER EVERY MOMENT WE DELAY! THE REALM? PFAH! THE OCEANS THEMSELVES, AND MORE!
I CONCUR, WISE ONE. AS WARLORD, I SHALL SPEAK TO ATTUKAR, AND--
HO, KRANG! THE SWIFT TIDE SAID THERE WAS NEWS...
AH, NAMOR! LADY DORMA! AND AMBROSE, OF COURSE.
HOW HAS YOUR DAY GONE? YOU MET THE TIDE?
NAMOR MET ATTUMA, TOO--AND THEY DIDN'T GET ALONG SO WELL!
PFF. HARDLY FAIR, DORMA.
I TRIED TO BE POLITE, BUT THAT PUMPED-UP PUFFERFISH IS SUCH A--

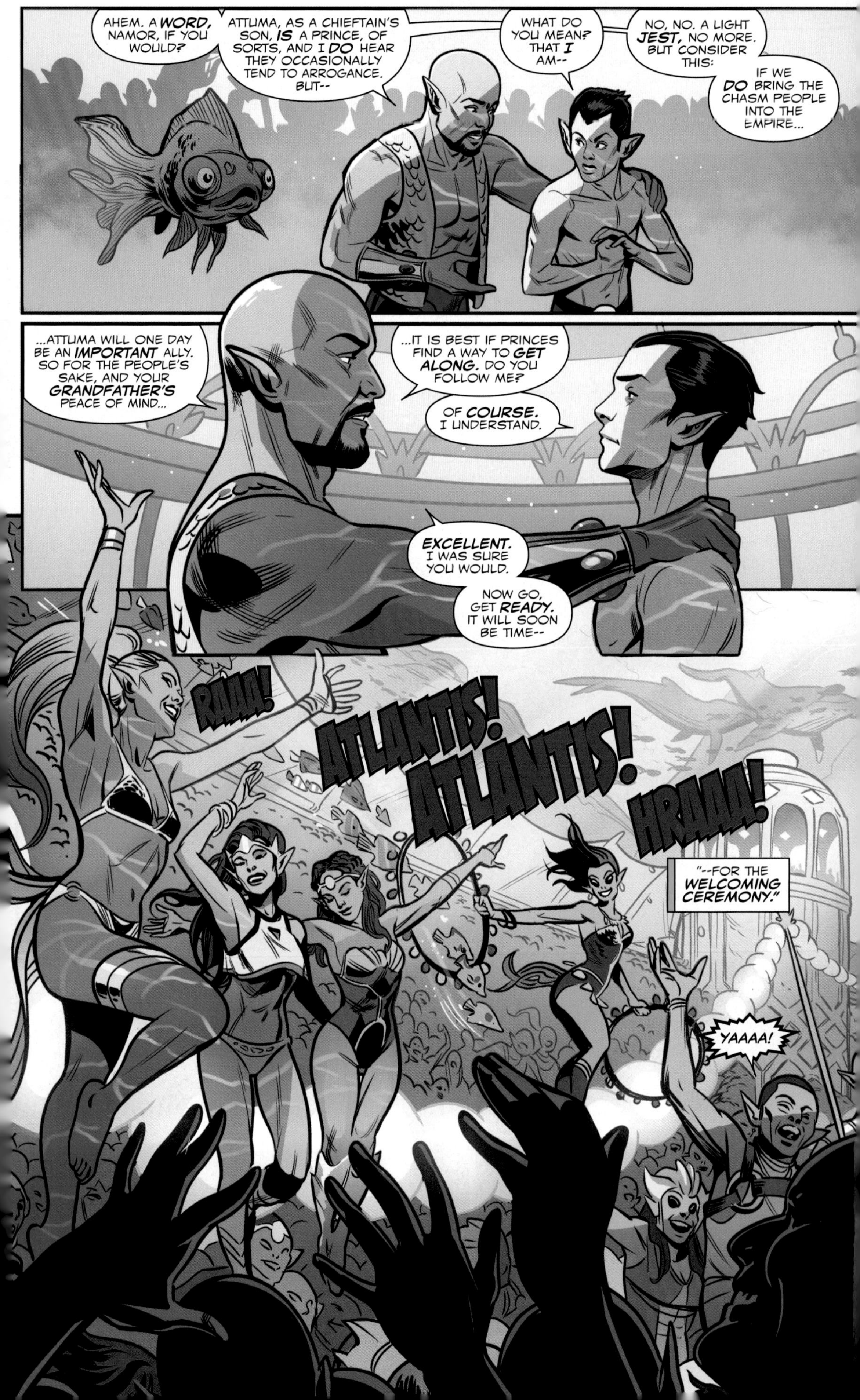
AHEM. A WORD, NAMOR, IF YOU WOULD?
ATTUMA, AS A CHIEFTAIN'S SON, IS A PRINCE, OF SORTS, AND I DO HEAR THEY OCCASIONALLY TEND TO ARROGANCE. BUT--
WHAT DO YOU MEAN? THAT I AM--
NO, NO. A LIGHT JEST, NO MORE. BUT CONSIDER THIS:
IF WE DO BRING THE CHASM PEOPLE INTO THE EMPIRE...
...ATTUMA WILL ONE DAY BE AN IMPORTANT ALLY. SO FOR THE PEOPLE'S SAKE, AND YOUR GRANDFATHER'S PEACE OF MIND...
...IT IS BEST IF PRINCES FIND A WAY TO GET ALONG. DO YOU FOLLOW ME?
OF COURSE. I UNDERSTAND.
EXCELLENT. I WAS SURE YOU WOULD.
NOW GO, GET READY. IT WILL SOON BE TIME--
RAAA!
ATLANTIS! ATLANTIS!
HRAAA!
"--FOR THE WELCOMING CEREMONY."
YAAAA!

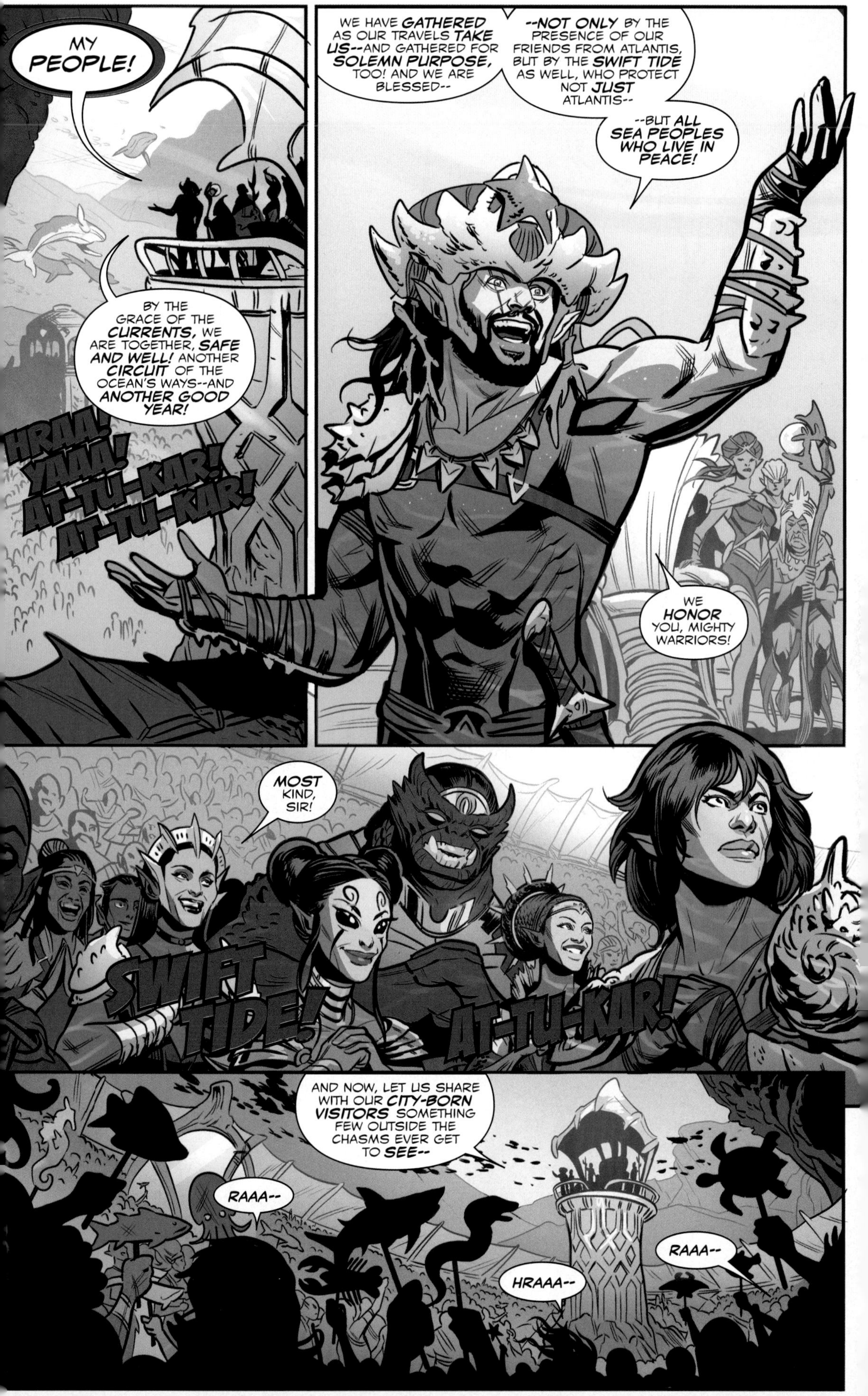
MY PEOPLE!
BY THE GRACE OF THE CURRENTS, WE ARE TOGETHER, SAFE AND WELL! ANOTHER CIRCUIT OF THE OCEAN'S WAYS--AND ANOTHER GOOD YEAR!
HRAA! YAAA! AT-TU-KAR! AT-TU-KAR!
WE HAVE GATHERED AS OUR TRAVELS TAKE US--AND GATHERED FOR SOLEMN PURPOSE, TOO! AND WE ARE BLESSED--
--NOT ONLY BY THE PRESENCE OF OUR FRIENDS FROM ATLANTIS, BUT BY THE SWIFT TIDE AS WELL, WHO PROTECT NOT JUST ATLANTIS--
--BUT ALL SEA PEOPLES WHO LIVE IN PEACE!
WE HONOR YOU, MIGHTY WARRIORS!
MOST KIND, SIR!
SWIFT TIDE!
AT-TU-KAR!
AND NOW, LET US SHARE WITH OUR CITY-BORN VISITORS SOMETHING FEW OUTSIDE THE CHASMS EVER GET TO SEE--
RAAA--
RAAA--
HRAAA--

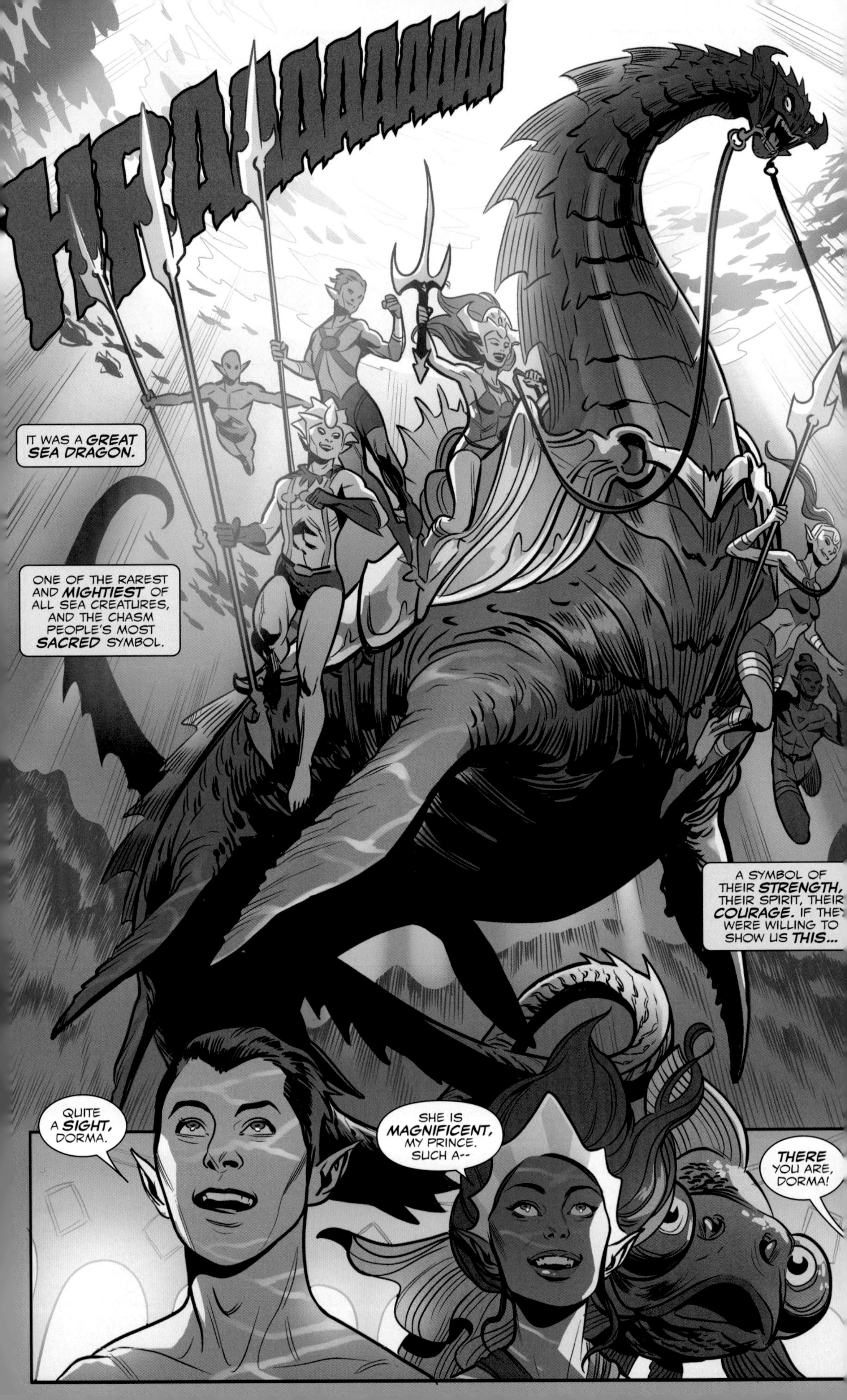
HRAAAAAAAAAA
IT WAS A GREAT SEA DRAGON.
ONE OF THE RAREST AND MIGHTIEST OF ALL SEA CREATURES, AND THE CHASM PEOPLE'S MOST SACRED SYMBOL.
A SYMBOL OF THEIR STRENGTH, THEIR SPIRIT, THEIR COURAGE. IF THEY WERE WILLING TO SHOW US THIS...
QUITE A SIGHT, DORMA.
SHE IS MAGNIFICENT, MY PRINCE. SUCH A--
THERE YOU ARE, DORMA!

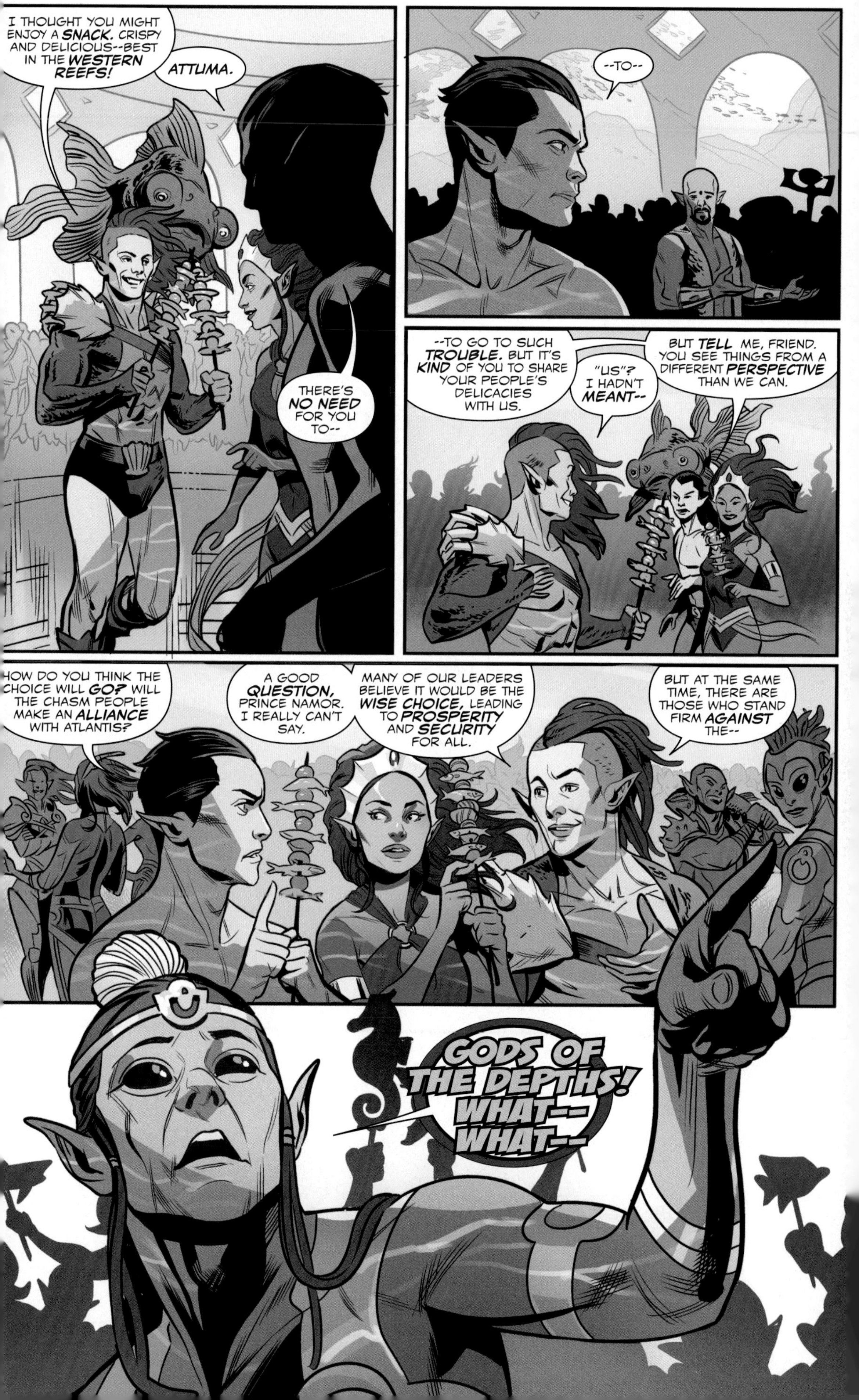
I THOUGHT YOU MIGHT ENJOY A SNACK. CRISPY AND DELICIOUS--BEST IN THE WESTERN REEFS!
ATTUMA.
THERE'S NO NEED FOR YOU TO--
--TO--
--TO GO TO SUCH TROUBLE. BUT IT'S KIND OF YOU TO SHARE YOUR PEOPLE'S DELICACIES WITH US.
"US"? I HADN'T MEANT--
BUT TELL ME, FRIEND. YOU SEE THINGS FROM A DIFFERENT PERSPECTIVE THAN WE CAN.
HOW DO YOU THINK THE CHOICE WILL GO? WILL THE CHASM PEOPLE MAKE AN ALLIANCE WITH ATLANTIS?
A GOOD QUESTION, PRINCE NAMOR. I REALLY CAN'T SAY.
MANY OF OUR LEADERS BELIEVE IT WOULD BE THE WISE CHOICE, LEADING TO PROSPERITY AND SECURITY FOR ALL.
BUT AT THE SAME TIME, THERE ARE THOSE WHO STAND FIRM AGAINST THE--
GODS OF THE DEPTHS! WHAT-- WHAT--

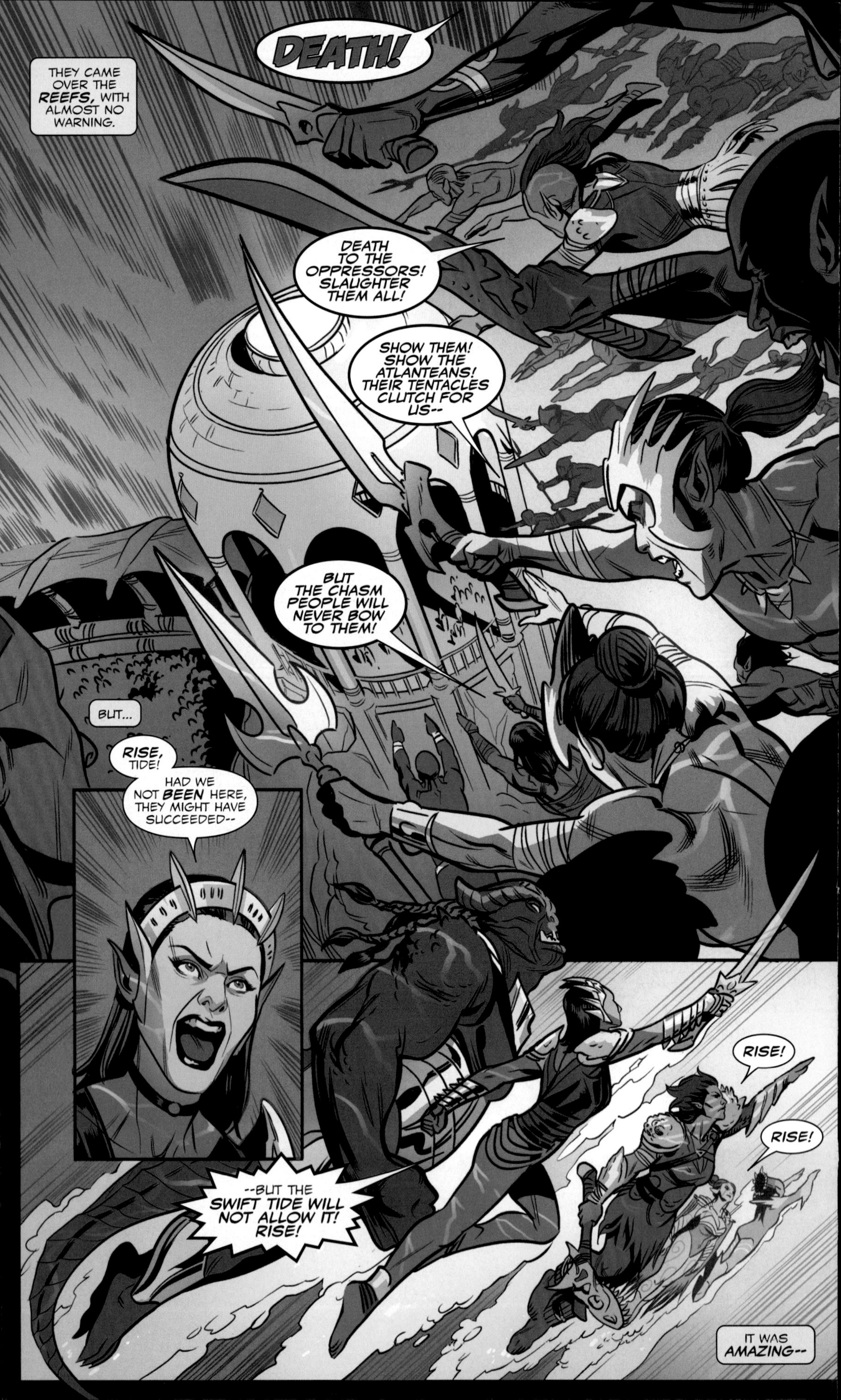

DEATH!
THEY CAME OVER THE REEFS, WITH ALMOST NO WARNING.
DEATH TO THE OPPRESSORS! SLAUGHTER THEM ALL!
SHOW THEM! SHOW THE ATLANTEANS! THEIR TENTACLES CLUTCH FOR US--
BUT THE CHASM PEOPLE WILL NEVER BOW TO THEM!
BUT...
RISE, TIDE!
HAD WE NOT BEEN HERE, THEY MIGHT HAVE SUCCEEDED--
--BUT THE SWIFT TIDE WILL NOT ALLOW IT! RISE!
RISE!
RISE!
IT WAS AMAZING--

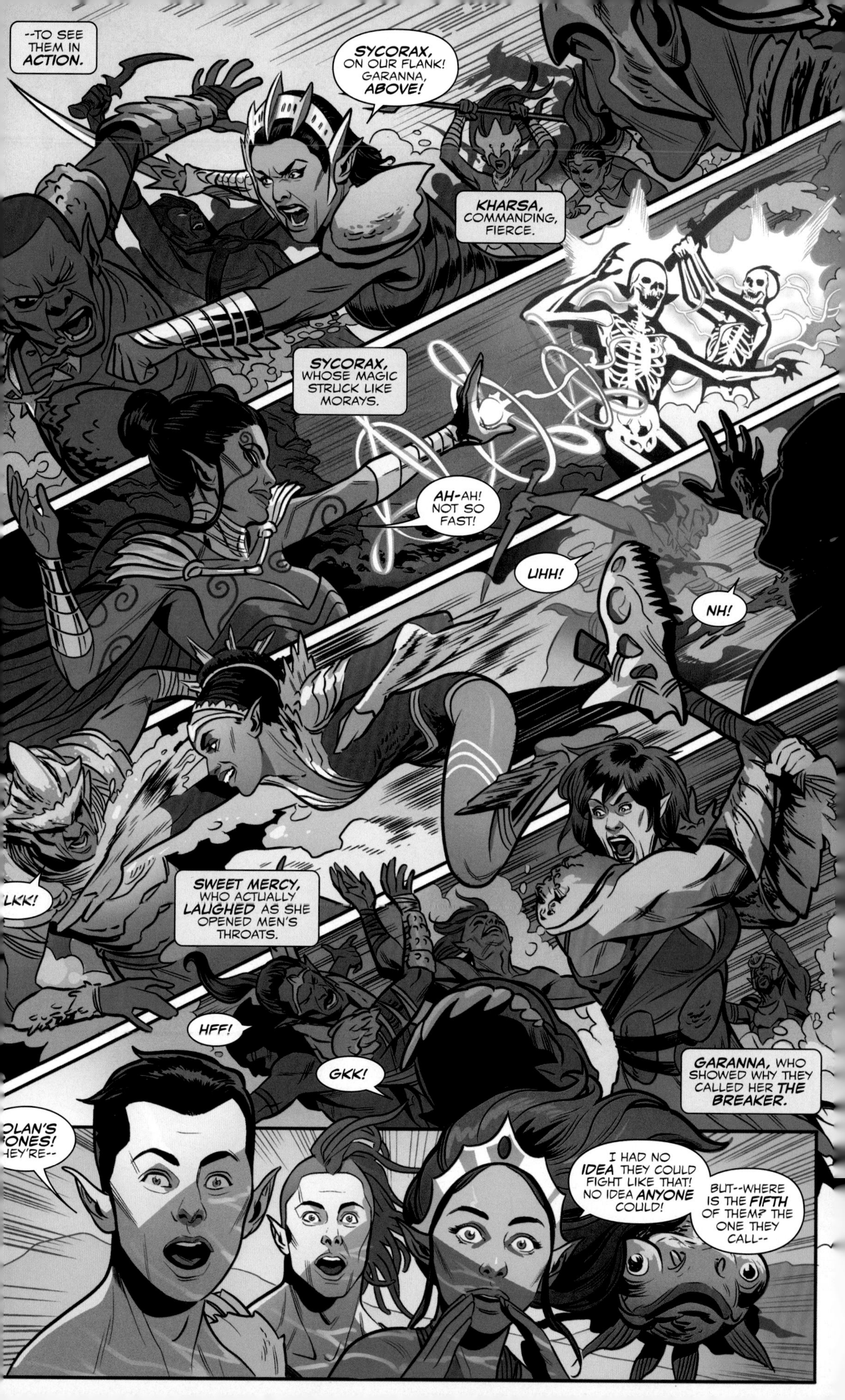
--TO SEE THEM IN ACTION.
SYCORAX, ON OUR FLANK! GARANNA, ABOVE!
KHARSA, COMMANDING, FIERCE.
SYCORAX, WHOSE MAGIC STRUCK LIKE MORAYS.
AH-AH! NOT SO FAST!
UHH!
NH!
SWEET MERCY, WHO ACTUALLY LAUGHED AS SHE OPENED MEN'S THROATS.
HFF!
GKK!
GARANNA, WHO SHOWED WHY THEY CALLED HER THE BREAKER.
I HAD NO IDEA THEY COULD FIGHT LIKE THAT! NO IDEA ANYONE COULD!
BUT--WHERE IS THE FIFTH OF THEM? THE ONE THEY CALL--

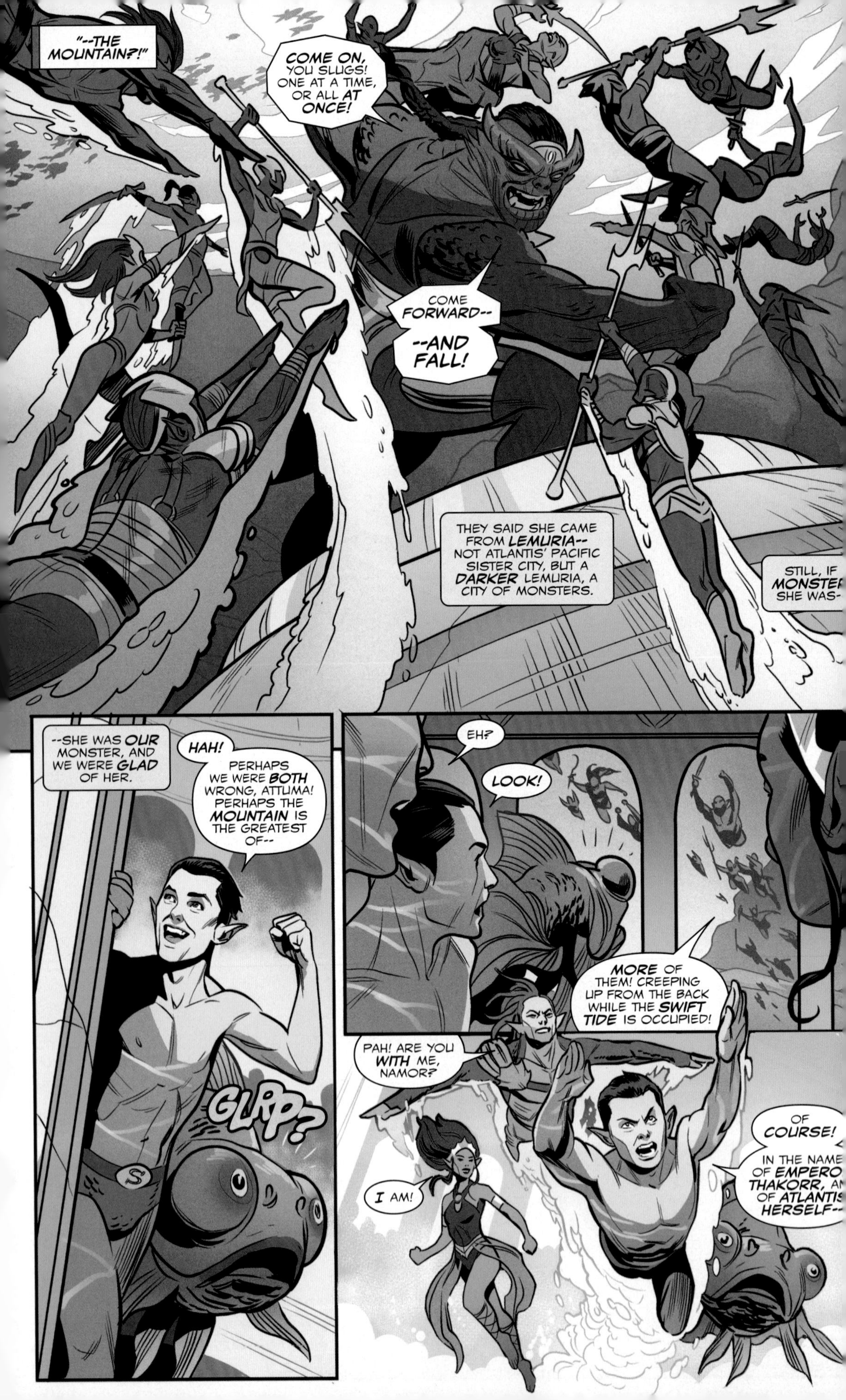
"--THE MOUNTAIN?!"
COME ON, YOU SLUGS! ONE AT A TIME, OR ALL AT ONCE!
COME FORWARD--
--AND FALL!
THEY SAID SHE CAME FROM LEMURIA-- NOT ATLANTIS' PACIFIC SISTER CITY, BUT A DARKER LEMURIA, A CITY OF MONSTERS.
STILL, IF MONSTER SHE WAS-
--SHE WAS OUR MONSTER, AND WE WERE GLAD OF HER.
HAH!
PERHAPS WE WERE BOTH WRONG, ATTUMA! PERHAPS THE MOUNTAIN IS THE GREATEST OF--
GLRP?
EH?
LOOK!
MORE OF THEM! CREEPING UP FROM THE BACK WHILE THE SWIFT TIDE IS OCCUPIED!
PAH! ARE YOU WITH ME, NAMOR?
I AM!
OF COURSE!
IN THE NAME OF EMPERO THAKORR, AN OF ATLANTIS HERSELF--

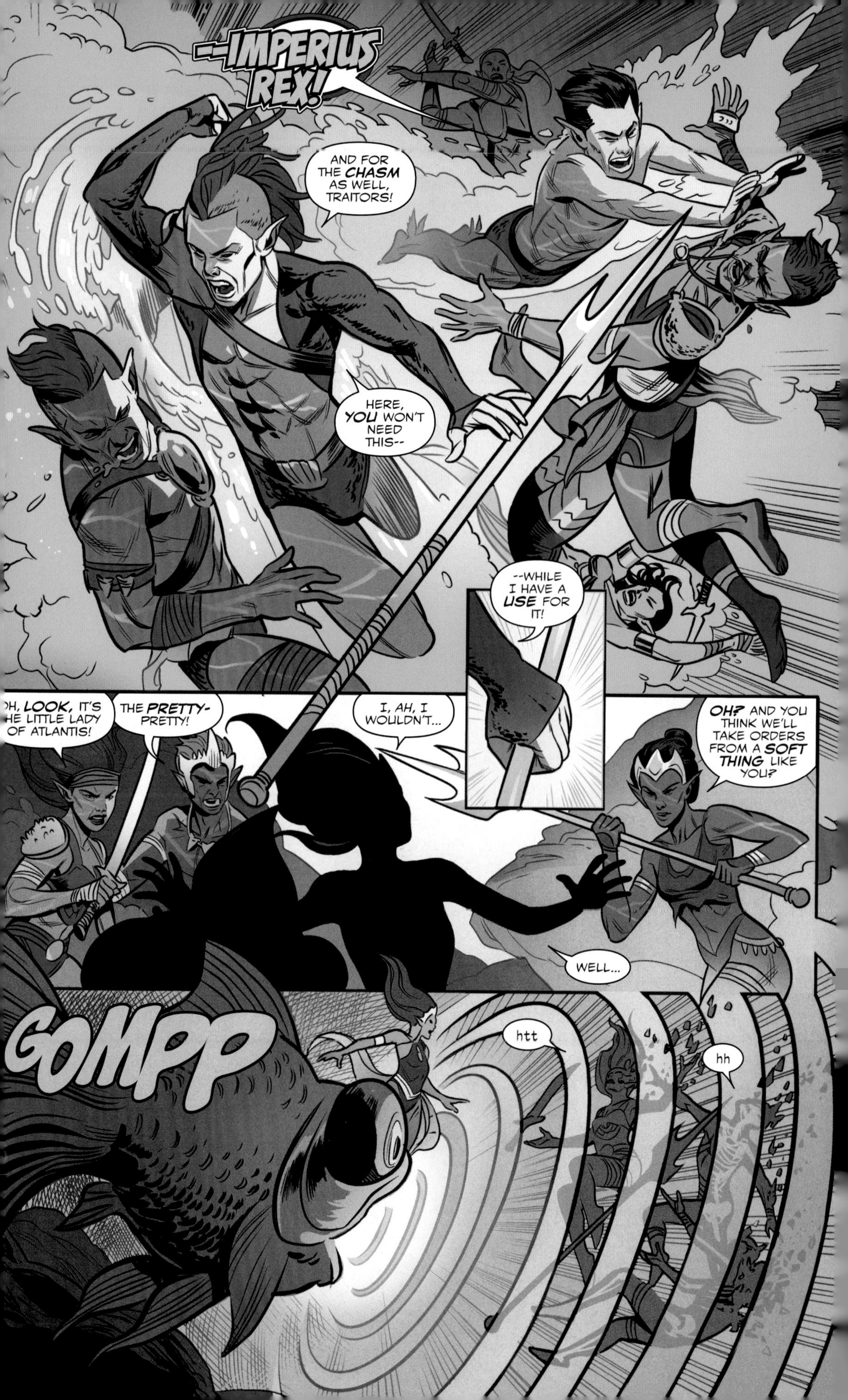
--IMPERIUS REX!
AND FOR THE CHASM AS WELL, TRAITORS!
HERE, YOU WON'T NEED THIS--
--WHILE I HAVE A USE FOR IT!
H, LOOK, IT'S HE LITTLE LADY OF ATLANTIS!
THE PRETTY-PRETTY!
I, AH, I WOULDN'T...
OH? AND YOU THINK WE'LL TAKE ORDERS FROM A SOFT THING LIKE YOU?
WELL...
GOMPP
htt
hh

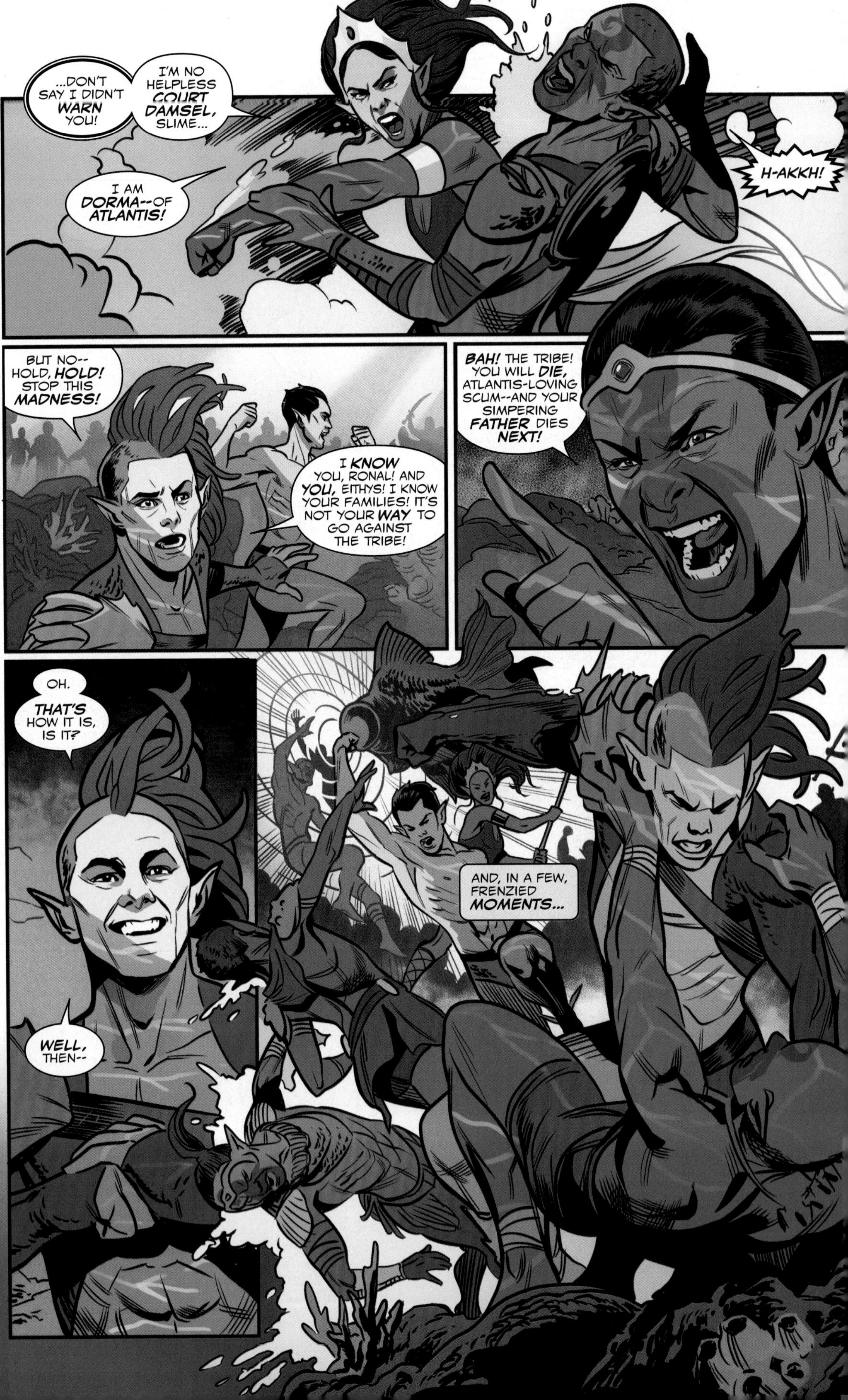

...DON'T SAY I DIDN'T WARN YOU!
I'M NO HELPLESS COURT DAMSEL, SLIME...
I AM DORMA--OF ATLANTIS!
H-AKKH!
BUT NO-- HOLD, HOLD! STOP THIS MADNESS!
I KNOW YOU, RONAL! AND YOU, EITHYS! I KNOW YOUR FAMILIES! IT'S NOT YOUR WAY TO GO AGAINST THE TRIBE!
BAH! THE TRIBE! YOU WILL DIE, ATLANTIS-LOVING SCUM--AND YOUR SIMPERING FATHER DIES NEXT!
OH. THAT'S HOW IT IS, IS IT?
WELL, THEN--
AND, IN A FEW, FRENZIED MOMENTS...

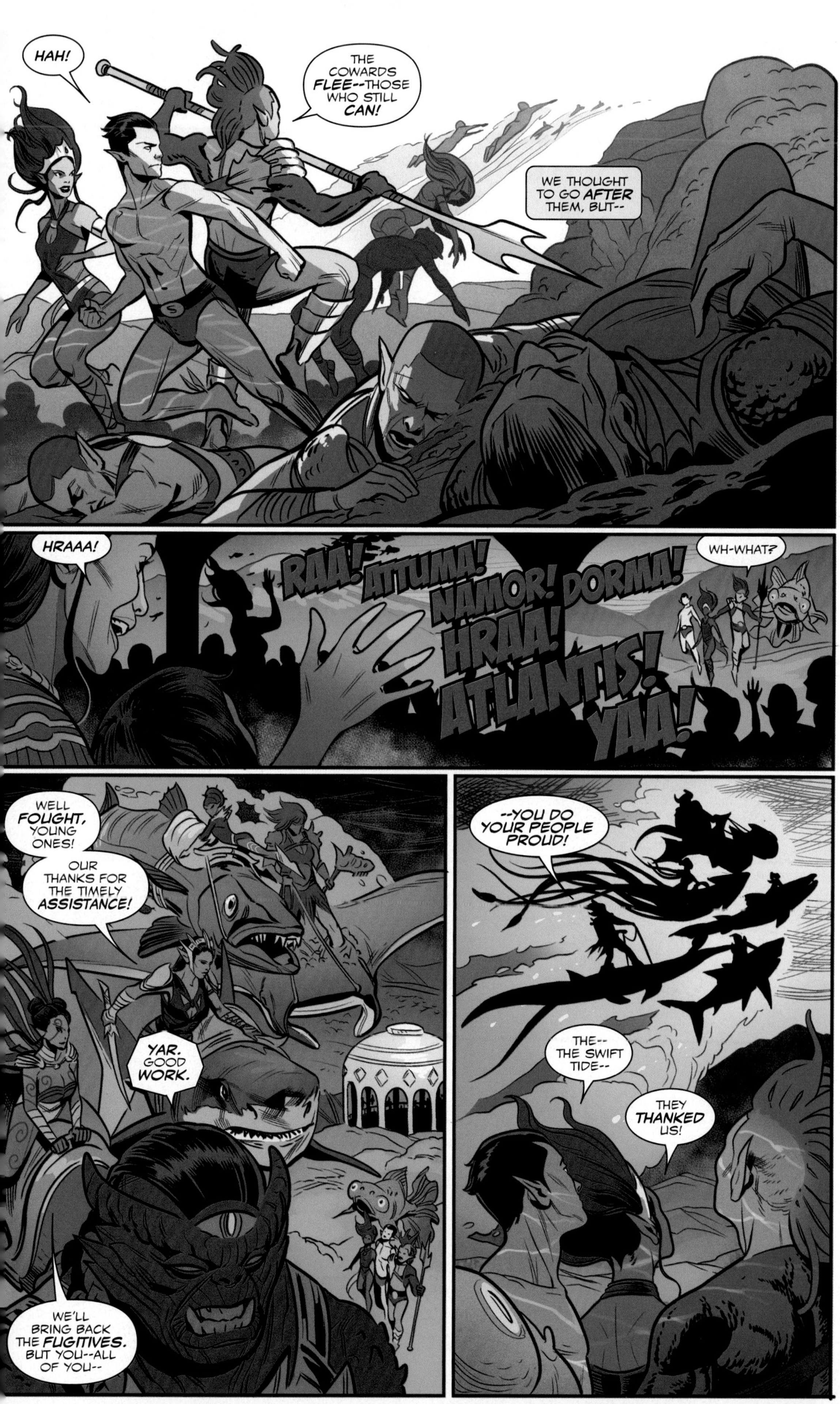
HAH!
THE COWARDS FLEE--THOSE WHO STILL CAN!
WE THOUGHT TO GO AFTER THEM, BUT--
HRAAA!
RAA! ATTUMA! NAMOR! DORMA! HRAA! ATLANTIS! YAA!
WH-WHAT?
WELL FOUGHT, YOUNG ONES!
OUR THANKS FOR THE TIMELY ASSISTANCE!
YAR. GOOD WORK.
WE'LL BRING BACK THE FUGITIVES. BUT YOU--ALL OF YOU--
--YOU DO YOUR PEOPLE PROUD!
THE-- THE SWIFT TIDE--
THEY THANKED US!

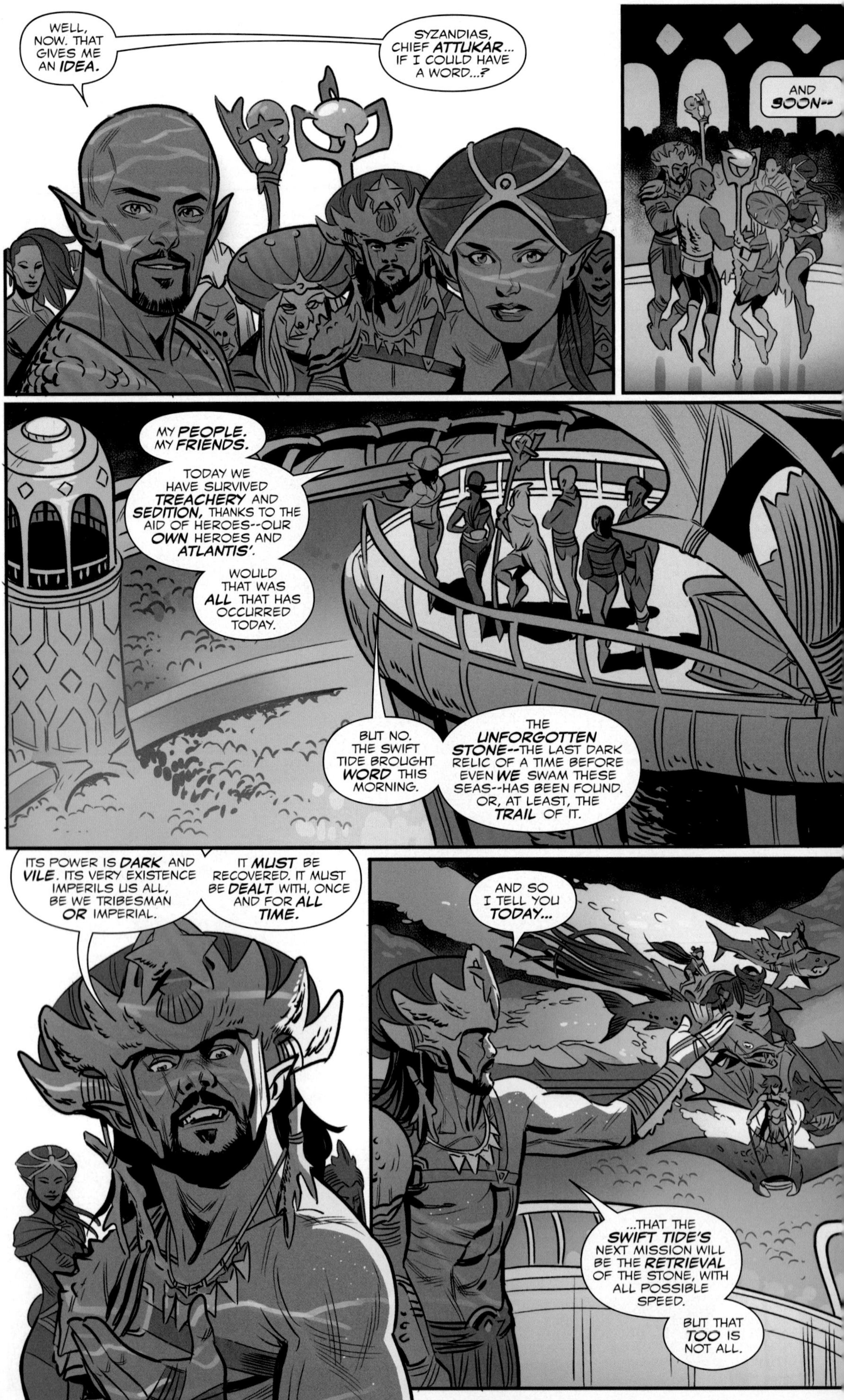
WELL, NOW. THAT GIVES ME AN IDEA.
SYZANDIAS, CHIEF ATTUKAR... IF I COULD HAVE A WORD...?
AND SOON--
MY PEOPLE. MY FRIENDS.
TODAY WE HAVE SURVIVED TREACHERY AND SEDITION, THANKS TO THE AID OF HEROES--OUR OWN HEROES AND ATLANTIS'.
WOULD THAT WAS ALL THAT HAS OCCURRED TODAY.
BUT NO. THE SWIFT TIDE BROUGHT WORD THIS MORNING.
THE UNFORGOTTEN STONE--THE LAST DARK RELIC OF A TIME BEFORE EVEN WE SWAM THESE SEAS--HAS BEEN FOUND. OR, AT LEAST, THE TRAIL OF IT.
ITS POWER IS DARK AND VILE. ITS VERY EXISTENCE IMPERILS US ALL, BE WE TRIBESMAN OR IMPERIAL.
IT MUST BE RECOVERED. IT MUST BE DEALT WITH, ONCE AND FOR ALL TIME.
AND SO I TELL YOU TODAY...
...THAT THE SWIFT TIDE'S NEXT MISSION WILL BE THE RETRIEVAL OF THE STONE, WITH ALL POSSIBLE SPEED.
BUT THAT TOO IS NOT ALL.

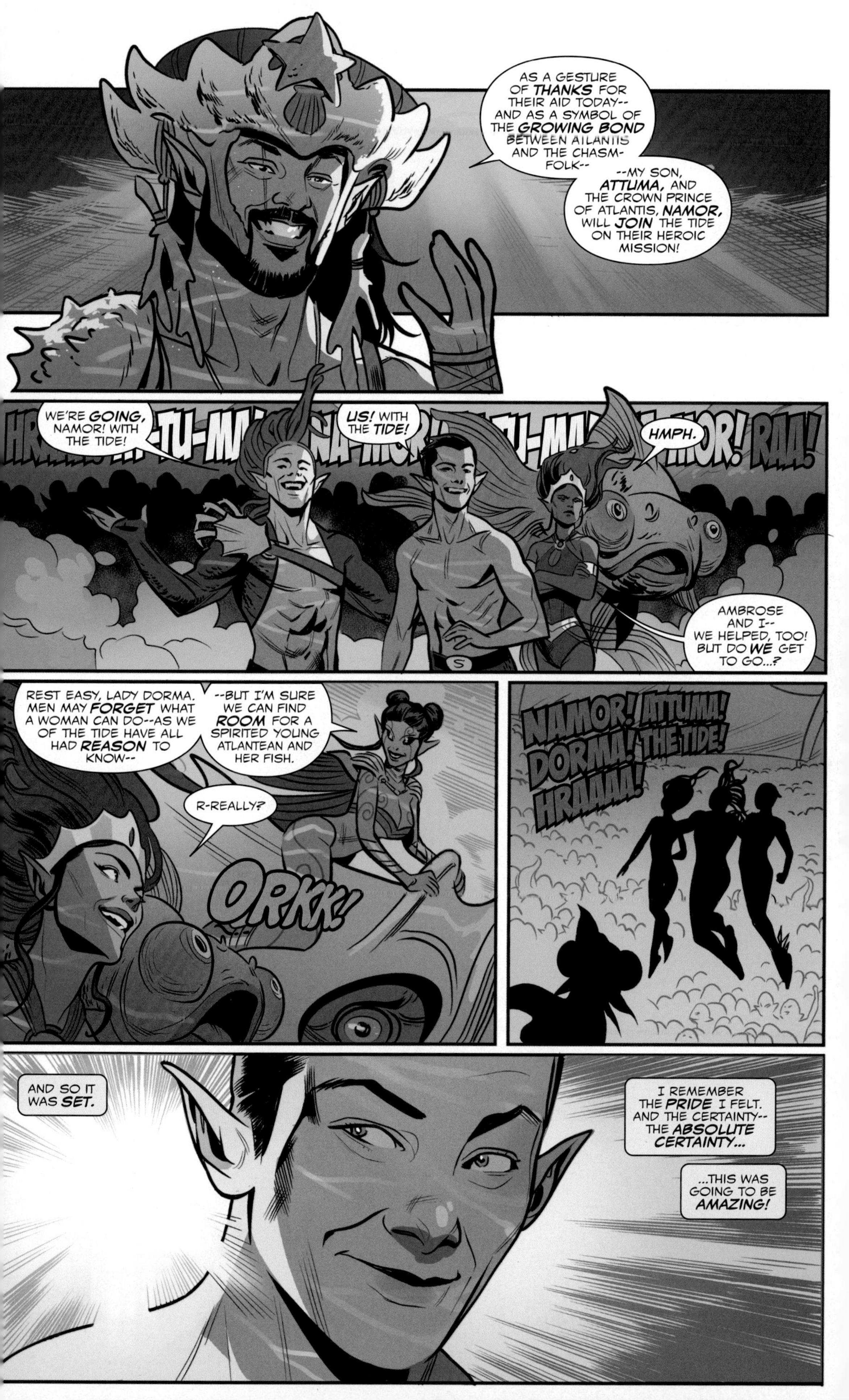
AS A GESTURE OF THANKS FOR THEIR AID TODAY-- AND AS A SYMBOL OF THE GROWING BOND BETWEEN ATLANTIS AND THE CHASM-FOLK--
--MY SON, ATTUMA, AND THE CROWN PRINCE OF ATLANTIS, NAMOR, WILL JOIN THE TIDE ON THEIR HEROIC MISSION!
WE'RE GOING, NAMOR! WITH THE TIDE!
US! WITH THE TIDE!
HMPH.
RAA!
AMBROSE AND I-- WE HELPED, TOO! BUT DO WE GET TO GO...?
REST EASY, LADY DORMA. MEN MAY FORGET WHAT A WOMAN CAN DO--AS WE OF THE TIDE HAVE ALL HAD REASON TO KNOW--
--BUT I'M SURE WE CAN FIND ROOM FOR A SPIRITED YOUNG ATLANTEAN AND HER FISH.
R-REALLY?
ORKK!
NAMOR! ATTUMA! DORMA! THE TIDE! HRAAAA!
AND SO IT WAS SET.
I REMEMBER THE PRIDE I FELT. AND THE CERTAINTY-- THE ABSOLUTE CERTAINTY...
...THIS WAS GOING TO BE AMAZING!

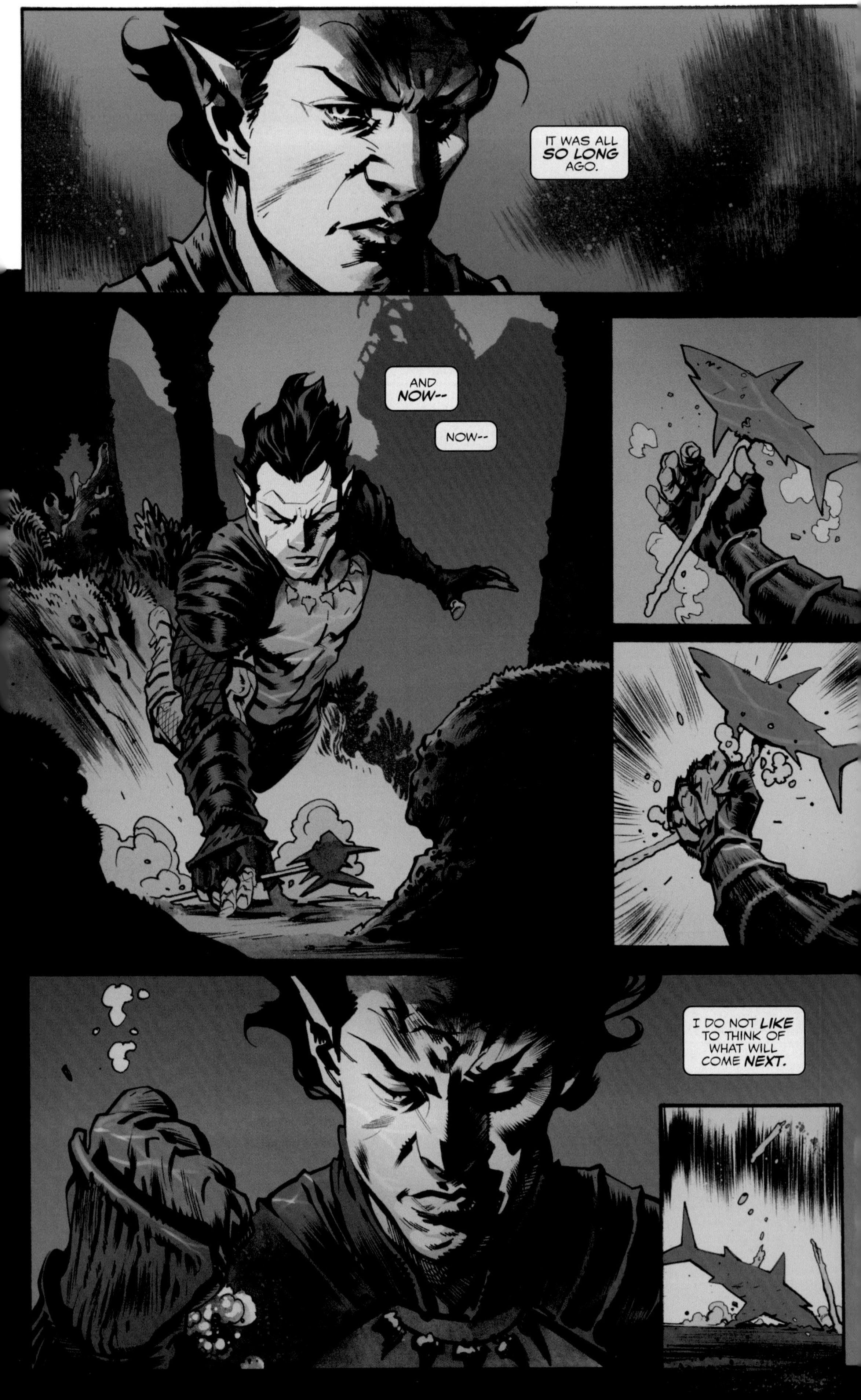
IT WAS ALL SO LONG AGO.
AND NOW--
NOW--
I DO NOT LIKE TO THINK OF WHAT WILL COME NEXT.

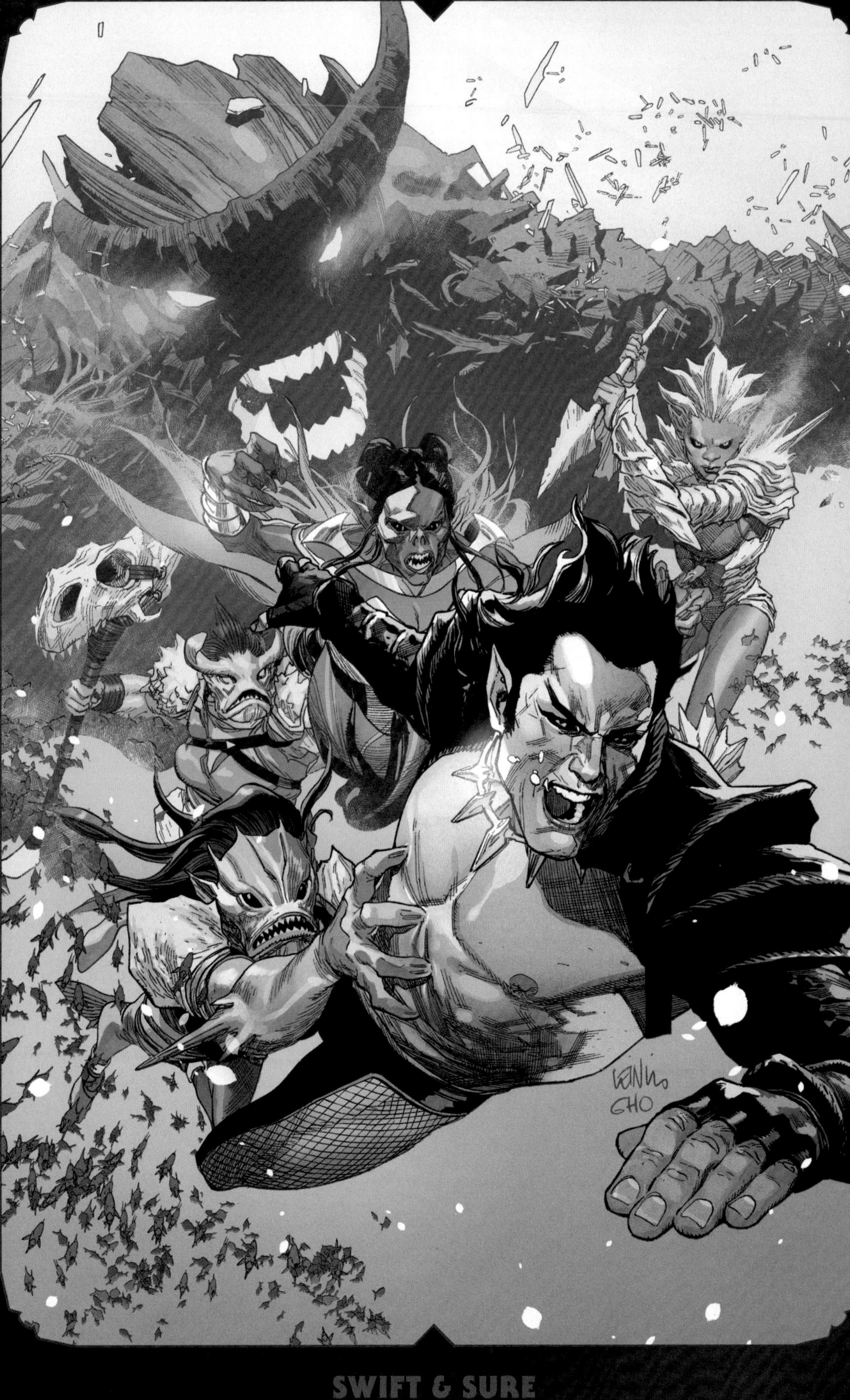

SWIFT & SURE

2

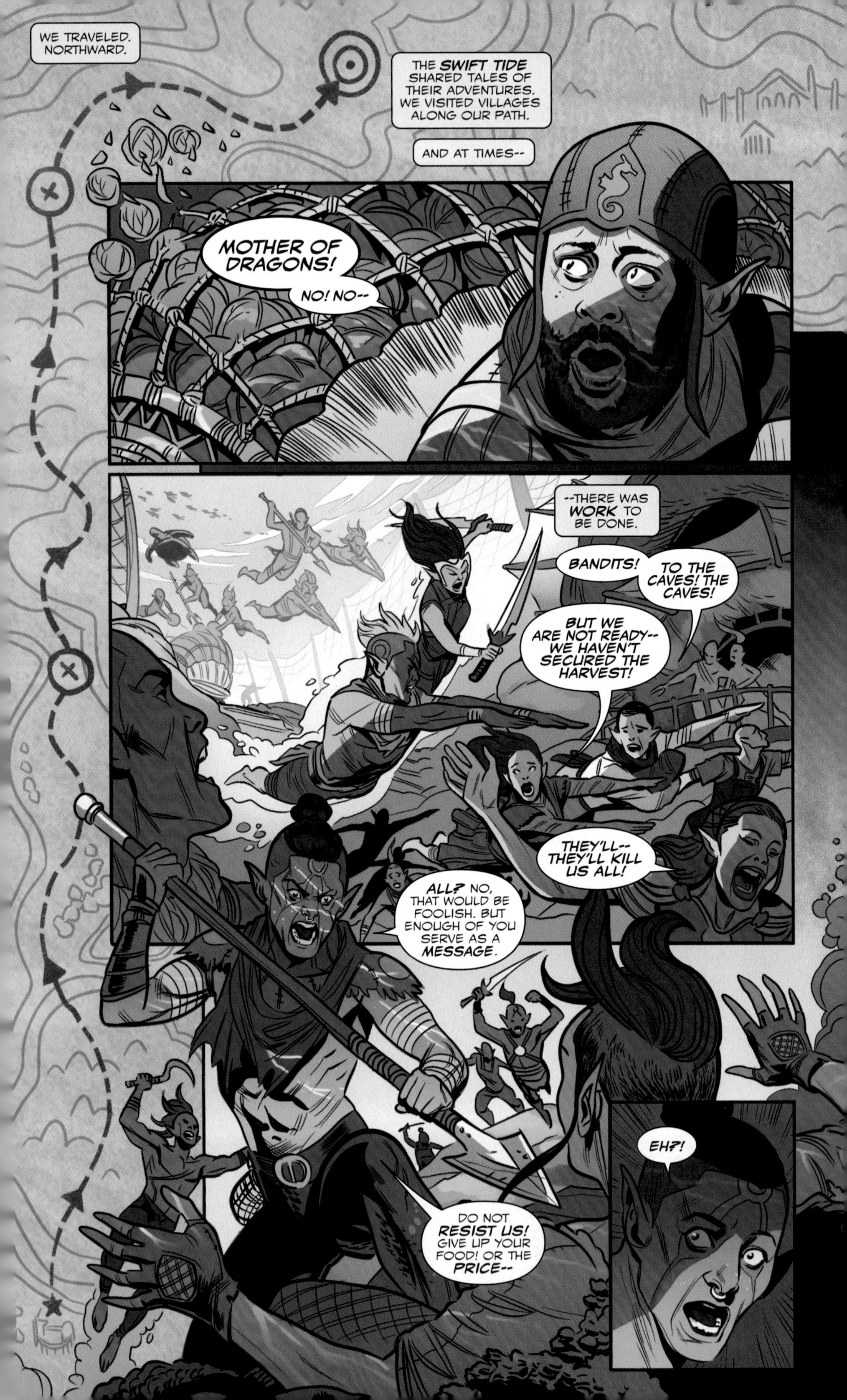

WE TRAVELED. NORTHWARD.
THE SWIFT TIDE SHARED TALES OF THEIR ADVENTURES. WE VISITED VILLAGES ALONG OUR PATH.
AND AT TIMES--
MOTHER OF DRAGONS!
NO! NO--
--THERE WAS WORK TO BE DONE.
BANDITS!
TO THE CAVES! THE CAVES!
BUT WE ARE NOT READY-- WE HAVEN'T SECURED THE HARVEST!
THEY'LL-- THEY'LL KILL US ALL!
ALL? NO, THAT WOULD BE FOOLISH. BUT ENOUGH OF YOU SERVE AS A MESSAGE.
DO NOT RESIST US! GIVE UP YOUR FOOD! OR THE PRICE--
EH?!

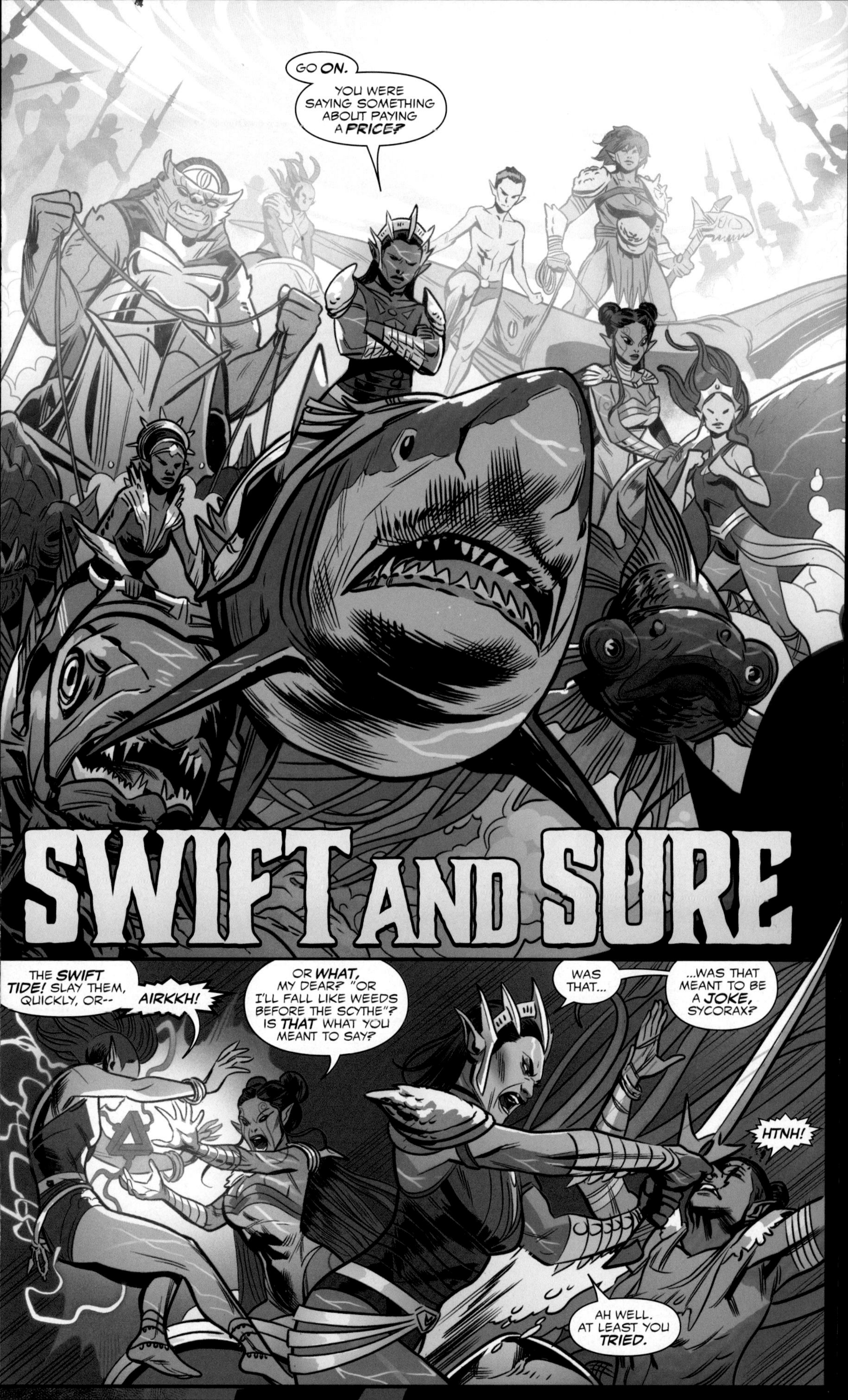
GO ON.
YOU WERE SAYING SOMETHING ABOUT PAYING A PRICE?
SWIFT AND SURE
THE SWIFT TIDE! SLAY THEM, QUICKLY, OR--
AIRKKH!
OR WHAT, MY DEAR? "OR I'LL FALL LIKE WEEDS BEFORE THE SCYTHE"? IS THAT WHAT YOU MEANT TO SAY?
WAS THAT...
...WAS THAT MEANT TO BE A JOKE, SYCORAX?
HTNH!
AH WELL. AT LEAST YOU TRIED.

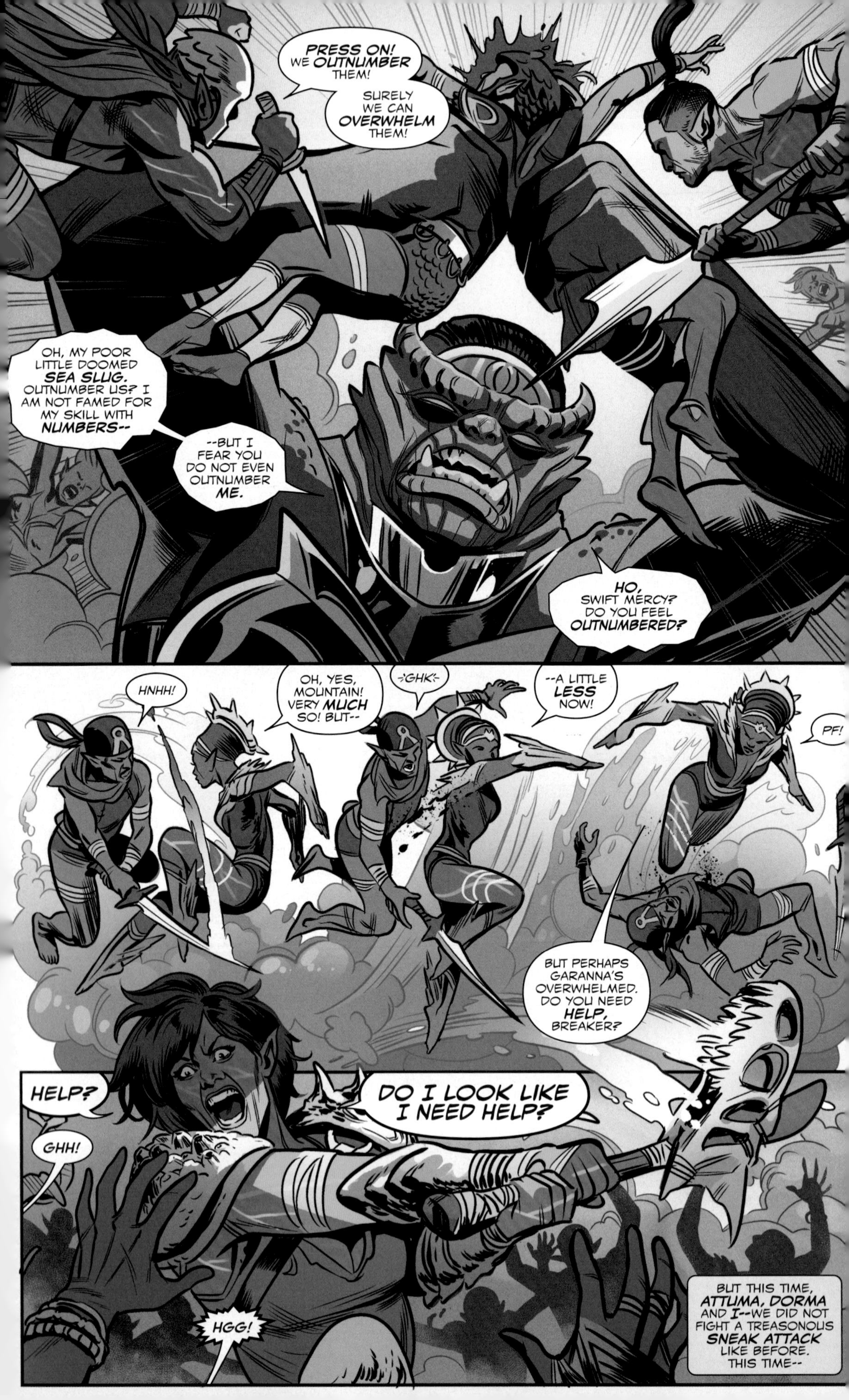
PRESS ON! WE OUTNUMBER THEM!
SURELY WE CAN OVERWHELM THEM!
OH, MY POOR LITTLE DOOMED SEA SLUG. OUTNUMBER US? I AM NOT FAMED FOR MY SKILL WITH NUMBERS--
--BUT I FEAR YOU DO NOT EVEN OUTNUMBER ME.
HO, SWIFT MERCY? DO YOU FEEL OUTNUMBERED?
HNHH!
OH, YES, MOUNTAIN! VERY MUCH SO! BUT--
GHK
--A LITTLE LESS NOW!
PF!
BUT PERHAPS GARANNA'S OVERWHELMED. DO YOU NEED HELP, BREAKER?
HELP?
DO I LOOK LIKE I NEED HELP?
GHH!
HGG!
BUT THIS TIME, ATTUMA, DORMA AND I--WE DID NOT FIGHT A TREASONOUS SNEAK ATTACK LIKE BEFORE. THIS TIME--

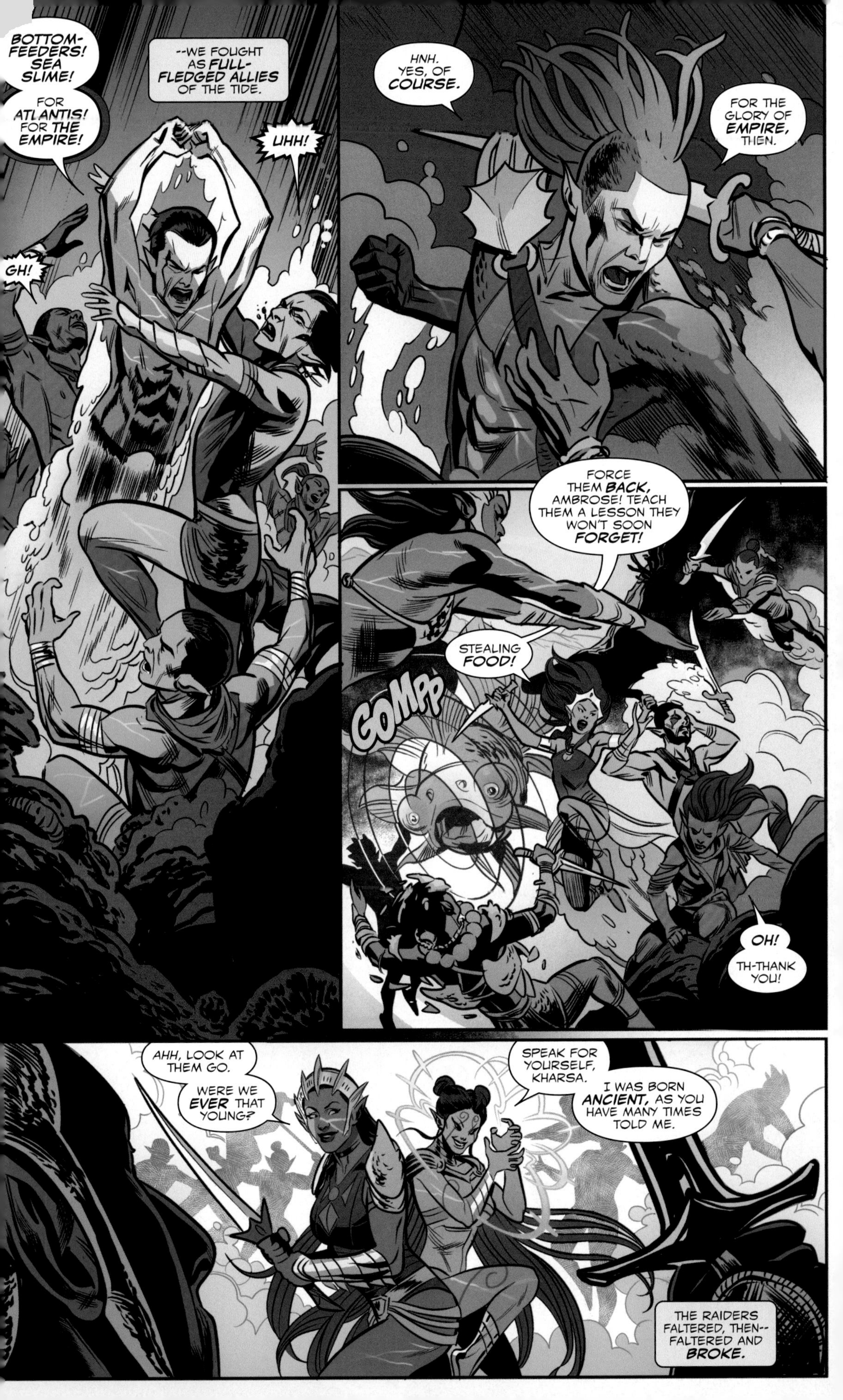

BOTTOM-FEEDERS! SEA SLIME!
FOR ATLANTIS! FOR THE EMPIRE!
--WE FOUGHT AS FULL-FLEDGED ALLIES OF THE TIDE.
UHH!
GH!
HNH. YES, OF COURSE.
FOR THE GLORY OF EMPIRE, THEN.
FORCE THEM BACK, AMBROSE! TEACH THEM A LESSON THEY WON'T SOON FORGET!
STEALING FOOD!
GOMPP
OH!
TH-THANK YOU!
AHH, LOOK AT THEM GO.
WERE WE EVER THAT YOUNG?
SPEAK FOR YOURSELF, KHARSA.
I WAS BORN ANCIENT, AS YOU HAVE MANY TIMES TOLD ME.
THE RAIDERS FALTERED, THEN-- FALTERED AND BROKE.

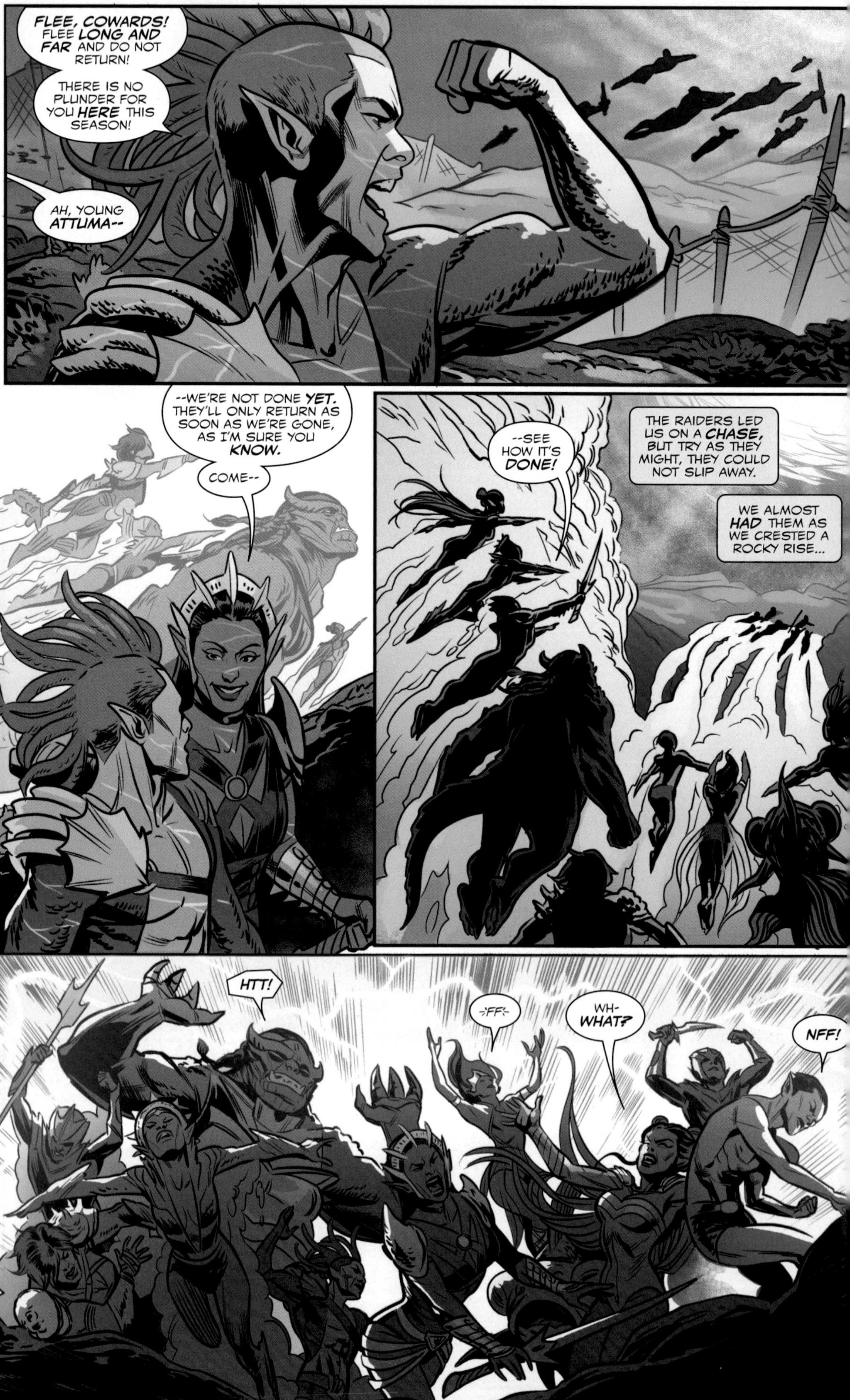
FLEE, COWARDS! FLEE LONG AND FAR AND DO NOT RETURN!
THERE IS NO PLUNDER FOR YOU HERE THIS SEASON!
AH, YOUNG ATTUMA--
--WE'RE NOT DONE YET. THEY'LL ONLY RETURN AS SOON AS WE'RE GONE, AS I'M SURE YOU KNOW.
COME--
--SEE HOW IT'S DONE!
THE RAIDERS LED US ON A CHASE, BUT TRY AS THEY MIGHT, THEY COULD NOT SLIP AWAY.
WE ALMOST HAD THEM AS WE CRESTED A ROCKY RISE...
HTT!
FF
WH- WHAT?
NFF!

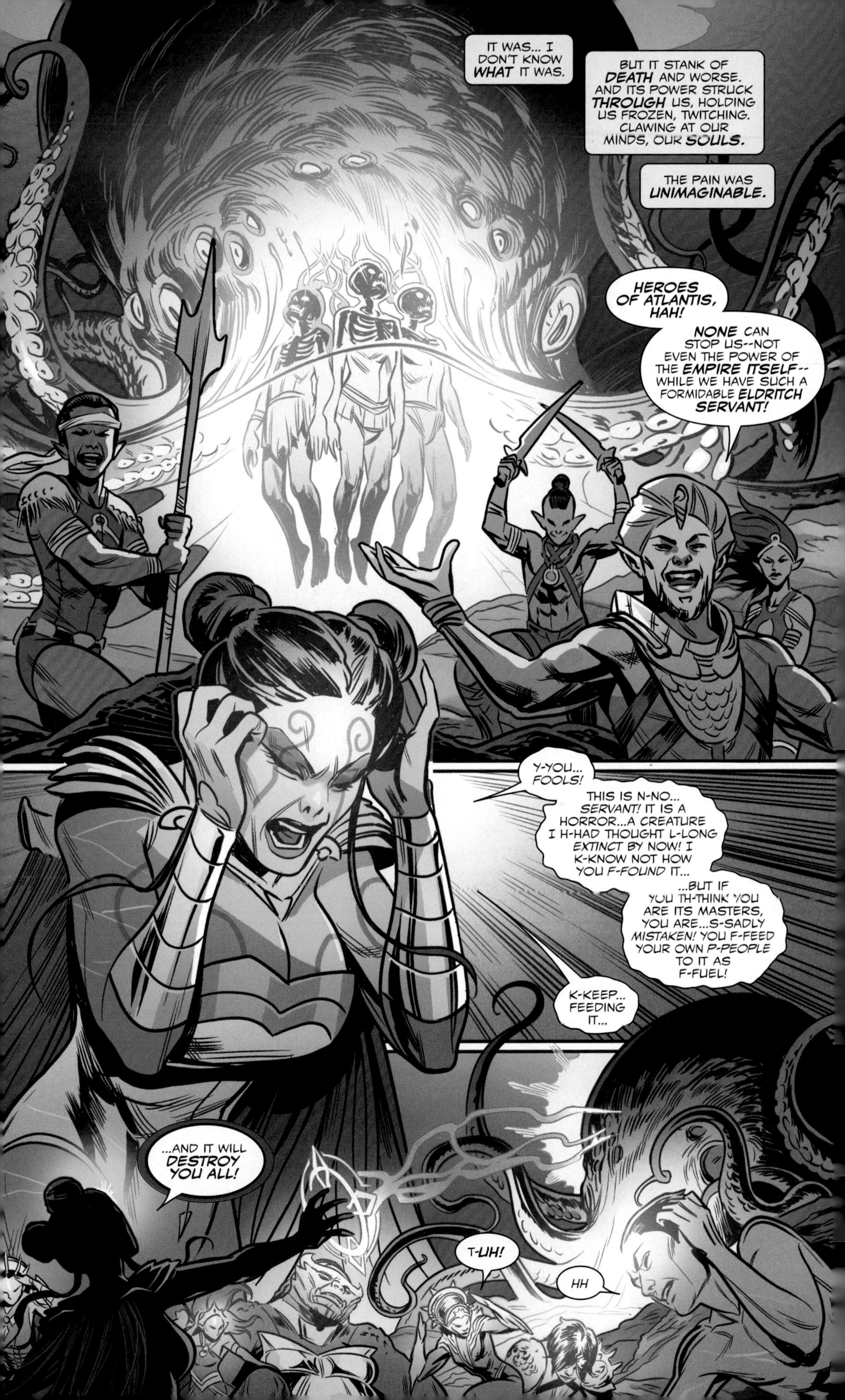
IT WAS... I DON'T KNOW **WHAT** IT WAS.
BUT IT STANK OF **DEATH** AND WORSE. AND ITS POWER STRUCK **THROUGH** US, HOLDING US FROZEN, TWITCHING. CLAWING AT OUR MINDS, OUR **SOULS.**
THE PAIN WAS **UNIMAGINABLE.**
HEROES OF ATLANTIS, HAH!
NONE CAN STOP US--NOT EVEN THE POWER OF THE **EMPIRE ITSELF**-- WHILE WE HAVE SUCH A FORMIDABLE **ELDRITCH SERVANT!**
Y-YOU... *FOOLS!*
THIS IS N-NO... *SERVANT!* IT IS A HORROR...A CREATURE I H-HAD THOUGHT L-LONG *EXTINCT* BY NOW! I K-KNOW NOT HOW YOU F-FOUND IT...
...BUT IF YOU TH-THINK YOU ARE ITS MASTERS, YOU ARE...S-SADLY *MISTAKEN!* YOU F-FEED YOUR OWN *P-PEOPLE* TO IT AS F-FUEL!
K-KEEP... FEEDING IT...
...AND IT WILL ***DESTROY YOU ALL!***
T-**UH!**
HH

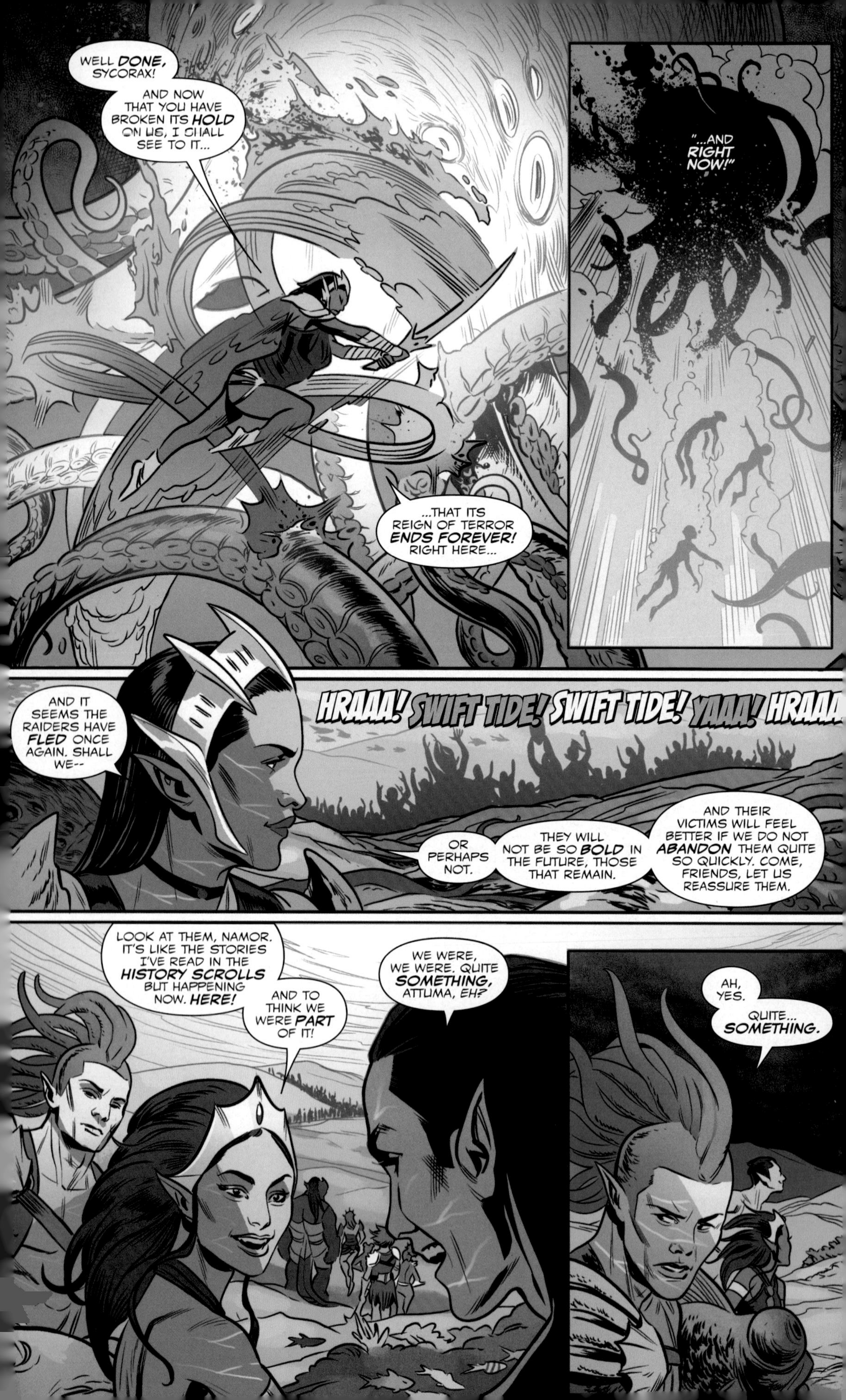
WELL DONE, SYCORAX!
AND NOW THAT YOU HAVE BROKEN ITS HOLD ON US, I SHALL SEE TO IT...
...THAT ITS REIGN OF TERROR ENDS FOREVER! RIGHT HERE...
"...AND RIGHT NOW!"
AND IT SEEMS THE RAIDERS HAVE FLED ONCE AGAIN. SHALL WE--
HRAAA! SWIFT TIDE! SWIFT TIDE! YAAA! HRAAA
OR PERHAPS NOT.
THEY WILL NOT BE SO BOLD IN THE FUTURE, THOSE THAT REMAIN.
AND THEIR VICTIMS WILL FEEL BETTER IF WE DO NOT ABANDON THEM QUITE SO QUICKLY. COME, FRIENDS, LET US REASSURE THEM.
LOOK AT THEM, NAMOR. IT'S LIKE THE STORIES I'VE READ IN THE HISTORY SCROLLS BUT HAPPENING NOW. HERE!
AND TO THINK WE WERE PART OF IT!
WE WERE, WE WERE. QUITE SOMETHING, ATTUMA, EH?
AH, YES.
QUITE... SOMETHING.

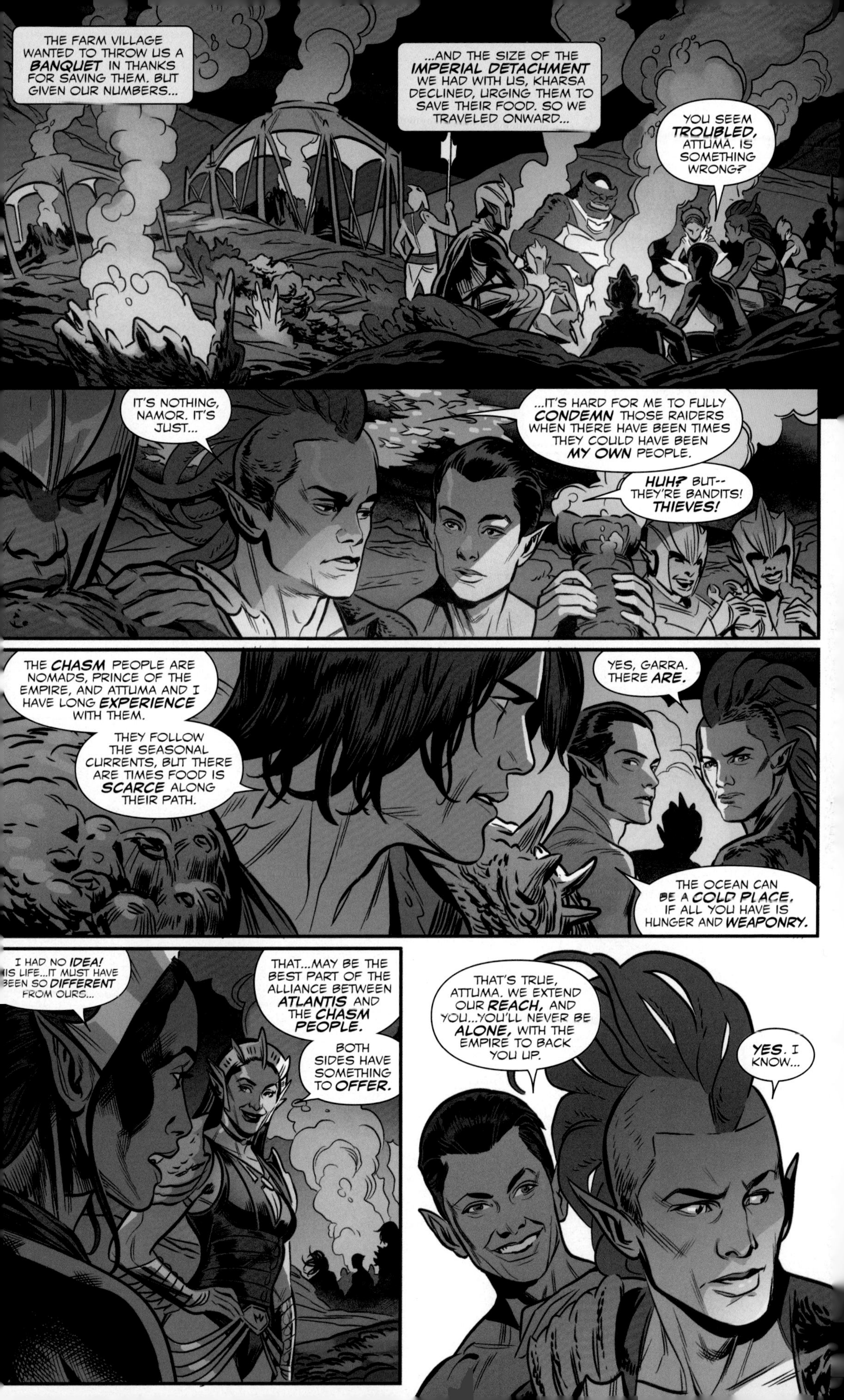
THE FARM VILLAGE WANTED TO THROW US A BANQUET IN THANKS FOR SAVING THEM. BUT GIVEN OUR NUMBERS...
...AND THE SIZE OF THE IMPERIAL DETACHMENT WE HAD WITH US, KHARSA DECLINED, URGING THEM TO SAVE THEIR FOOD. SO WE TRAVELED ONWARD...
YOU SEEM TROUBLED, ATTUMA. IS SOMETHING WRONG?
IT'S NOTHING, NAMOR. IT'S JUST...
...IT'S HARD FOR ME TO FULLY CONDEMN THOSE RAIDERS WHEN THERE HAVE BEEN TIMES THEY COULD HAVE BEEN MY OWN PEOPLE.
HUH? BUT-- THEY'RE BANDITS! THIEVES!
THE CHASM PEOPLE ARE NOMADS, PRINCE OF THE EMPIRE, AND ATTUMA AND I HAVE LONG EXPERIENCE WITH THEM.
THEY FOLLOW THE SEASONAL CURRENTS, BUT THERE ARE TIMES FOOD IS SCARCE ALONG THEIR PATH.
YES, GARRA. THERE ARE.
THE OCEAN CAN BE A COLD PLACE, IF ALL YOU HAVE IS HUNGER AND WEAPONRY.
I HAD NO IDEA! HIS LIFE...IT MUST HAVE BEEN SO DIFFERENT FROM OURS...
THAT...MAY BE THE BEST PART OF THE ALLIANCE BETWEEN ATLANTIS AND THE CHASM PEOPLE.
BOTH SIDES HAVE SOMETHING TO OFFER.
THAT'S TRUE, ATTUMA. WE EXTEND OUR REACH, AND YOU...YOU'LL NEVER BE ALONE, WITH THE EMPIRE TO BACK YOU UP.
YES. I KNOW...

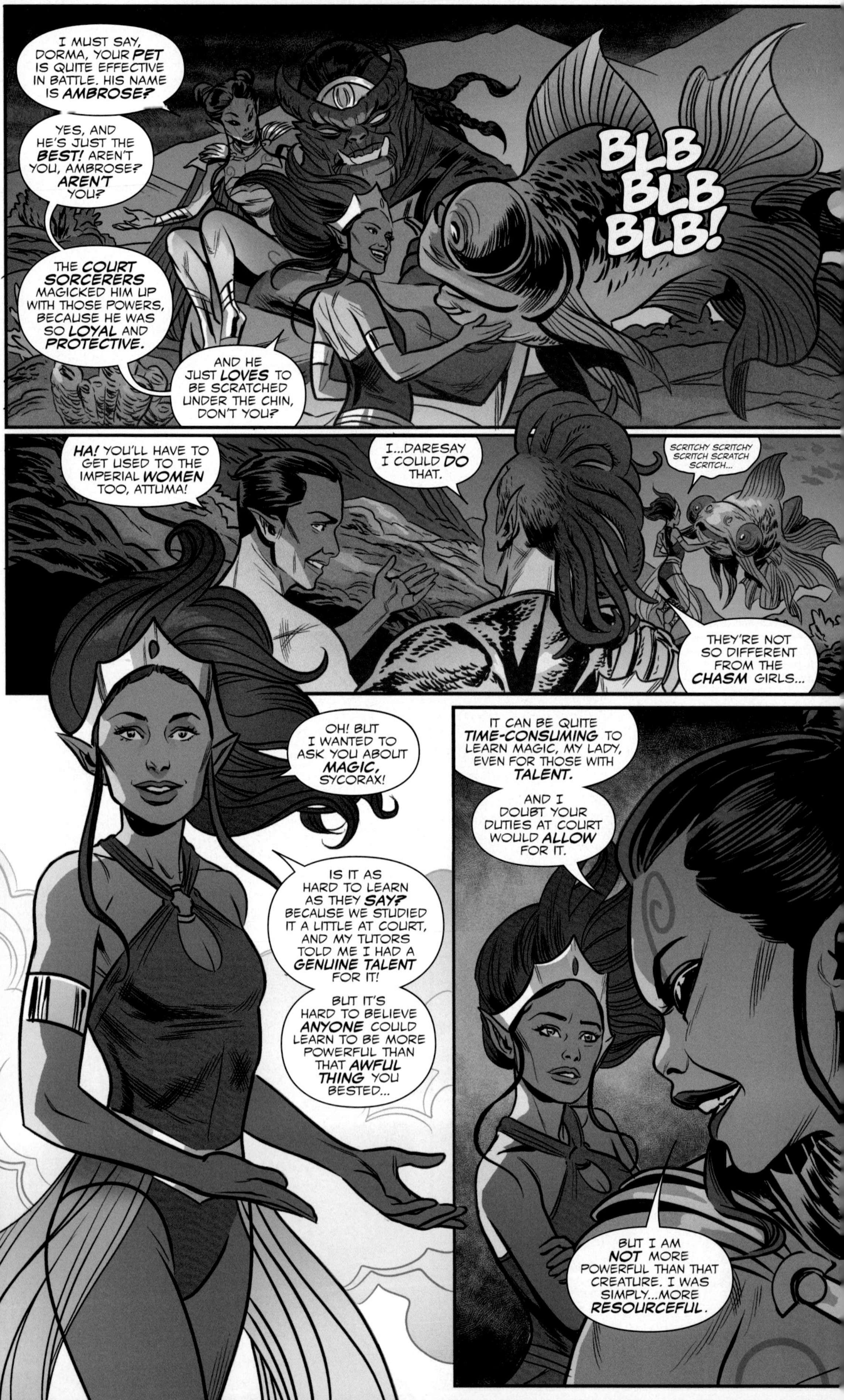
I MUST SAY, DORMA, YOUR PET IS QUITE EFFECTIVE IN BATTLE. HIS NAME IS AMBROSE?
YES, AND HE'S JUST THE BEST! AREN'T YOU, AMBROSE? AREN'T YOU?
THE COURT SORCERERS MAGICKED HIM UP WITH THOSE POWERS, BECAUSE HE WAS SO LOYAL AND PROTECTIVE.
AND HE JUST LOVES TO BE SCRATCHED UNDER THE CHIN, DON'T YOU?
BLB BLB BLB!
HA! YOU'LL HAVE TO GET USED TO THE IMPERIAL WOMEN TOO, ATTUMA!
I...DARESAY I COULD DO THAT.
SCRITCHY SCRITCHY SCRITCH SCRATCH SCRITCH...
THEY'RE NOT SO DIFFERENT FROM THE CHASM GIRLS...
OH! BUT I WANTED TO ASK YOU ABOUT MAGIC, SYCORAX!
IS IT AS HARD TO LEARN AS THEY SAY? BECAUSE WE STUDIED IT A LITTLE AT COURT, AND MY TUTORS TOLD ME I HAD A GENUINE TALENT FOR IT!
BUT IT'S HARD TO BELIEVE ANYONE COULD LEARN TO BE MORE POWERFUL THAN THAT AWFUL THING YOU BESTED...
IT CAN BE QUITE TIME-CONSUMING TO LEARN MAGIC, MY LADY, EVEN FOR THOSE WITH TALENT.
AND I DOUBT YOUR DUTIES AT COURT WOULD ALLOW FOR IT.
BUT I AM NOT MORE POWERFUL THAN THAT CREATURE. I WAS SIMPLY...MORE RESOURCEFUL.

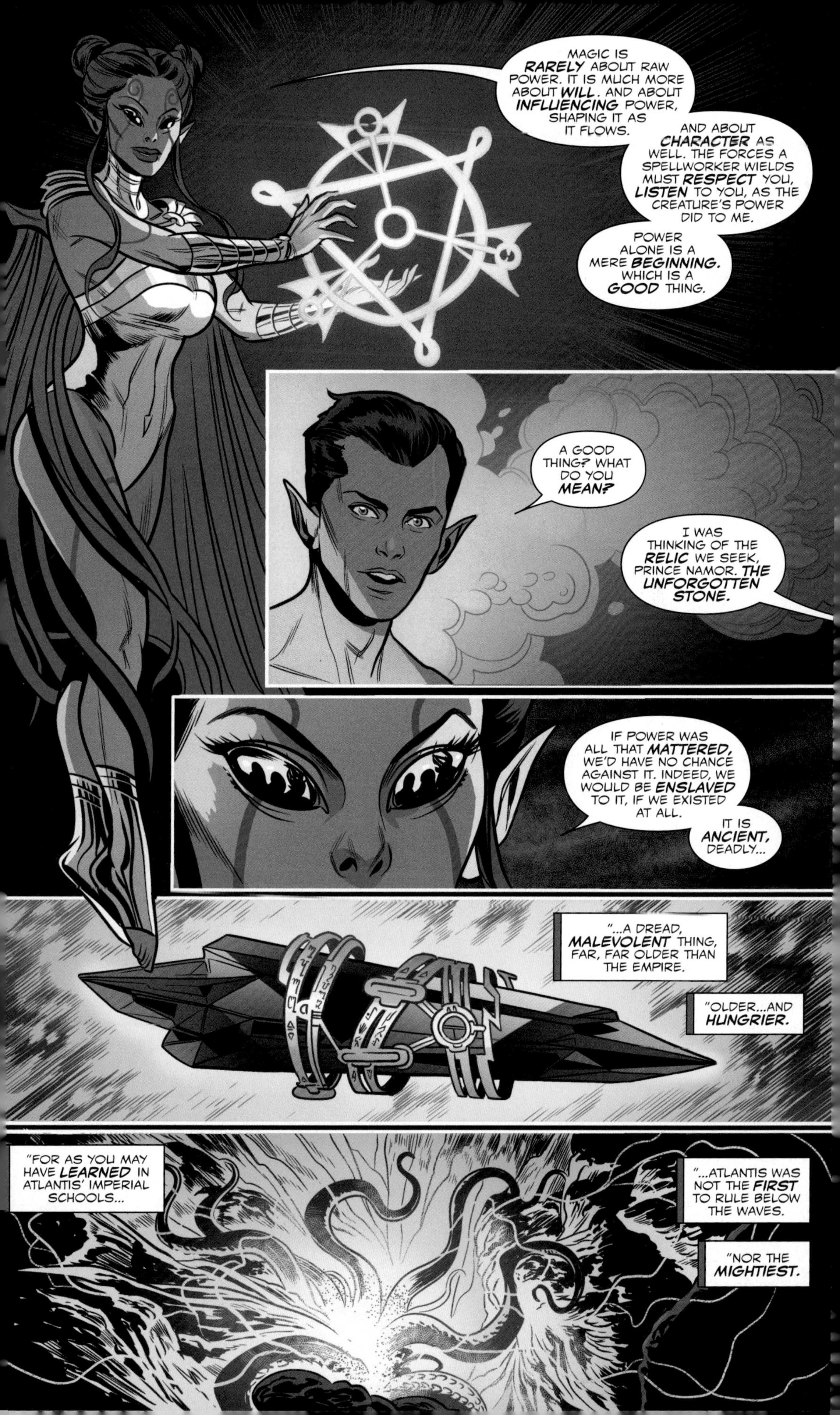
MAGIC IS RARELY ABOUT RAW POWER. IT IS MUCH MORE ABOUT WILL. AND ABOUT INFLUENCING POWER, SHAPING IT AS IT FLOWS.
AND ABOUT CHARACTER AS WELL. THE FORCES A SPELLWORKER WIELDS MUST RESPECT YOU, LISTEN TO YOU, AS THE CREATURE'S POWER DID TO ME.
POWER ALONE IS A MERE BEGINNING. WHICH IS A GOOD THING.
A GOOD THING? WHAT DO YOU MEAN?
I WAS THINKING OF THE RELIC WE SEEK, PRINCE NAMOR. THE UNFORGOTTEN STONE.
IF POWER WAS ALL THAT MATTERED, WE'D HAVE NO CHANCE AGAINST IT. INDEED, WE WOULD BE ENSLAVED TO IT, IF WE EXISTED AT ALL.
IT IS ANCIENT, DEADLY...
"...A DREAD, MALEVOLENT THING, FAR, FAR OLDER THAN THE EMPIRE.
"OLDER...AND HUNGRIER.
"FOR AS YOU MAY HAVE LEARNED IN ATLANTIS' IMPERIAL SCHOOLS...
"...ATLANTIS WAS NOT THE FIRST TO RULE BELOW THE WAVES.
"NOR THE MIGHTIEST.

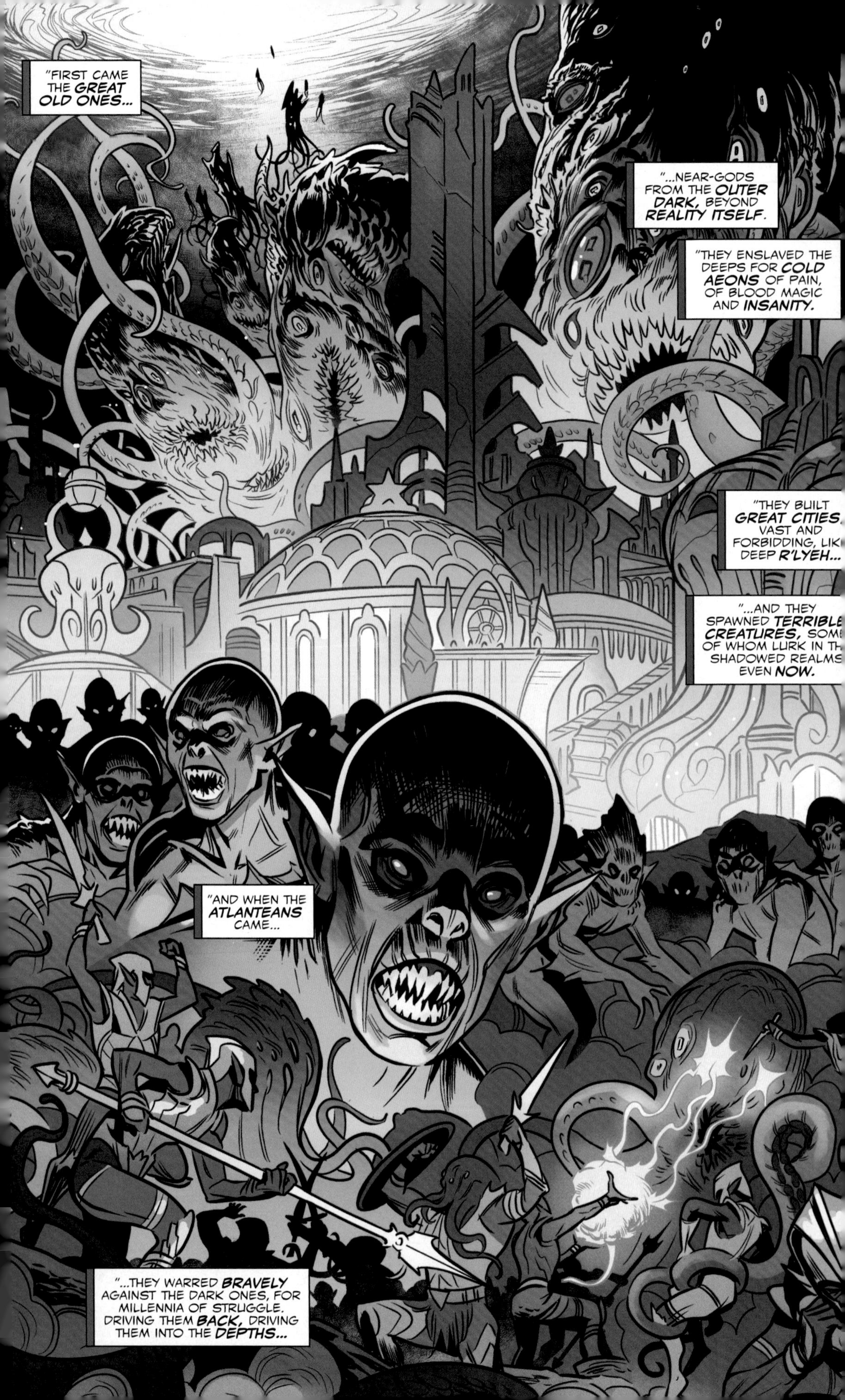
"FIRST CAME THE GREAT OLD ONES...
"...NEAR-GODS FROM THE OUTER DARK, BEYOND REALITY ITSELF.
"THEY ENSLAVED THE DEEPS FOR COLD AEONS OF PAIN, OF BLOOD MAGIC AND INSANITY.
"THEY BUILT GREAT CITIES, VAST AND FORBIDDING, LIKE DEEP R'LYEH...
"...AND THEY SPAWNED TERRIBLE CREATURES, SOME OF WHOM LURK IN THE SHADOWED REALMS EVEN NOW.
"AND WHEN THE ATLANTEANS CAME...
"...THEY WARRED BRAVELY AGAINST THE DARK ONES, FOR MILLENNIA OF STRUGGLE. DRIVING THEM BACK, DRIVING THEM INTO THE DEPTHS...

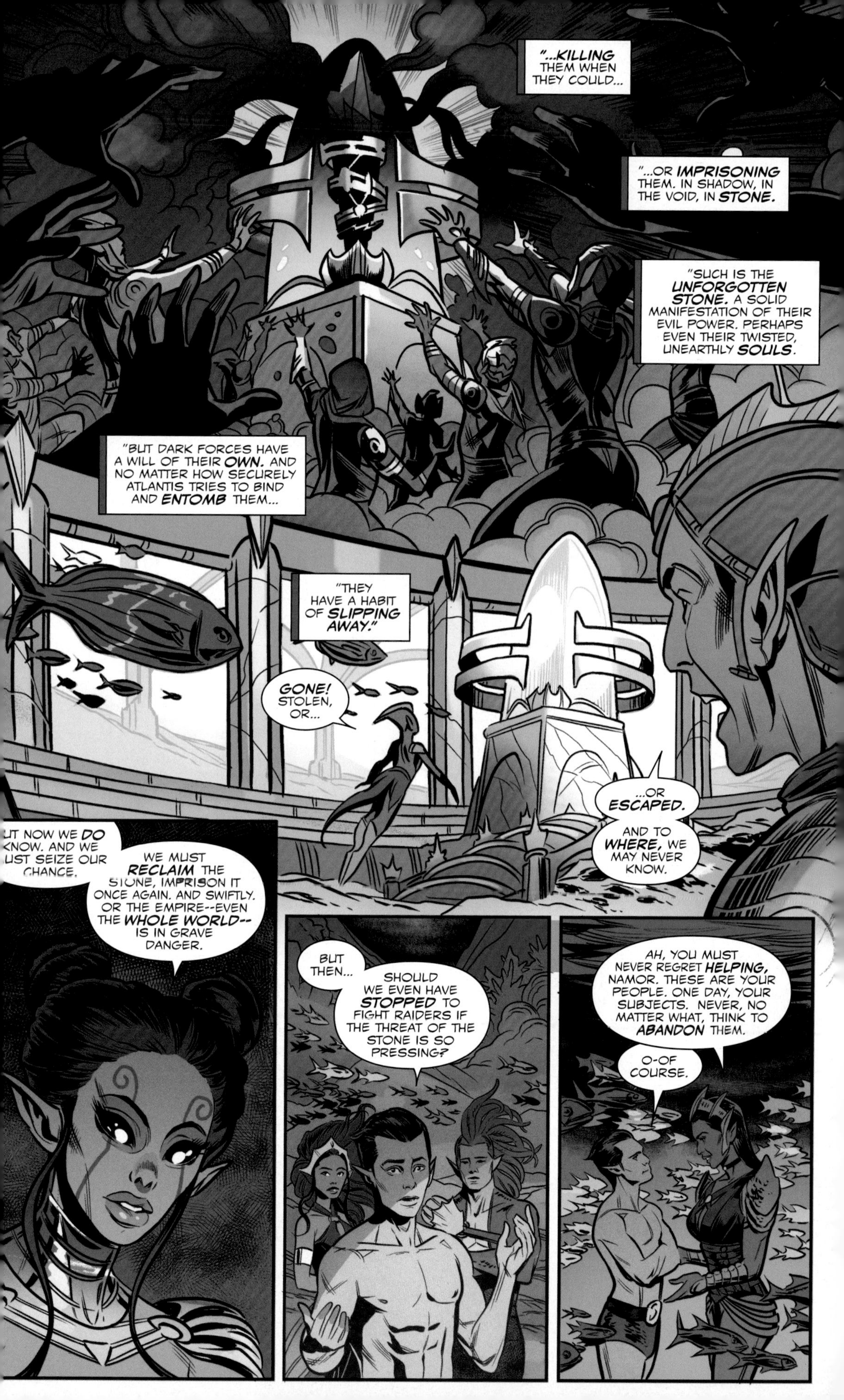
"...KILLING THEM WHEN THEY COULD...
"...OR IMPRISONING THEM. IN SHADOW, IN THE VOID, IN STONE.
"SUCH IS THE UNFORGOTTEN STONE. A SOLID MANIFESTATION OF THEIR EVIL POWER. PERHAPS EVEN THEIR TWISTED, UNEARTHLY SOULS.
"BUT DARK FORCES HAVE A WILL OF THEIR OWN. AND NO MATTER HOW SECURELY ATLANTIS TRIES TO BIND AND ENTOMB THEM...
"THEY HAVE A HABIT OF SLIPPING AWAY."
GONE! STOLEN, OR...
...OR ESCAPED.
AND TO WHERE, WE MAY NEVER KNOW.
UT NOW WE DO KNOW. AND WE UST SEIZE OUR CHANCE.
WE MUST RECLAIM THE STONE, IMPRISON IT ONCE AGAIN. AND SWIFTLY. OR THE EMPIRE--EVEN THE WHOLE WORLD--IS IN GRAVE DANGER.
BUT THEN...
SHOULD WE EVEN HAVE STOPPED TO FIGHT RAIDERS IF THE THREAT OF THE STONE IS SO PRESSING?
AH, YOU MUST NEVER REGRET HELPING, NAMOR. THESE ARE YOUR PEOPLE. ONE DAY, YOUR SUBJECTS. NEVER, NO MATTER WHAT, THINK TO ABANDON THEM.
O-OF COURSE.

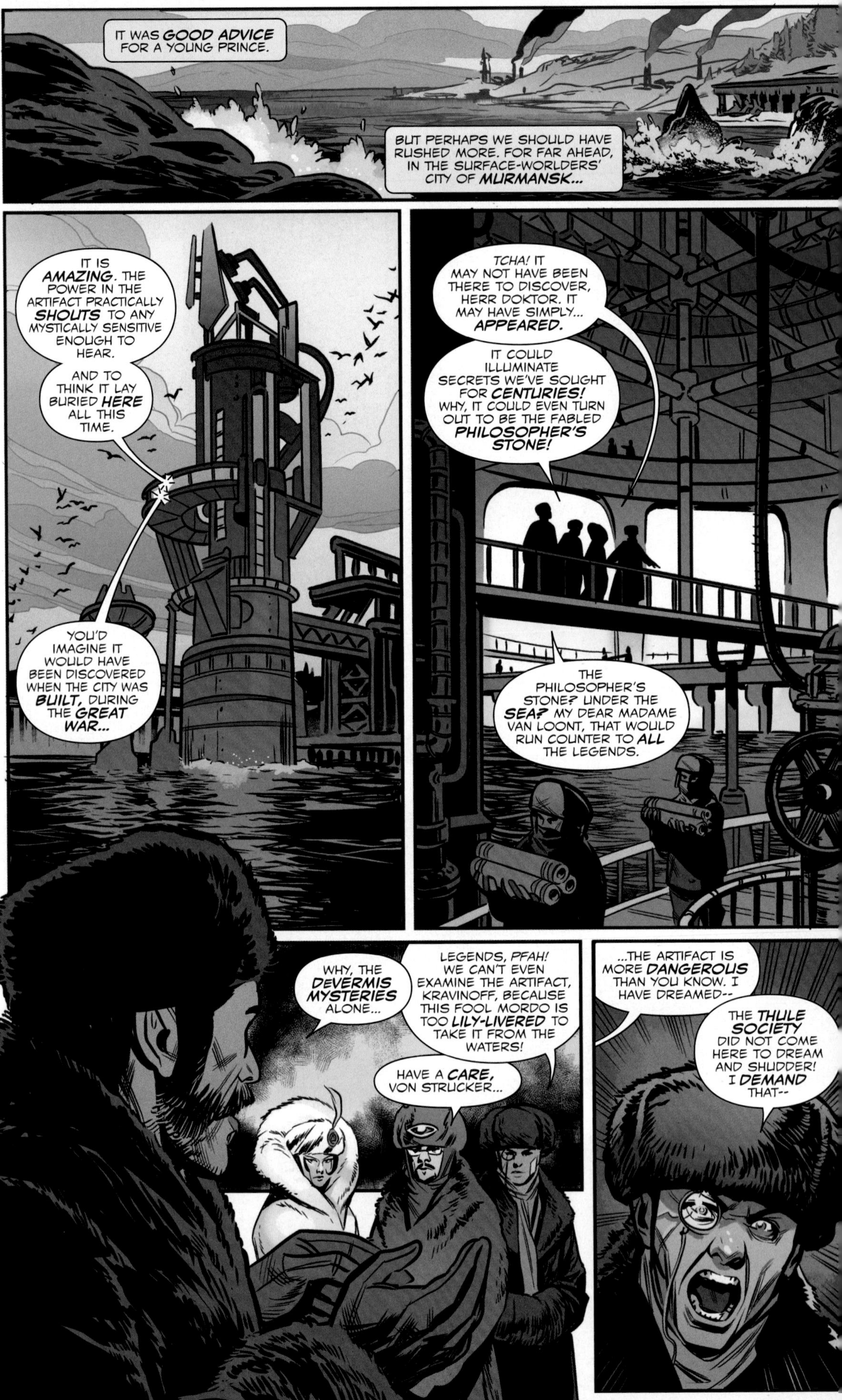
IT WAS GOOD ADVICE FOR A YOUNG PRINCE.
BUT PERHAPS WE SHOULD HAVE RUSHED MORE. FOR FAR AHEAD, IN THE SURFACE-WORLDERS' CITY OF MURMANSK...
IT IS AMAZING. THE POWER IN THE ARTIFACT PRACTICALLY SHOUTS TO ANY MYSTICALLY SENSITIVE ENOUGH TO HEAR.
AND TO THINK IT LAY BURIED HERE ALL THIS TIME.
YOU'D IMAGINE IT WOULD HAVE BEEN DISCOVERED WHEN THE CITY WAS BUILT, DURING THE GREAT WAR...
TCHA! IT MAY NOT HAVE BEEN THERE TO DISCOVER, HERR DOKTOR. IT MAY HAVE SIMPLY... APPEARED.
IT COULD ILLUMINATE SECRETS WE'VE SOUGHT FOR CENTURIES! WHY, IT COULD EVEN TURN OUT TO BE THE FABLED PHILOSOPHER'S STONE!
THE PHILOSOPHER'S STONE? UNDER THE SEA? MY DEAR MADAME VAN LOONT, THAT WOULD RUN COUNTER TO ALL THE LEGENDS.
WHY, THE DEVERMIS MYSTERIES ALONE...
LEGENDS, PFAH! WE CAN'T EVEN EXAMINE THE ARTIFACT, KRAVINOFF, BECAUSE THIS FOOL MORDO IS TOO LILY-LIVERED TO TAKE IT FROM THE WATERS!
HAVE A CARE, VON STRUCKER...
...THE ARTIFACT IS MORE DANGEROUS THAN YOU KNOW. I HAVE DREAMED--
THE THULE SOCIETY DID NOT COME HERE TO DREAM AND SHUDDER! I DEMAND THAT--

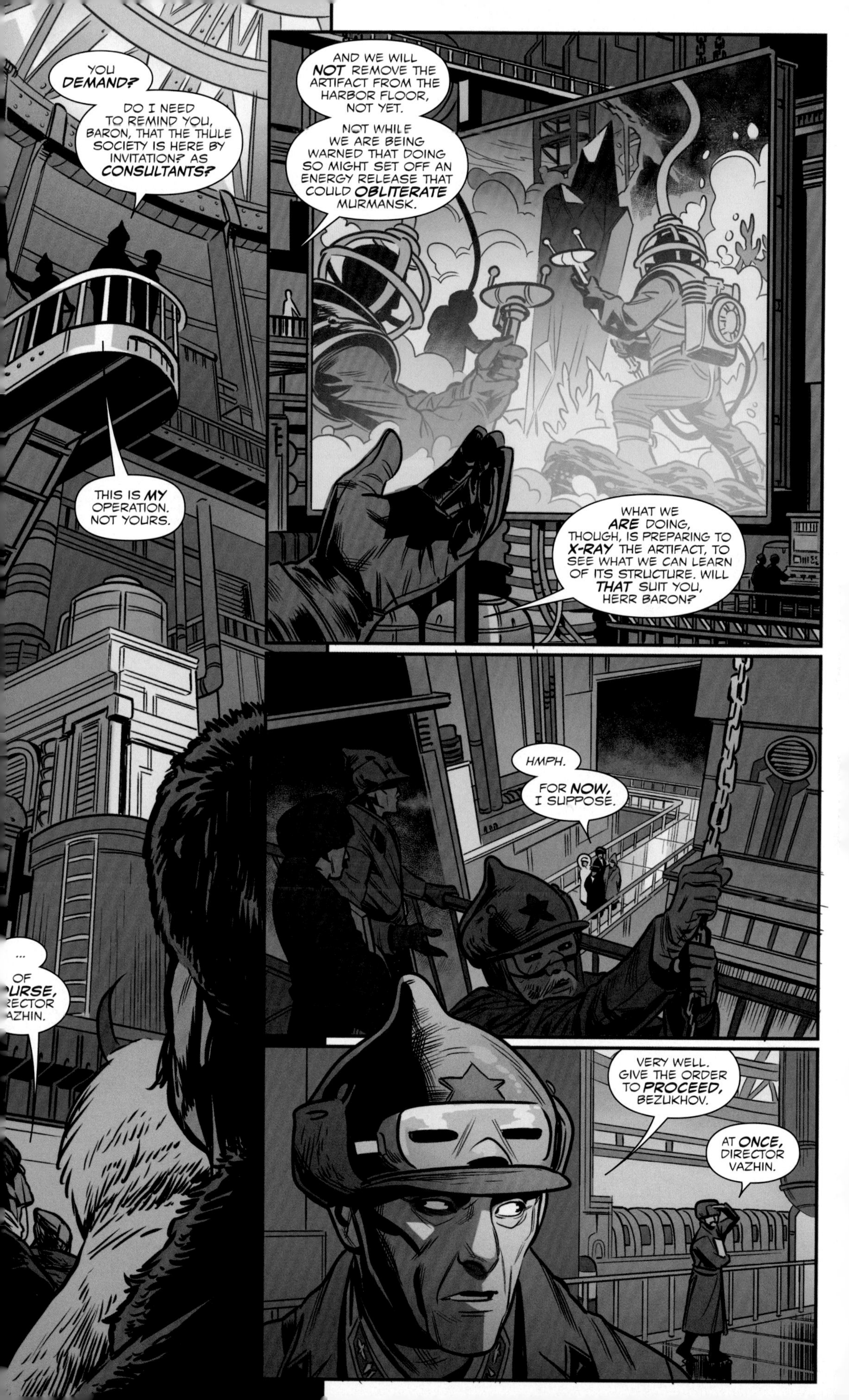
YOU DEMAND?
DO I NEED TO REMIND YOU, BARON, THAT THE THULE SOCIETY IS HERE BY INVITATION? AS CONSULTANTS?
THIS IS MY OPERATION. NOT YOURS.
AND WE WILL NOT REMOVE THE ARTIFACT FROM THE HARBOR FLOOR, NOT YET.
NOT WHILE WE ARE BEING WARNED THAT DOING SO MIGHT SET OFF AN ENERGY RELEASE THAT COULD OBLITERATE MURMANSK.
WHAT WE ARE DOING, THOUGH, IS PREPARING TO X-RAY THE ARTIFACT, TO SEE WHAT WE CAN LEARN OF ITS STRUCTURE. WILL THAT SUIT YOU, HERR BARON?
HMPH.
FOR NOW, I SUPPOSE.
...
OF
URSE,
RECTOR
AZHIN.
VERY WELL. GIVE THE ORDER TO PROCEED, BEZUKHOV.
AT ONCE, DIRECTOR VAZHIN.

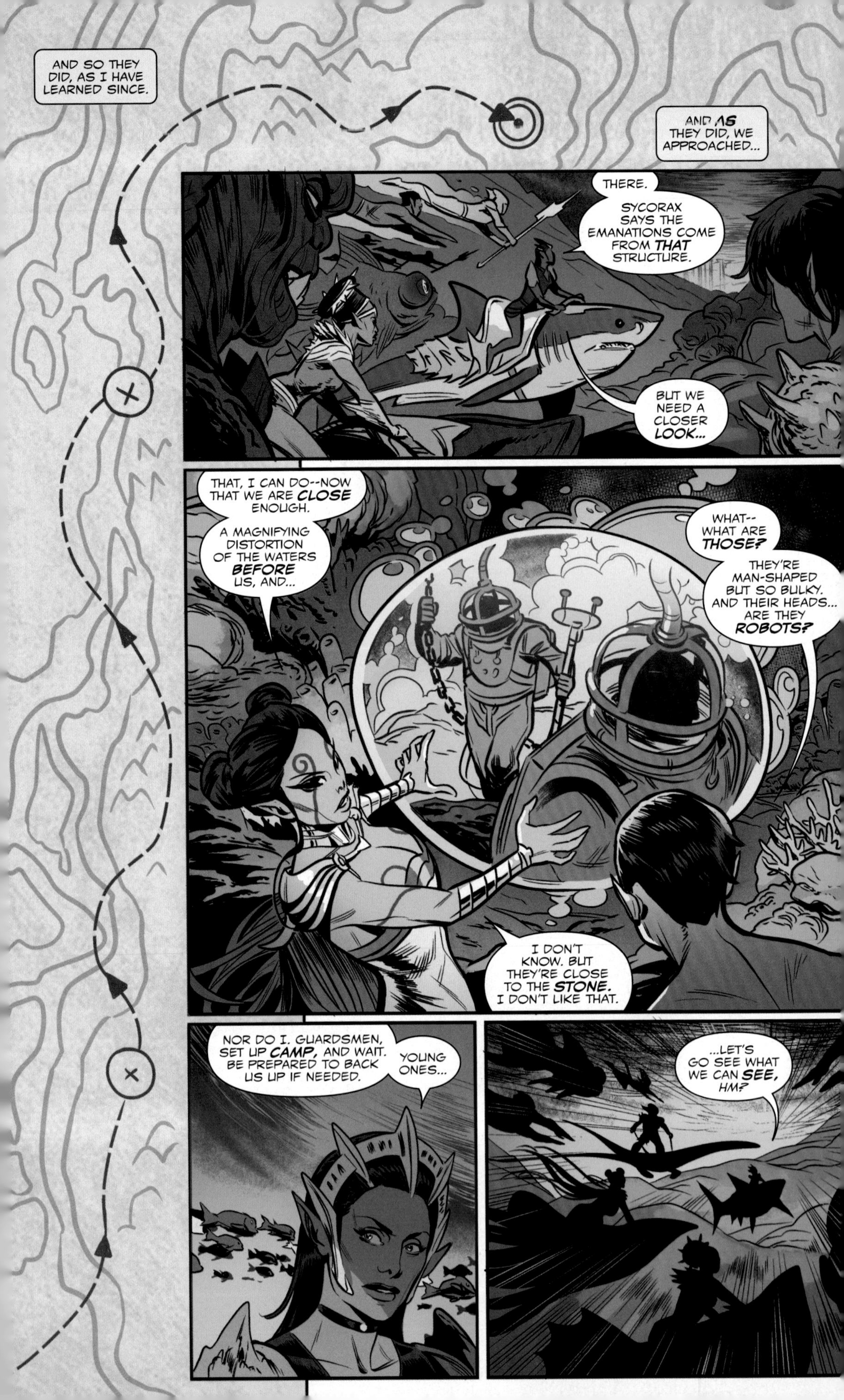
AND SO THEY DID, AS I HAVE LEARNED SINCE.
AND AS THEY DID, WE APPROACHED...
THERE.
SYCORAX SAYS THE EMANATIONS COME FROM THAT STRUCTURE.
BUT WE NEED A CLOSER LOOK...
THAT, I CAN DO--NOW THAT WE ARE CLOSE ENOUGH.
A MAGNIFYING DISTORTION OF THE WATERS BEFORE US, AND...
WHAT-- WHAT ARE THOSE?
THEY'RE MAN-SHAPED BUT SO BULKY. AND THEIR HEADS... ARE THEY ROBOTS?
I DON'T KNOW. BUT THEY'RE CLOSE TO THE STONE. I DON'T LIKE THAT.
NOR DO I. GUARDSMEN, SET UP CAMP, AND WAIT. BE PREPARED TO BACK US UP IF NEEDED.
YOUNG ONES...
...LET'S GO SEE WHAT WE CAN SEE, HM?

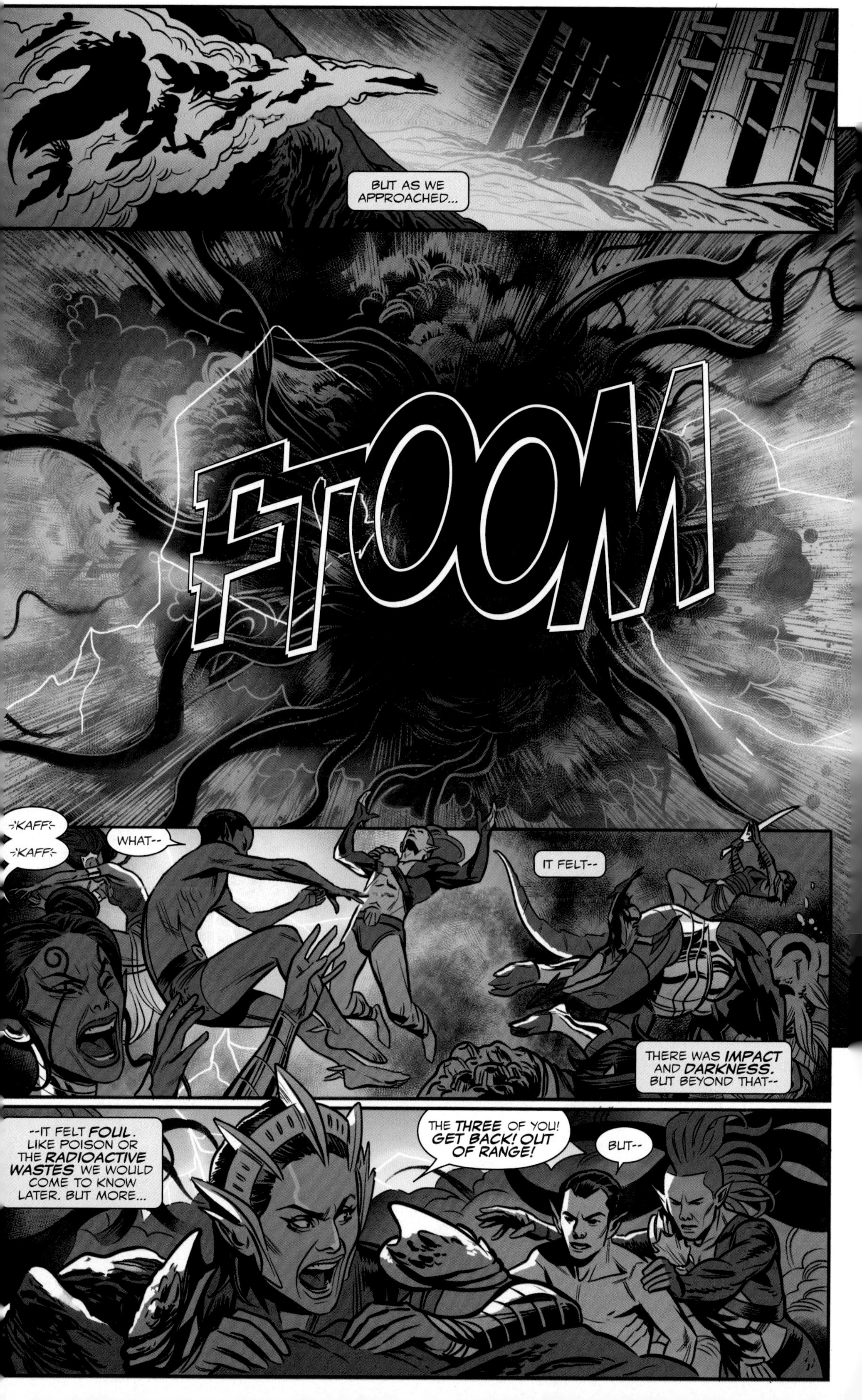

BUT AS WE APPROACHED...
FTOOM
-KAFF-
-KAFF-
WHAT--
IT FELT--
THERE WAS IMPACT AND DARKNESS. BUT BEYOND THAT--
--IT FELT FOUL. LIKE POISON OR THE RADIOACTIVE WASTES WE WOULD COME TO KNOW LATER. BUT MORE...
THE THREE OF YOU! GET BACK! OUT OF RANGE!
BUT--

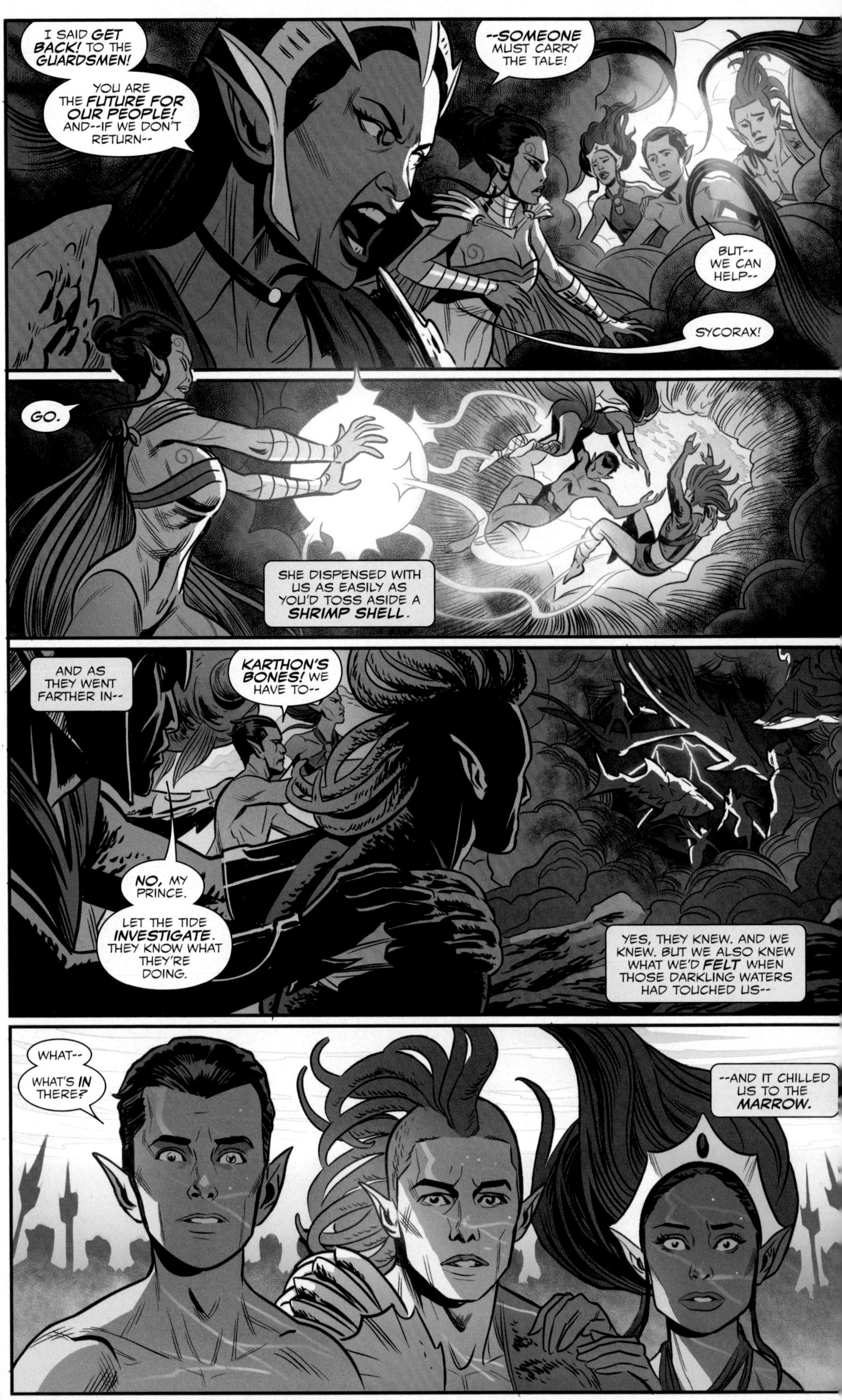
I SAID GET BACK! TO THE GUARDSMEN!
YOU ARE THE FUTURE FOR OUR PEOPLE! AND--IF WE DON'T RETURN--
--SOMEONE MUST CARRY THE TALE!
BUT-- WE CAN HELP--
SYCORAX!
GO.
SHE DISPENSED WITH US AS EASILY AS YOU'D TOSS ASIDE A SHRIMP SHELL.
AND AS THEY WENT FARTHER IN--
KARTHON'S BONES! WE HAVE TO--
NO, MY PRINCE.
LET THE TIDE INVESTIGATE. THEY KNOW WHAT THEY'RE DOING.
YES, THEY KNEW. AND WE KNEW. BUT WE ALSO KNEW WHAT WE'D FELT WHEN THOSE DARKLING WATERS HAD TOUCHED US--
WHAT--
WHAT'S IN THERE?
--AND IT CHILLED US TO THE MARROW.

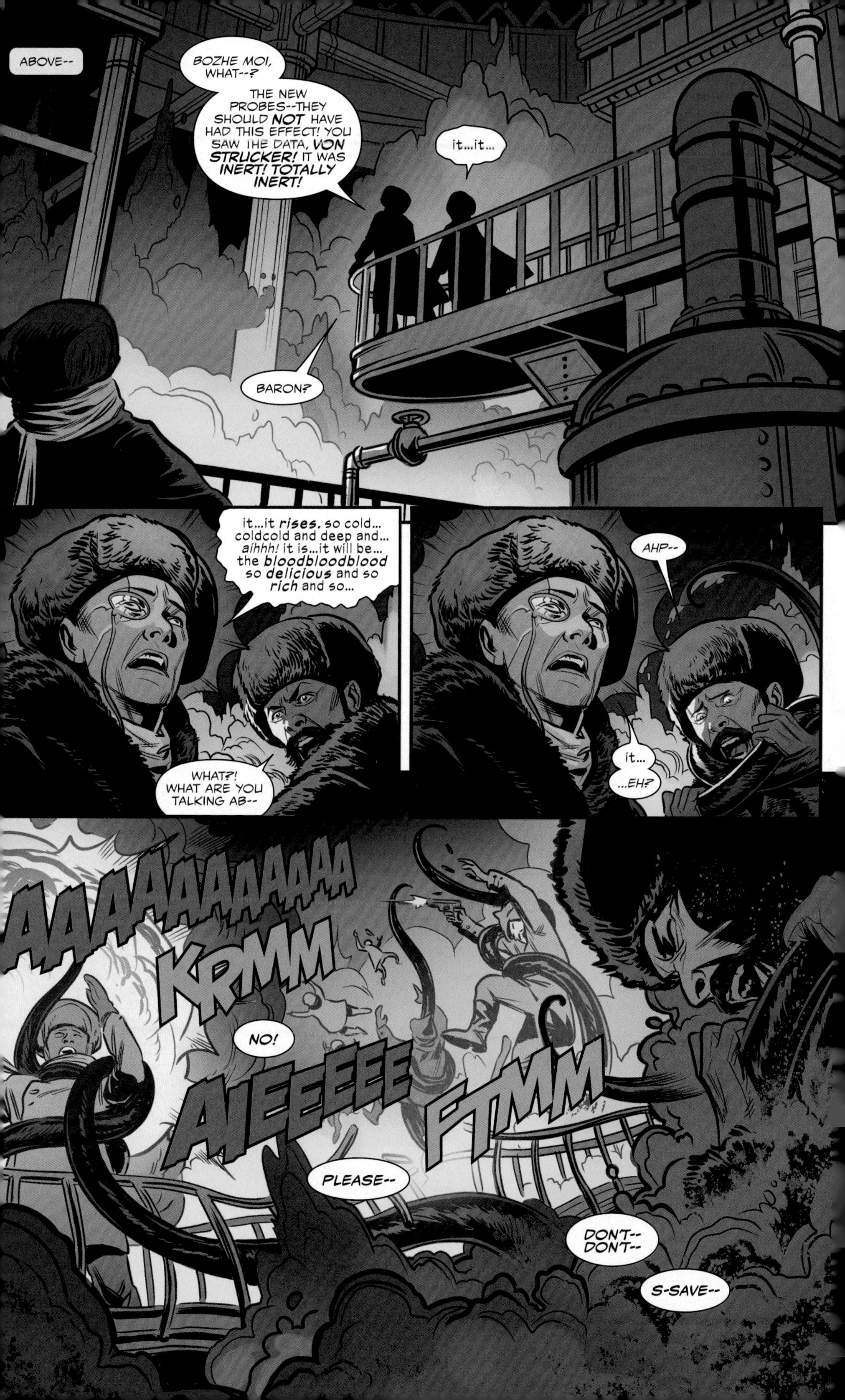
ABOVE--
BOZHE MOI, WHAT--?
THE NEW PROBES--THEY SHOULD NOT HAVE HAD THIS EFFECT! YOU SAW THE DATA, VON STRUCKER! IT WAS INERT! TOTALLY INERT!
it...it...
BARON?
it...it rises. so cold... coldcold and deep and... aihhh! it is...it will be... the bloodbloodblood so delicious and so rich and so...
WHAT?! WHAT ARE YOU TALKING AB--
AHP--
it...
...EH?
AAAAAAAAA
KRMM
NO!
AIEEEEE
FTMM
PLEASE--
DON'T-- DON'T--
S-SAVE--

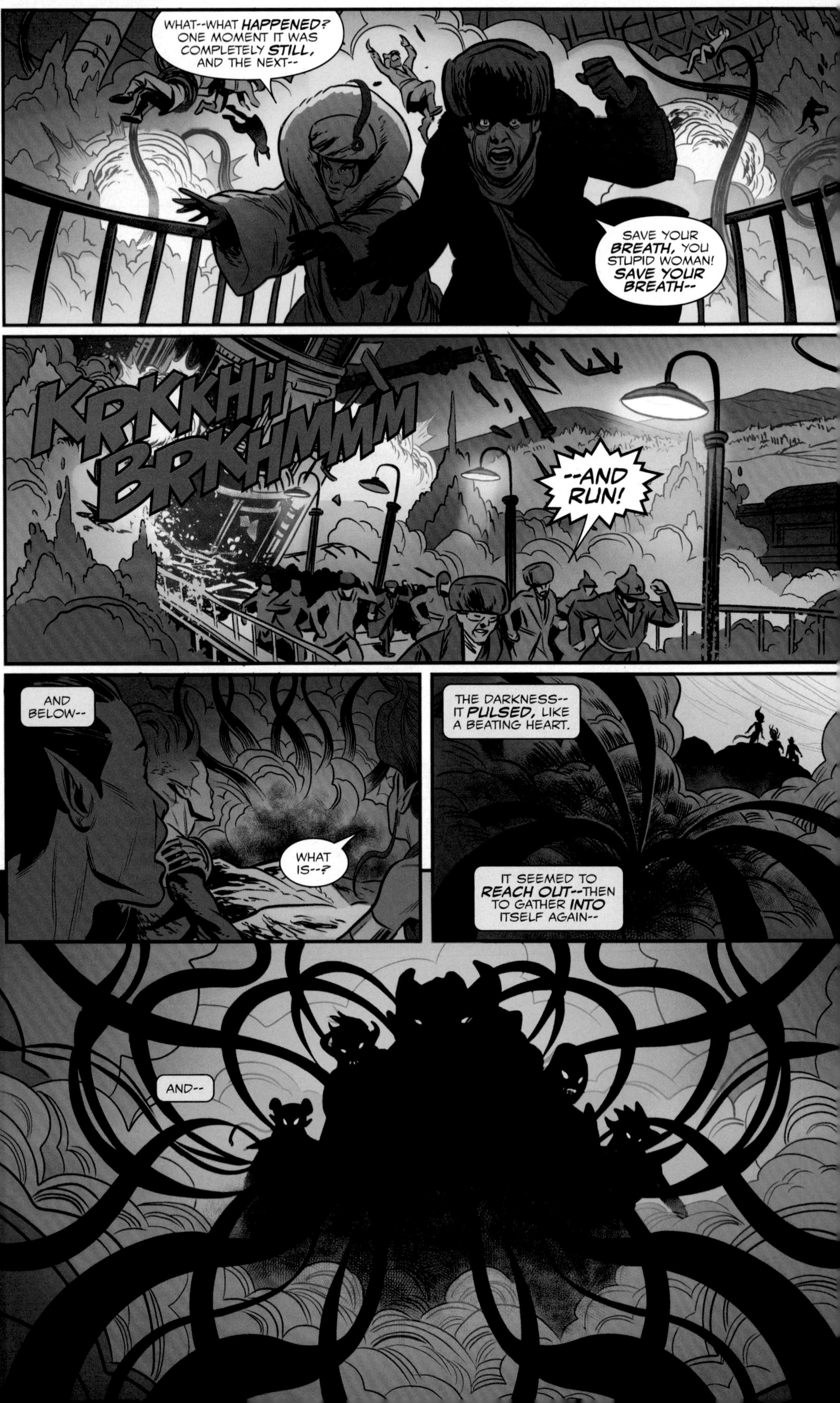
WHAT--WHAT HAPPENED? ONE MOMENT IT WAS COMPLETELY STILL, AND THE NEXT--
SAVE YOUR BREATH, YOU STUPID WOMAN! SAVE YOUR BREATH--
KRKKHH BRKHMMM
--AND RUN!
AND BELOW--
WHAT IS--?
THE DARKNESS-- IT PULSED, LIKE A BEATING HEART.
IT SEEMED TO REACH OUT--THEN TO GATHER INTO ITSELF AGAIN--
AND--

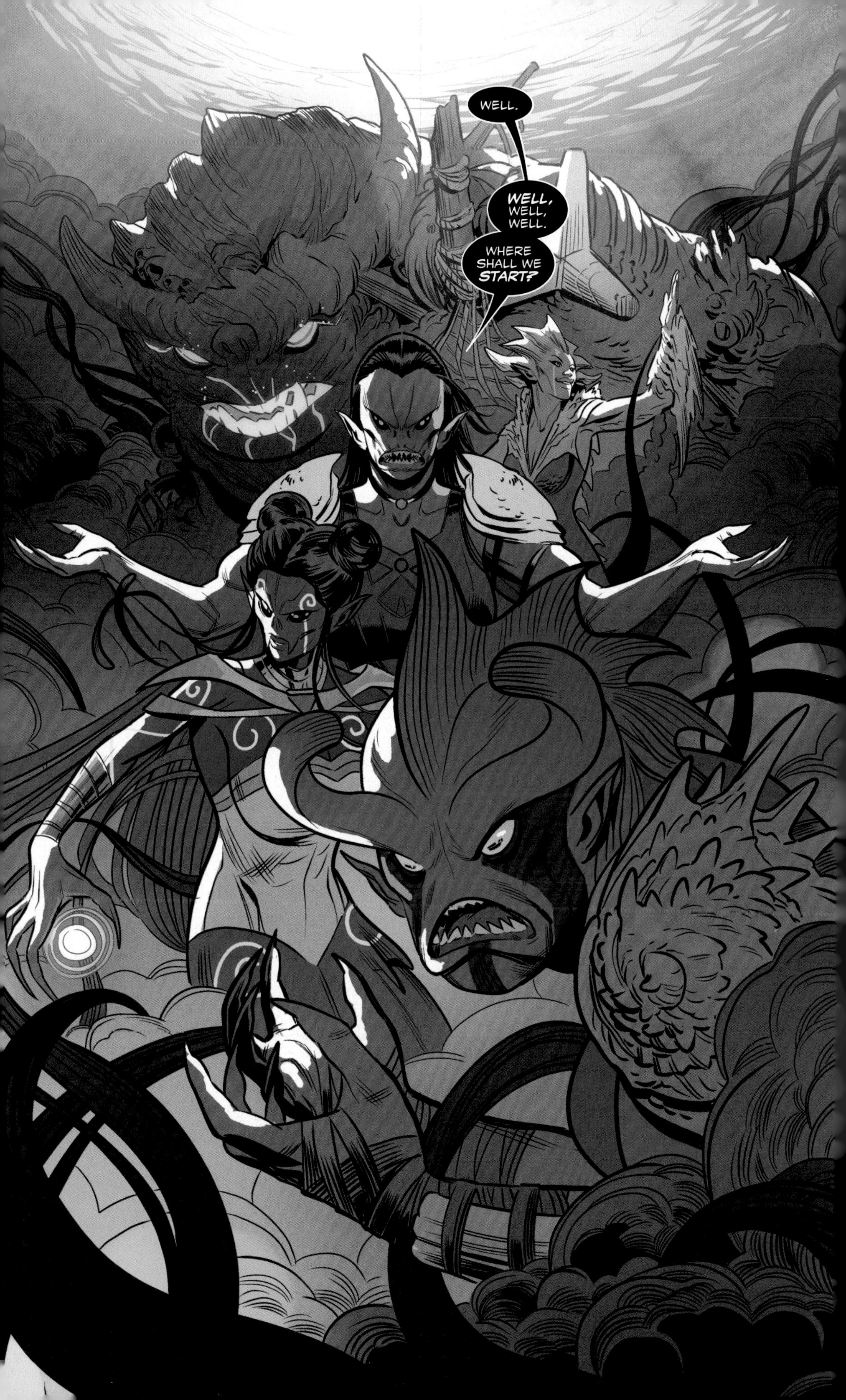
WELL.
WELL, WELL, WELL.
WHERE SHALL WE START?

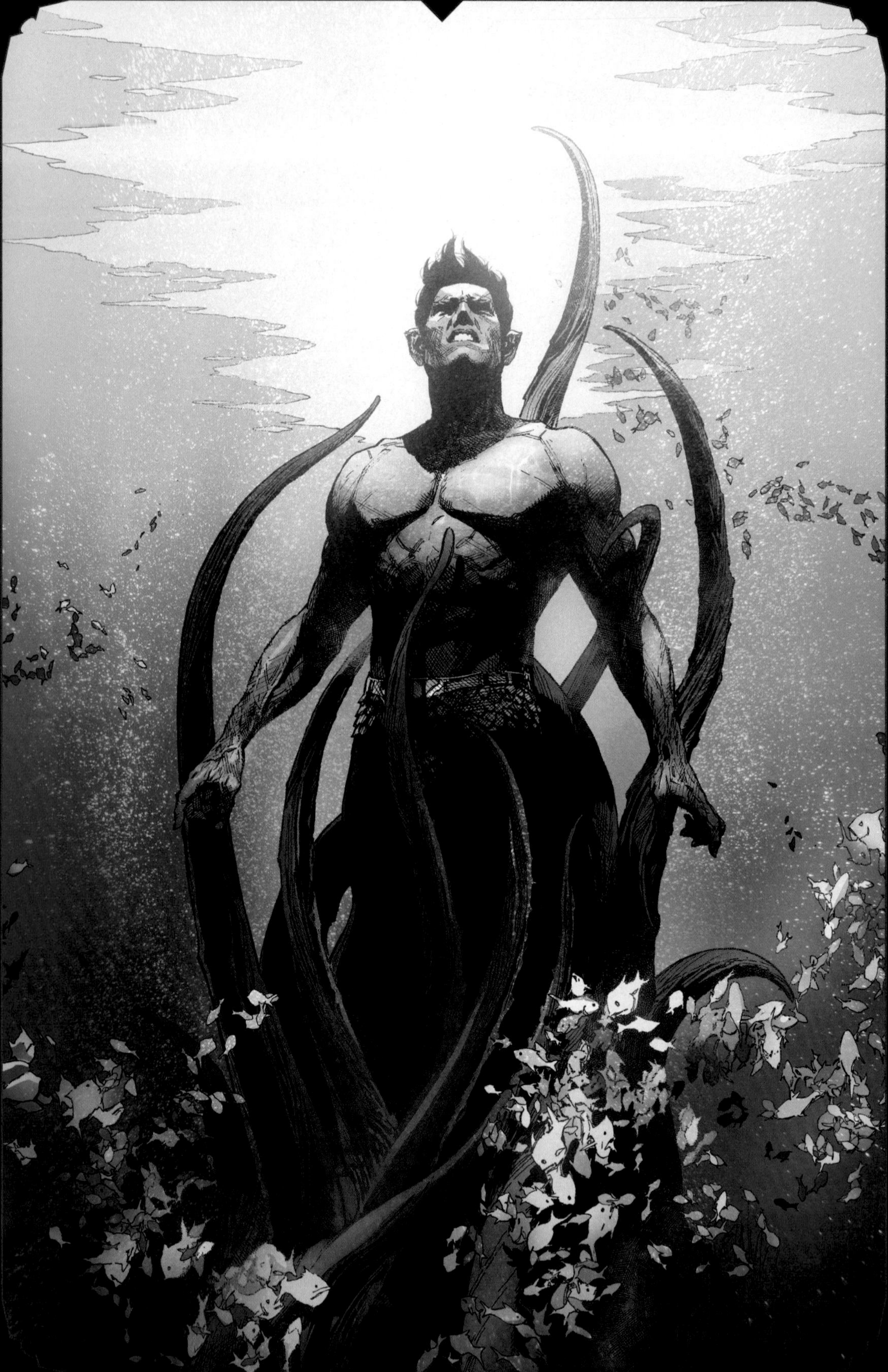

THE TIDE IS TURNED

3

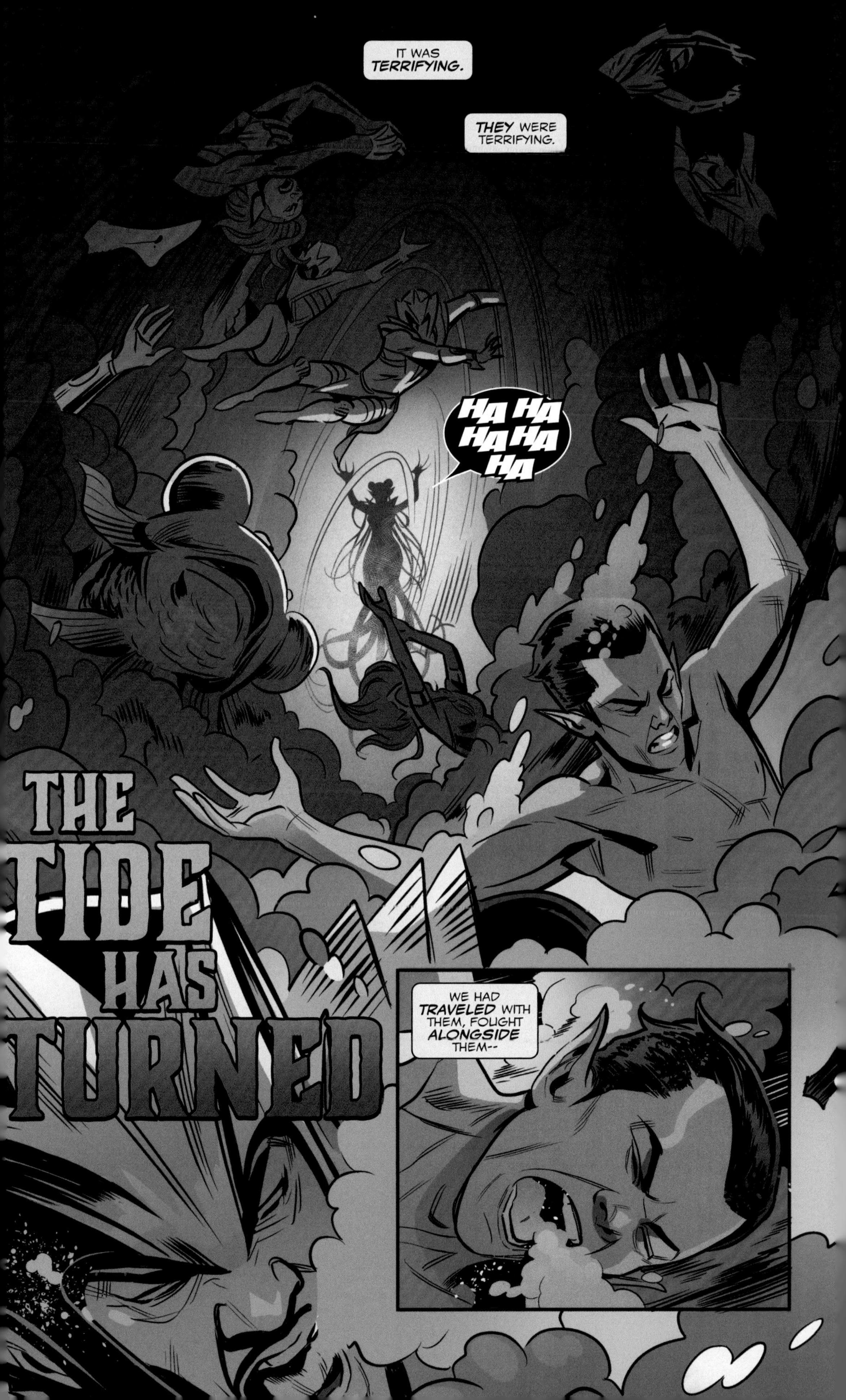
IT WAS TERRIFYING.
THEY WERE TERRIFYING.
HA HA HA HA HA
THE TIDE HAS TURNED
WE HAD TRAVELED WITH THEM, FOUGHT ALONGSIDE THEM--

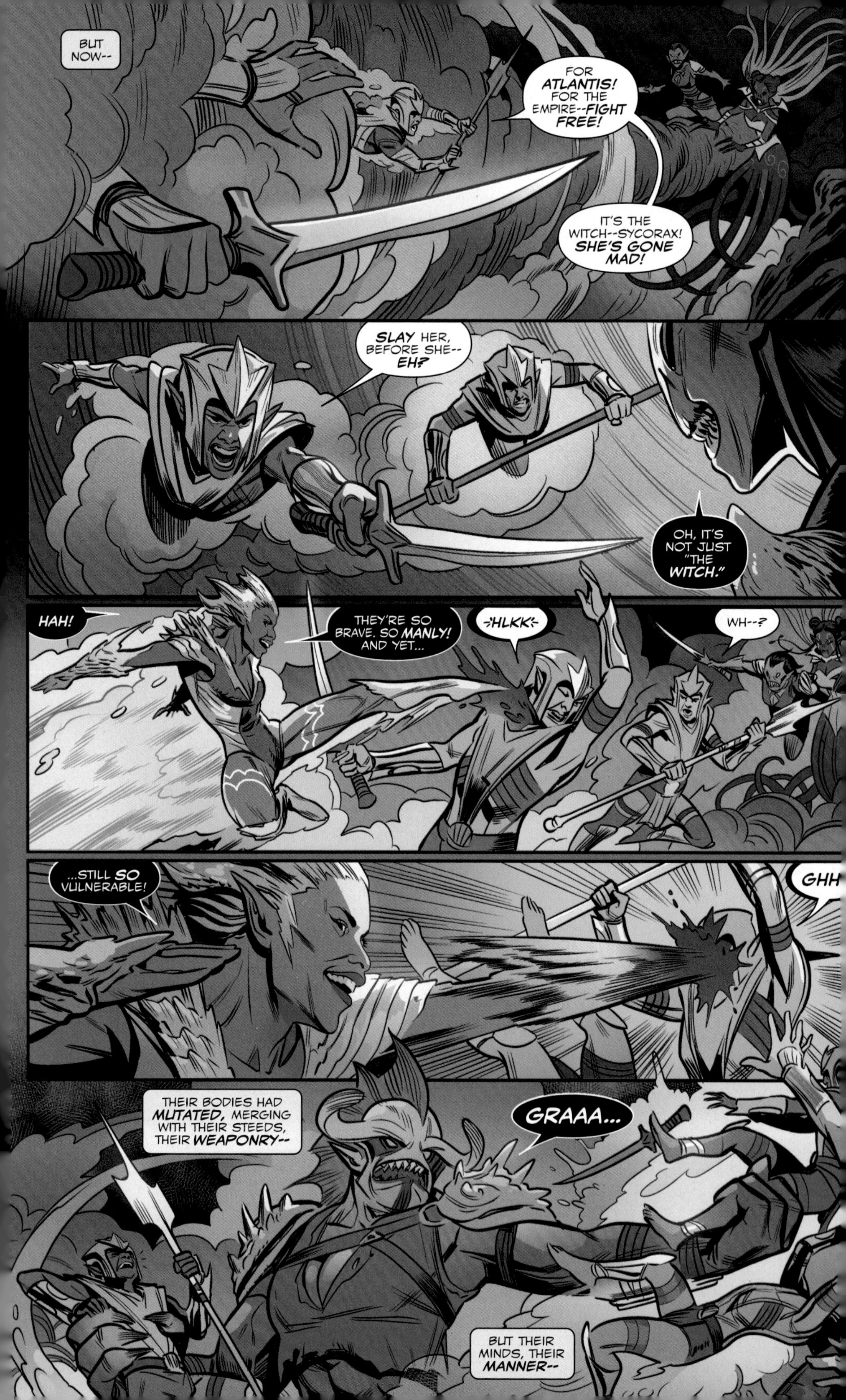
BUT NOW--
FOR ATLANTIS! FOR THE EMPIRE--FIGHT FREE!
IT'S THE WITCH--SYCORAX! SHE'S GONE MAD!
SLAY HER, BEFORE SHE-- EH?
OH, IT'S NOT JUST "THE WITCH."
HAH!
THEY'RE SO BRAVE. SO MANLY! AND YET...
HLKK
WH--?
...STILL SO VULNERABLE!
GHH
THEIR BODIES HAD MUTATED, MERGING WITH THEIR STEEDS, THEIR WEAPONRY--
GRAAA...
BUT THEIR MINDS, THEIR MANNER--

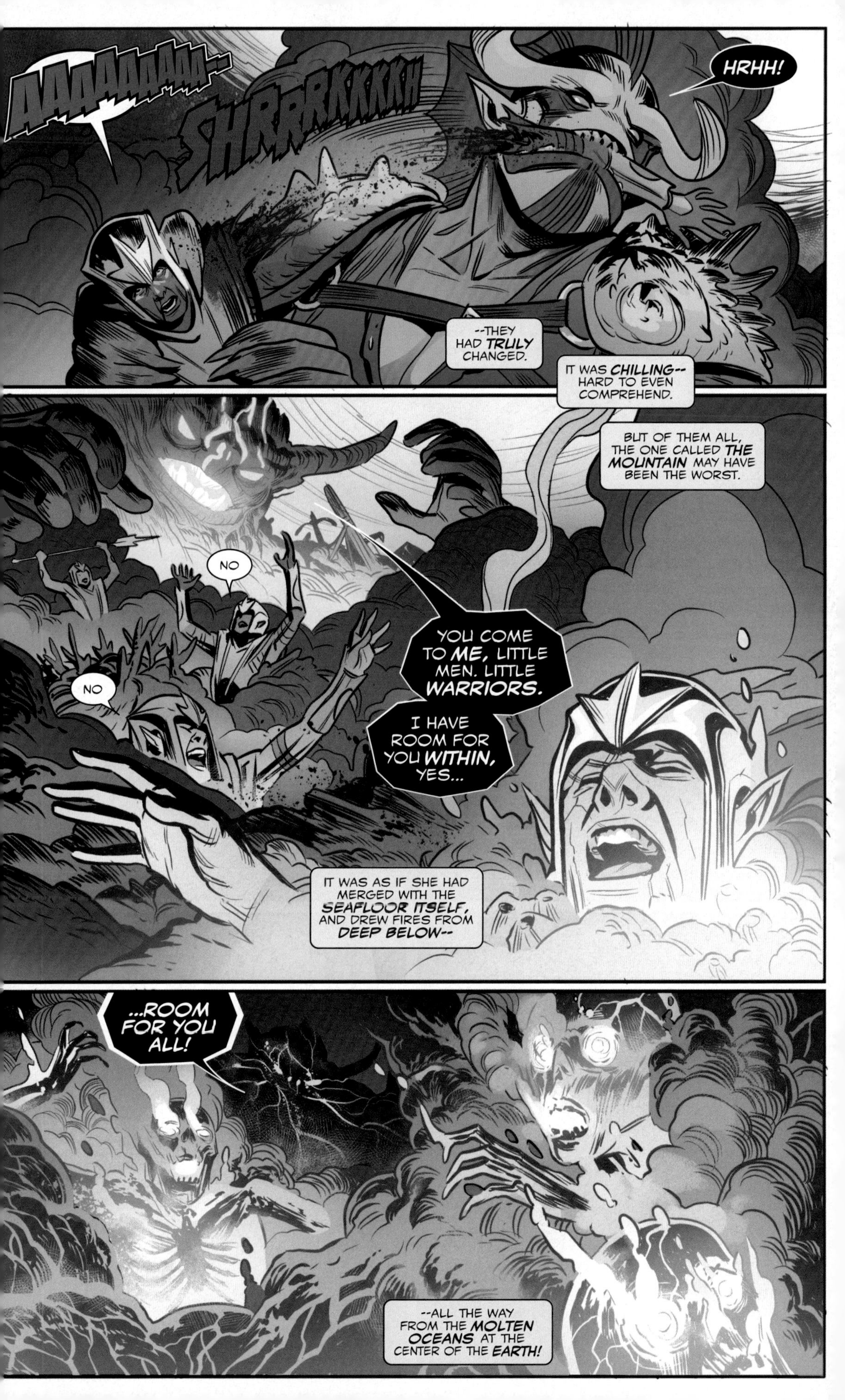
AAAAAAAA--
SHRRRKKKKH
HRHH!
--THEY HAD TRULY CHANGED.
IT WAS CHILLING-- HARD TO EVEN COMPREHEND.
BUT OF THEM ALL, THE ONE CALLED THE MOUNTAIN MAY HAVE BEEN THE WORST.
NO
NO
YOU COME TO ME, LITTLE MEN. LITTLE WARRIORS.
I HAVE ROOM FOR YOU WITHIN, YES...
IT WAS AS IF SHE HAD MERGED WITH THE SEAFLOOR ITSELF, AND DREW FIRES FROM DEEP BELOW--
...ROOM FOR YOU ALL!
--ALL THE WAY FROM THE MOLTEN OCEANS AT THE CENTER OF THE EARTH!

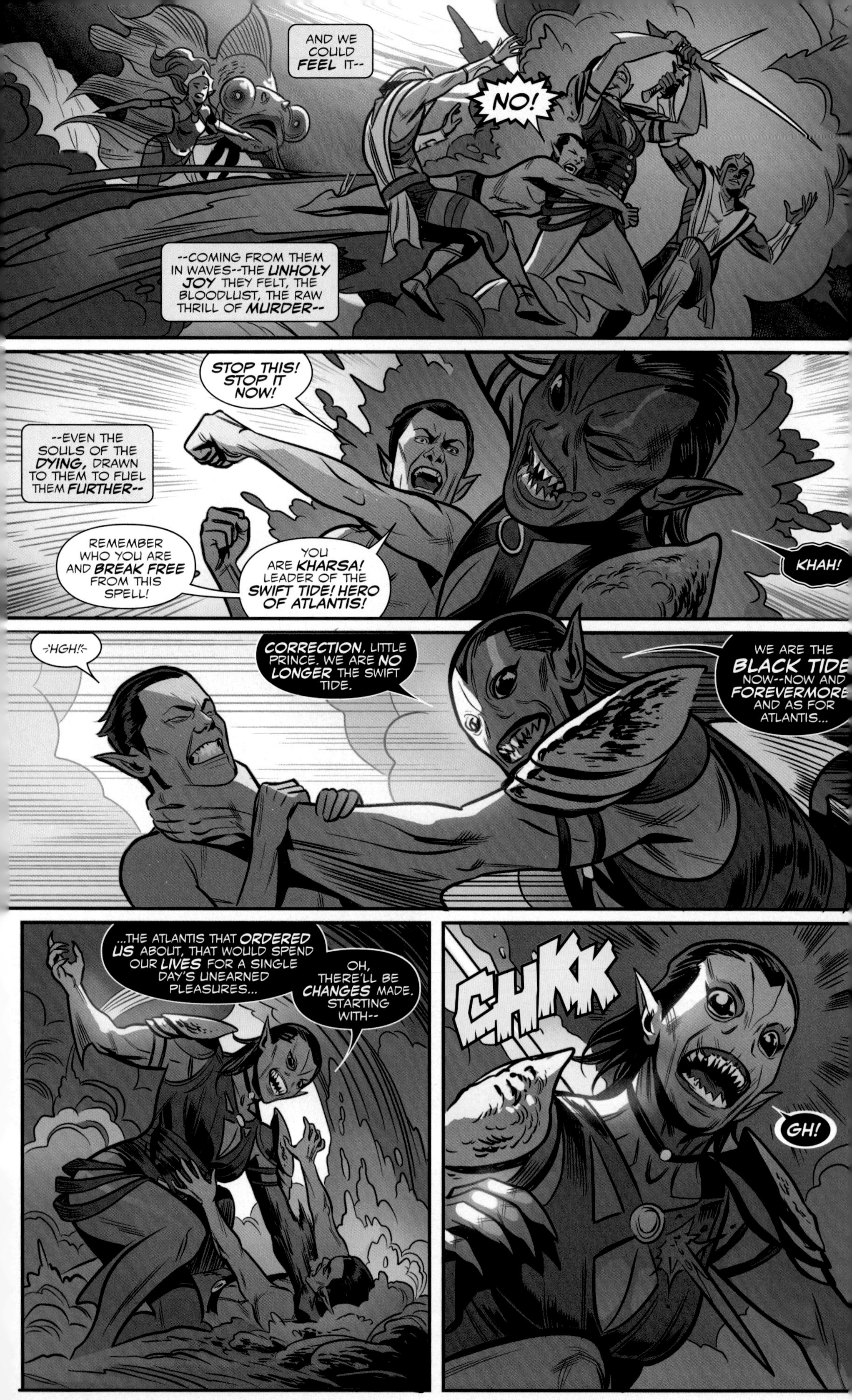

AND WE COULD FEEL IT--
NO!
--COMING FROM THEM IN WAVES--THE UNHOLY JOY THEY FELT, THE BLOODLUST, THE RAW THRILL OF MURDER--
STOP THIS! STOP IT NOW!
--EVEN THE SOULS OF THE DYING, DRAWN TO THEM TO FUEL THEM FURTHER--
REMEMBER WHO YOU ARE AND BREAK FREE FROM THIS SPELL!
YOU ARE KHARSA! LEADER OF THE SWIFT TIDE! HERO OF ATLANTIS!
KHAH!
HGH!
CORRECTION, LITTLE PRINCE. WE ARE NO LONGER THE SWIFT TIDE.
WE ARE THE BLACK TIDE NOW--NOW AND FOREVERMORE AND AS FOR ATLANTIS...
...THE ATLANTIS THAT ORDERED US ABOUT, THAT WOULD SPEND OUR LIVES FOR A SINGLE DAY'S UNEARNED PLEASURES...
OH, THERE'LL BE CHANGES MADE. STARTING WITH--
CHKK
GH!

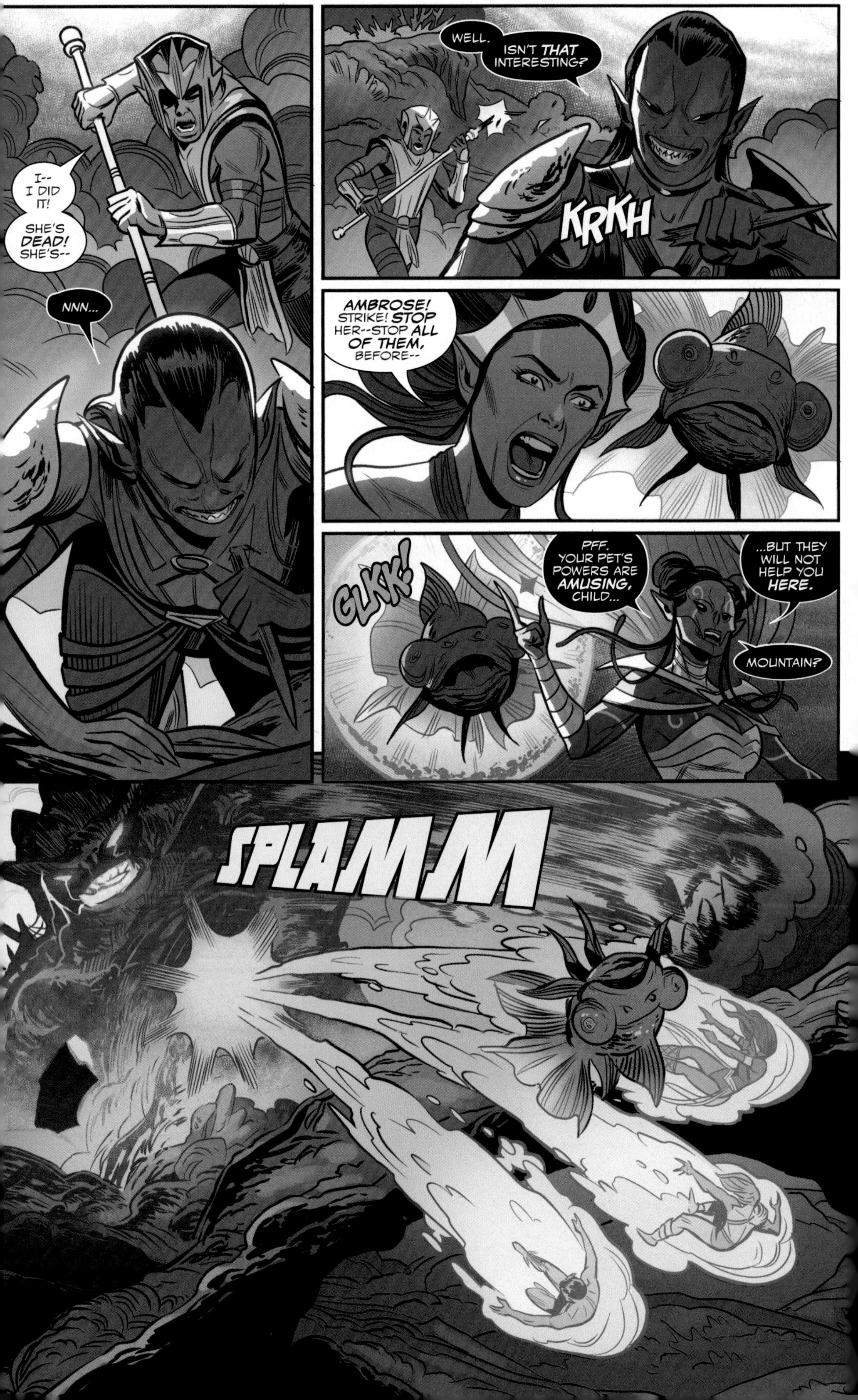
I--
I DID
IT!
SHE'S
DEAD!
SHE'S--
NNN...
WELL.
ISN'T THAT
INTERESTING?
KRKH
AMBROSE!
STRIKE! STOP
HER--STOP ALL
OF THEM,
BEFORE--
GLKK!
PFF.
YOUR PET'S
POWERS ARE
AMUSING,
CHILD...
...BUT THEY
WILL NOT
HELP YOU
HERE.
MOUNTAIN?
SPLAMM

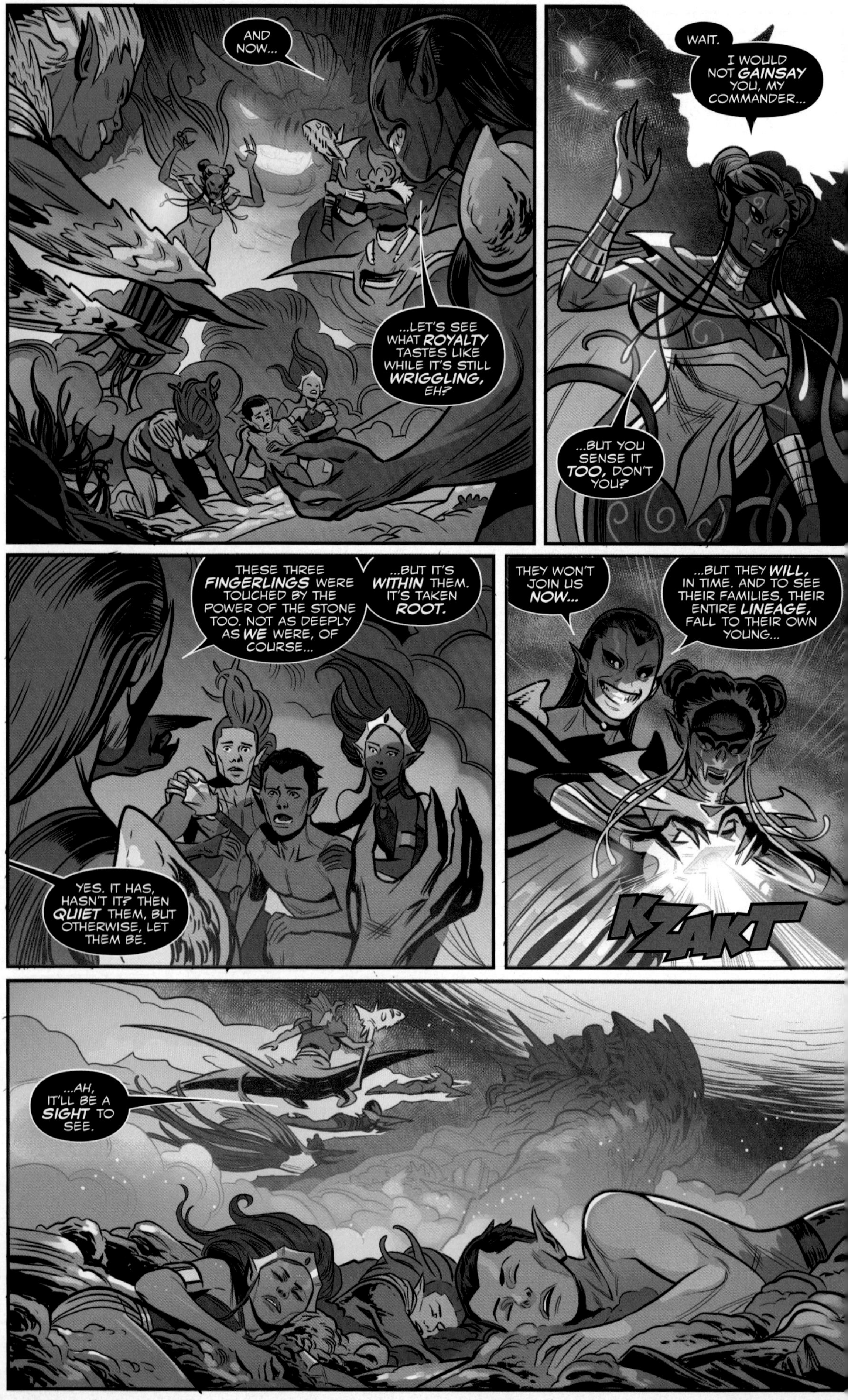
AND NOW...
...LET'S SEE WHAT ROYALTY TASTES LIKE WHILE IT'S STILL WRIGGLING, EH?
WAIT.
I WOULD NOT GAINSAY YOU, MY COMMANDER...
...BUT YOU SENSE IT TOO, DON'T YOU?
THESE THREE FINGERLINGS WERE TOUCHED BY THE POWER OF THE STONE TOO. NOT AS DEEPLY AS WE WERE, OF COURSE...
...BUT IT'S WITHIN THEM. IT'S TAKEN ROOT.
YES. IT HAS, HASN'T IT? THEN QUIET THEM, BUT OTHERWISE, LET THEM BE.
THEY WON'T JOIN US NOW...
...BUT THEY WILL, IN TIME. AND TO SEE THEIR FAMILIES, THEIR ENTIRE LINEAGE, FALL TO THEIR OWN YOUNG...
KZAKT
...AH, IT'LL BE A SIGHT TO SEE.

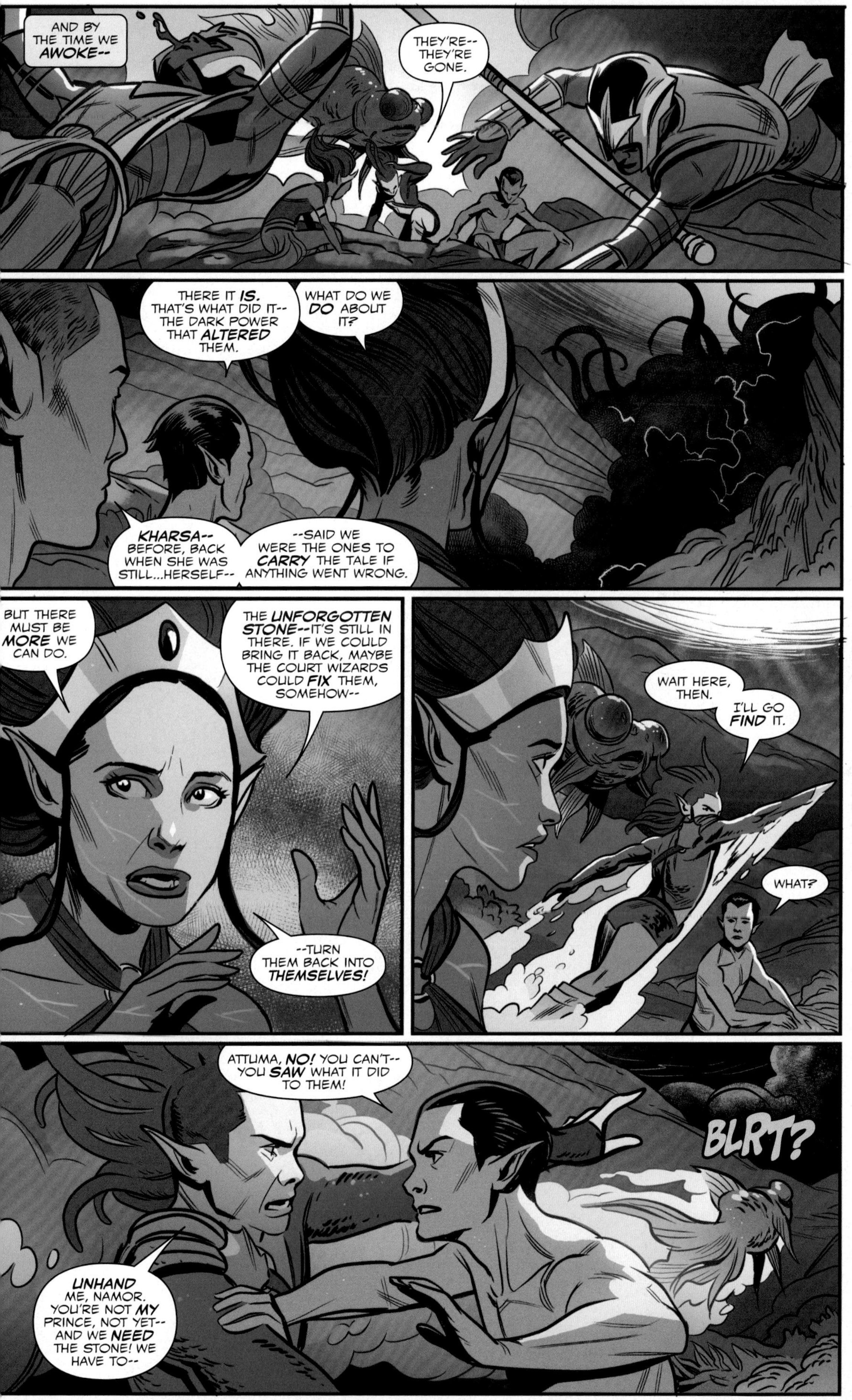
AND BY THE TIME WE AWOKE--
THEY'RE-- THEY'RE GONE.
THERE IT IS. THAT'S WHAT DID IT-- THE DARK POWER THAT ALTERED THEM.
WHAT DO WE DO ABOUT IT?
KHARSA-- BEFORE, BACK WHEN SHE WAS STILL...HERSELF--
--SAID WE WERE THE ONES TO CARRY THE TALE IF ANYTHING WENT WRONG.
BUT THERE MUST BE MORE WE CAN DO.
THE UNFORGOTTEN STONE--IT'S STILL IN THERE. IF WE COULD BRING IT BACK, MAYBE THE COURT WIZARDS COULD FIX THEM, SOMEHOW--
--TURN THEM BACK INTO THEMSELVES!
WAIT HERE, THEN.
I'LL GO FIND IT.
WHAT?
ATTUMA, NO! YOU CAN'T-- YOU SAW WHAT IT DID TO THEM!
BLRT?
UNHAND ME, NAMOR. YOU'RE NOT MY PRINCE, NOT YET-- AND WE NEED THE STONE! WE HAVE TO--

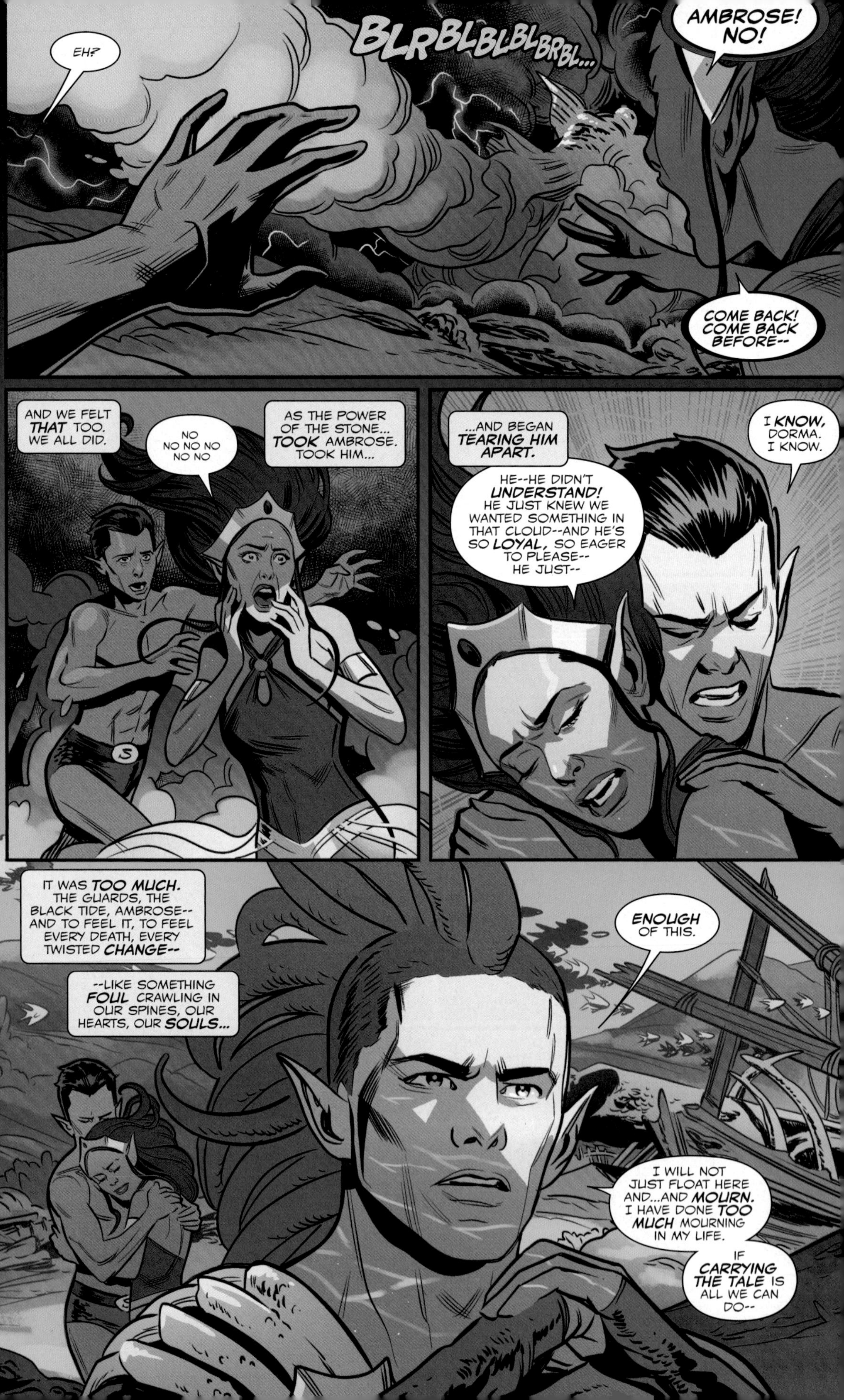

EH?
BLRBLBLBLBRBL...
AMBROSE! NO!
COME BACK! COME BACK BEFORE--
AND WE FELT THAT TOO. WE ALL DID.
NO NO NO NO NO NO
AS THE POWER OF THE STONE... TOOK AMBROSE. TOOK HIM...
...AND BEGAN TEARING HIM APART.
HE--HE DIDN'T UNDERSTAND! HE JUST KNEW WE WANTED SOMETHING IN THAT CLOUD--AND HE'S SO LOYAL, SO EAGER TO PLEASE-- HE JUST--
I KNOW, DORMA. I KNOW.
IT WAS TOO MUCH. THE GUARDS, THE BLACK TIDE, AMBROSE-- AND TO FEEL IT, TO FEEL EVERY DEATH, EVERY TWISTED CHANGE--
--LIKE SOMETHING FOUL CRAWLING IN OUR SPINES, OUR HEARTS, OUR SOULS...
ENOUGH OF THIS.
I WILL NOT JUST FLOAT HERE AND...AND MOURN. I HAVE DONE TOO MUCH MOURNING IN MY LIFE.
IF CARRYING THE TALE IS ALL WE CAN DO--

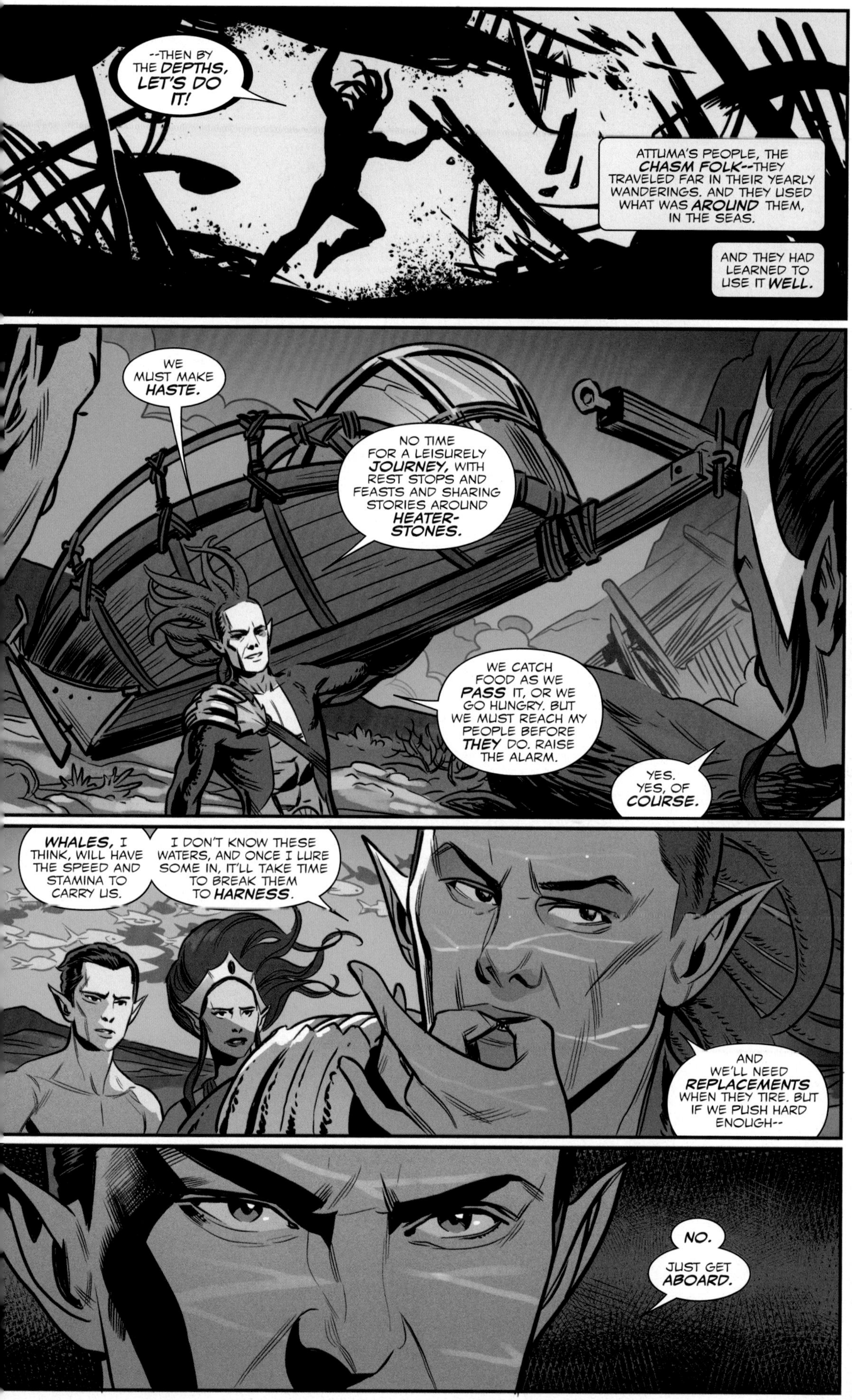

--THEN BY THE DEPTHS, LET'S DO IT!
ATTUMA'S PEOPLE, THE CHASM FOLK--THEY TRAVELED FAR IN THEIR YEARLY WANDERINGS. AND THEY USED WHAT WAS AROUND THEM, IN THE SEAS.
AND THEY HAD LEARNED TO USE IT WELL.
WE MUST MAKE HASTE.
NO TIME FOR A LEISURELY JOURNEY, WITH REST STOPS AND FEASTS AND SHARING STORIES AROUND HEATER-STONES.
WE CATCH FOOD AS WE PASS IT, OR WE GO HUNGRY. BUT WE MUST REACH MY PEOPLE BEFORE THEY DO. RAISE THE ALARM.
YES. YES, OF COURSE.
WHALES, I THINK, WILL HAVE THE SPEED AND STAMINA TO CARRY US.
I DON'T KNOW THESE WATERS, AND ONCE I LURE SOME IN, IT'LL TAKE TIME TO BREAK THEM TO HARNESS.
AND WE'LL NEED REPLACEMENTS WHEN THEY TIRE. BUT IF WE PUSH HARD ENOUGH--
NO.
JUST GET ABOARD.

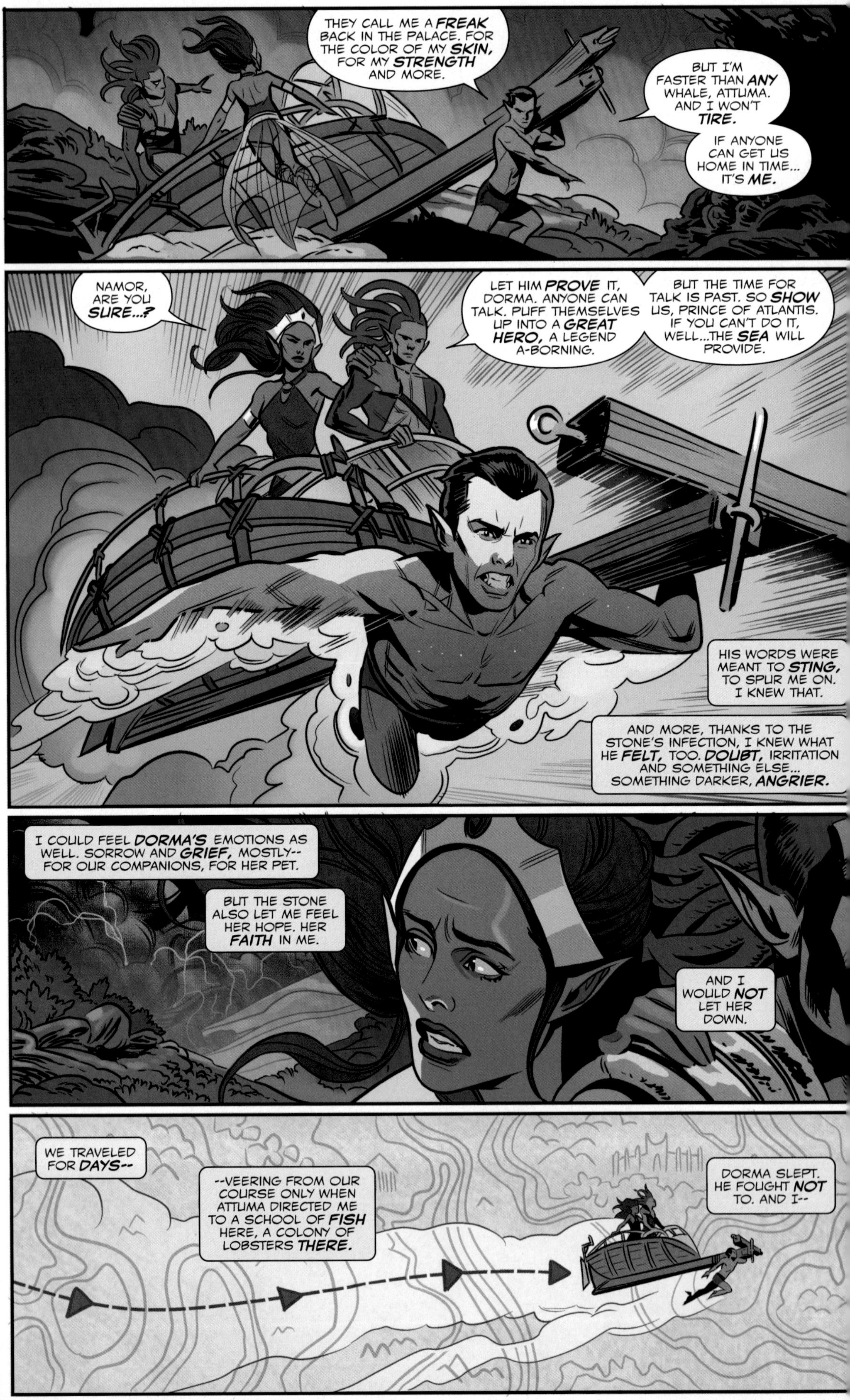
THEY CALL ME A FREAK BACK IN THE PALACE. FOR THE COLOR OF MY SKIN, FOR MY STRENGTH AND MORE.
BUT I'M FASTER THAN ANY WHALE, ATTUMA. AND I WON'T TIRE.
IF ANYONE CAN GET US HOME IN TIME... IT'S ME.
NAMOR, ARE YOU SURE...?
LET HIM PROVE IT, DORMA. ANYONE CAN TALK. PUFF THEMSELVES UP INTO A GREAT HERO, A LEGEND A-BORNING.
BUT THE TIME FOR TALK IS PAST. SO SHOW US, PRINCE OF ATLANTIS. IF YOU CAN'T DO IT, WELL...THE SEA WILL PROVIDE.
HIS WORDS WERE MEANT TO STING, TO SPUR ME ON. I KNEW THAT.
AND MORE, THANKS TO THE STONE'S INFECTION, I KNEW WHAT HE FELT, TOO. DOUBT, IRRITATION AND SOMETHING ELSE... SOMETHING DARKER, ANGRIER.
I COULD FEEL DORMA'S EMOTIONS AS WELL. SORROW AND GRIEF, MOSTLY-- FOR OUR COMPANIONS, FOR HER PET.
BUT THE STONE ALSO LET ME FEEL HER HOPE. HER FAITH IN ME.
AND I WOULD NOT LET HER DOWN.
WE TRAVELED FOR DAYS--
--VEERING FROM OUR COURSE ONLY WHEN ATTUMA DIRECTED ME TO A SCHOOL OF FISH HERE, A COLONY OF LOBSTERS THERE.
DORMA SLEPT. HE FOUGHT NOT TO. AND I--

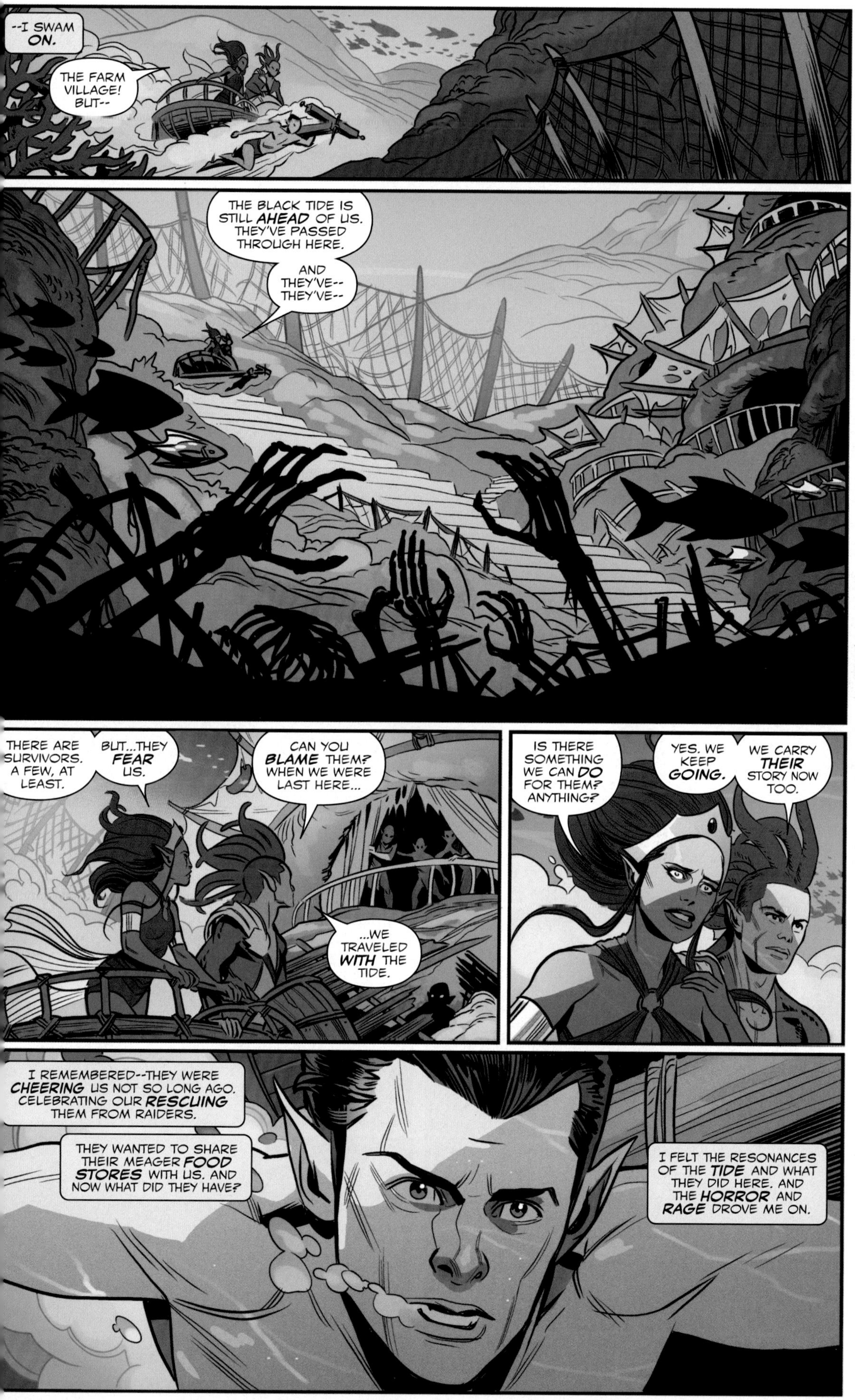
--I SWAM ON.
THE FARM VILLAGE! BUT--
THE BLACK TIDE IS STILL AHEAD OF US. THEY'VE PASSED THROUGH HERE.
AND THEY'VE-- THEY'VE--
THERE ARE SURVIVORS. A FEW, AT LEAST.
BUT...THEY FEAR US.
CAN YOU BLAME THEM? WHEN WE WERE LAST HERE...
...WE TRAVELED WITH THE TIDE.
IS THERE SOMETHING WE CAN DO FOR THEM? ANYTHING?
YES. WE KEEP GOING.
WE CARRY THEIR STORY NOW TOO.
I REMEMBERED--THEY WERE CHEERING US NOT SO LONG AGO. CELEBRATING OUR RESCUING THEM FROM RAIDERS.
THEY WANTED TO SHARE THEIR MEAGER FOOD STORES WITH US. AND NOW WHAT DID THEY HAVE?
I FELT THE RESONANCES OF THE TIDE AND WHAT THEY DID HERE. AND THE HORROR AND RAGE DROVE ME ON.

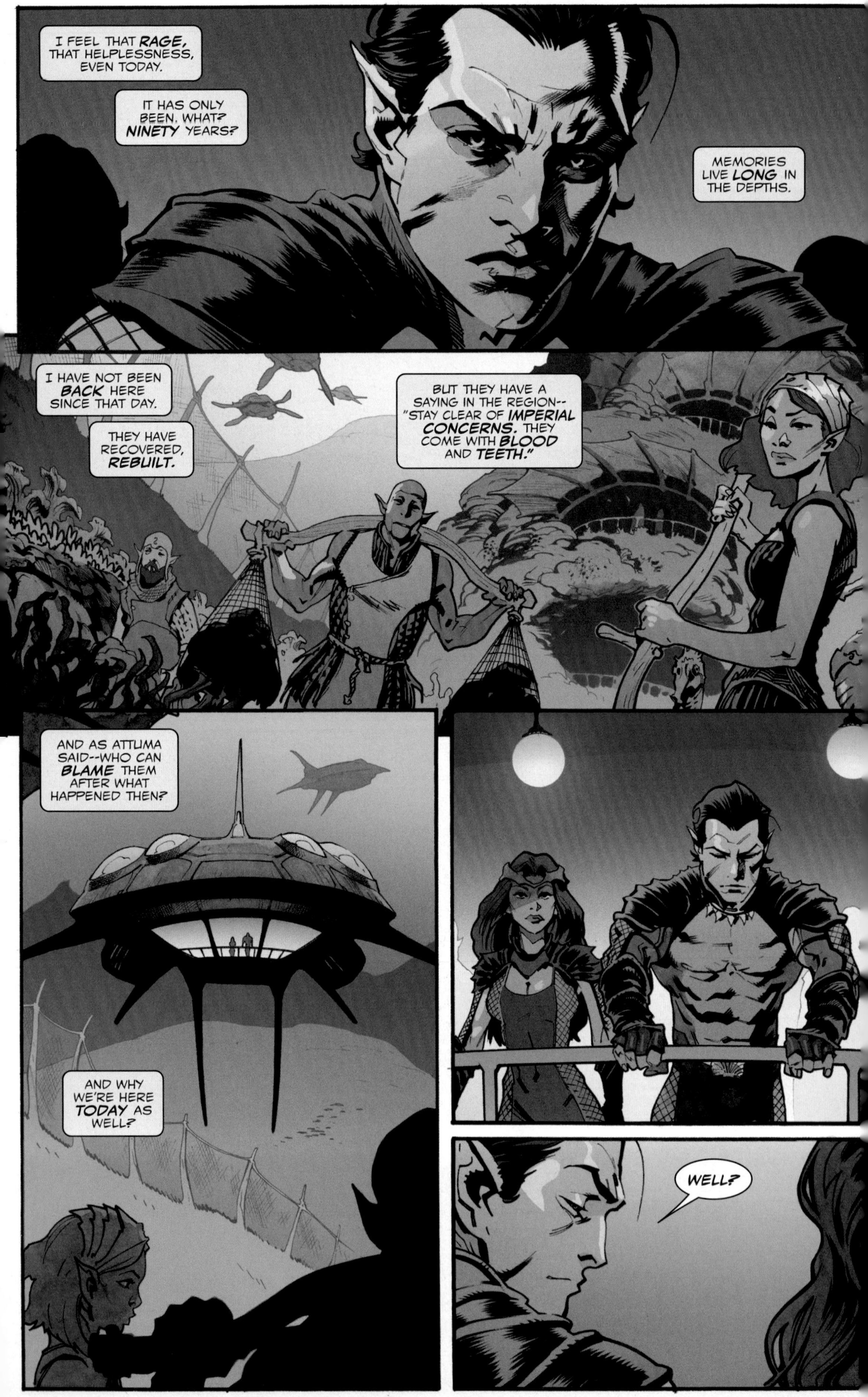

I FEEL THAT RAGE, THAT HELPLESSNESS, EVEN TODAY.
IT HAS ONLY BEEN. WHAT? NINETY YEARS?
MEMORIES LIVE LONG IN THE DEPTHS.
I HAVE NOT BEEN BACK HERE SINCE THAT DAY.
THEY HAVE RECOVERED, REBUILT.
BUT THEY HAVE A SAYING IN THE REGION--"STAY CLEAR OF IMPERIAL CONCERNS. THEY COME WITH BLOOD AND TEETH."
AND AS ATTUMA SAID--WHO CAN BLAME THEM AFTER WHAT HAPPENED THEN?
AND WHY WE'RE HERE TODAY AS WELL?
WELL?

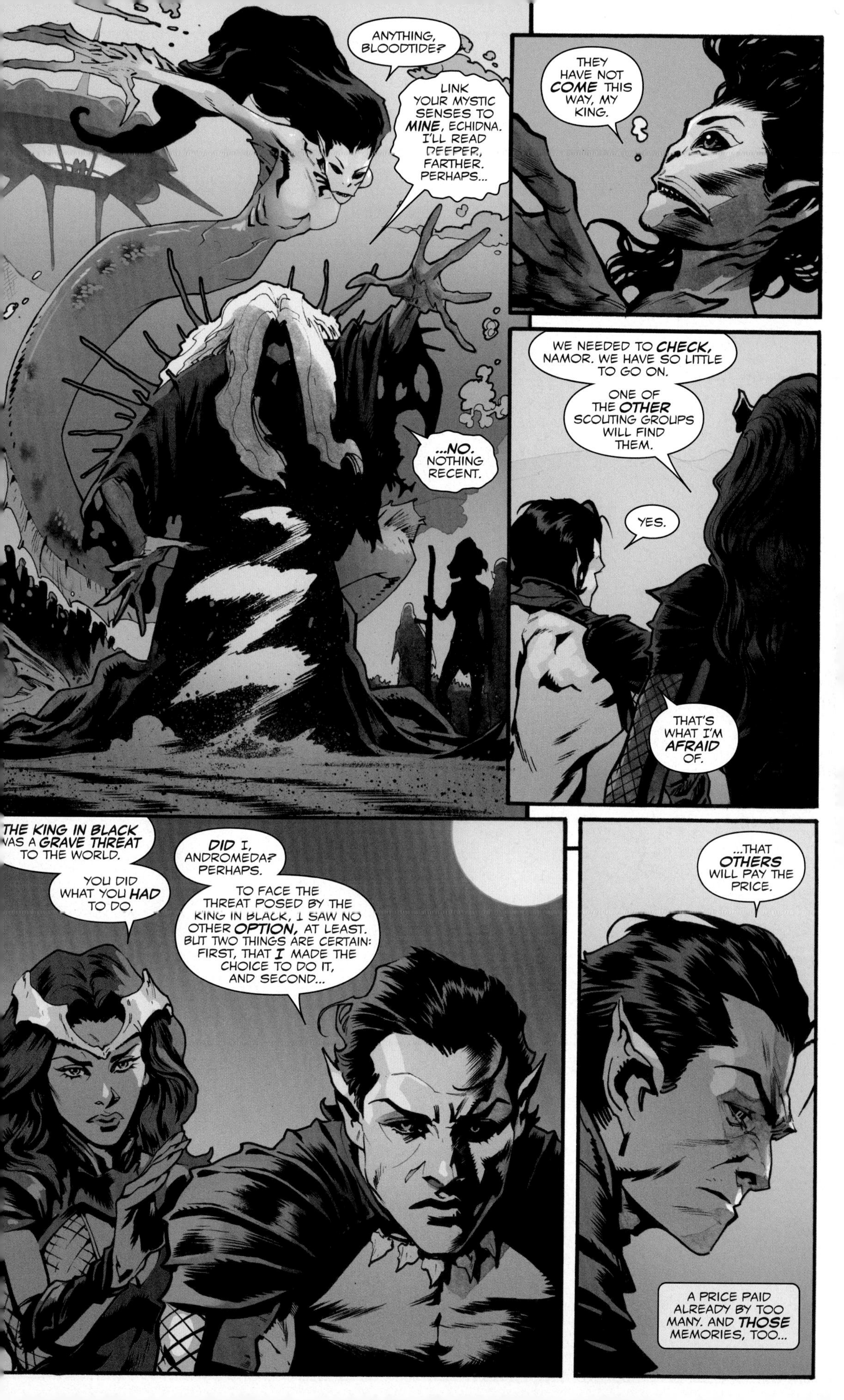
ANYTHING, BLOODTIDE?
LINK YOUR MYSTIC SENSES TO MINE, ECHIDNA. I'LL READ DEEPER, FARTHER. PERHAPS...
THEY HAVE NOT COME THIS WAY, MY KING.
...NO. NOTHING RECENT.
WE NEEDED TO CHECK, NAMOR. WE HAVE SO LITTLE TO GO ON.
ONE OF THE OTHER SCOUTING GROUPS WILL FIND THEM.
YES.
THAT'S WHAT I'M AFRAID OF.
THE KING IN BLACK WAS A GRAVE THREAT TO THE WORLD.
YOU DID WHAT YOU HAD TO DO.
DID I, ANDROMEDA? PERHAPS.
TO FACE THE THREAT POSED BY THE KING IN BLACK, I SAW NO OTHER OPTION, AT LEAST. BUT TWO THINGS ARE CERTAIN: FIRST, THAT I MADE THE CHOICE TO DO IT, AND SECOND...
...THAT OTHERS WILL PAY THE PRICE.
A PRICE PAID ALREADY BY TOO MANY. AND THOSE MEMORIES, TOO...

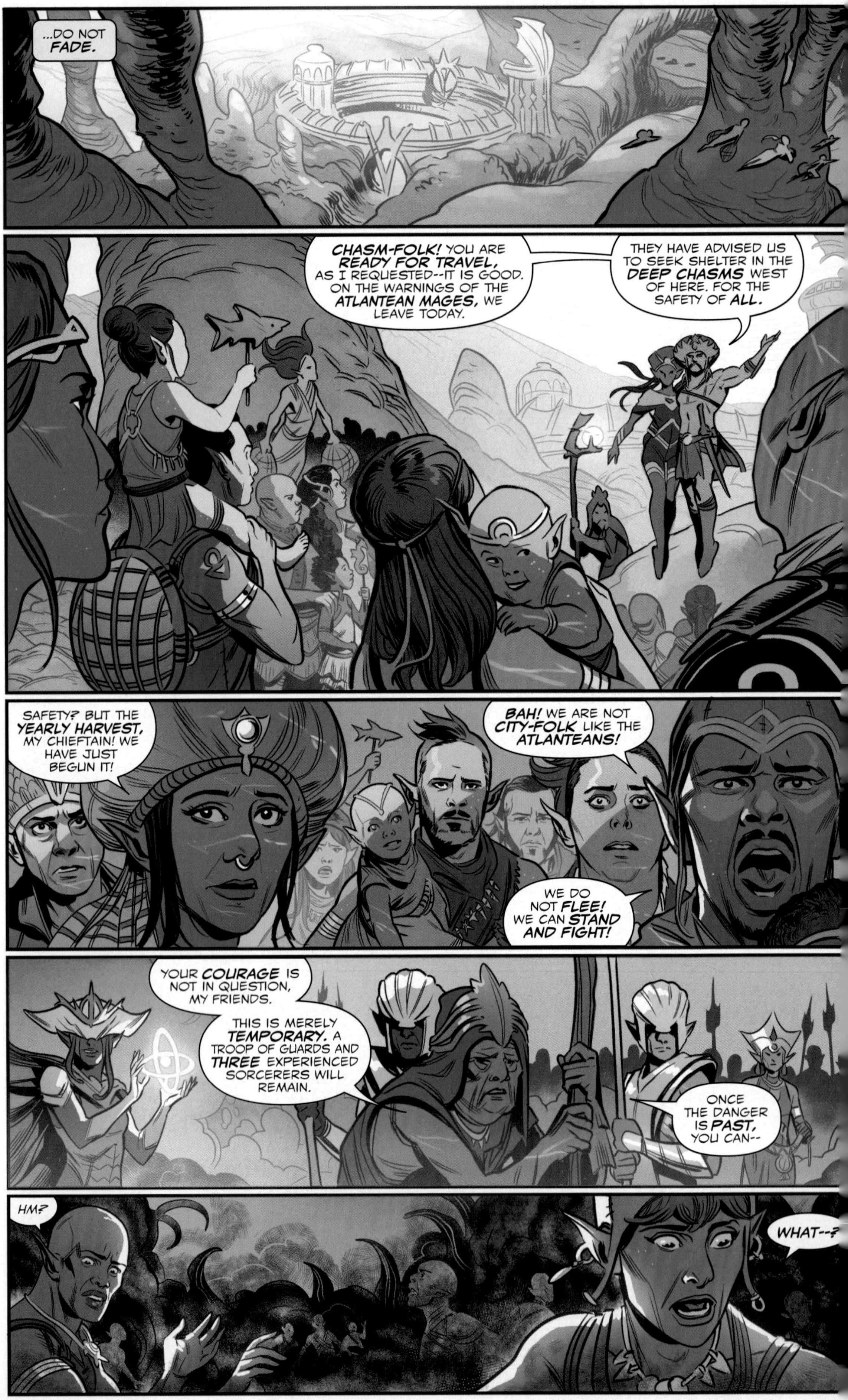
...DO NOT FADE.
CHASM-FOLK! YOU ARE READY FOR TRAVEL, AS I REQUESTED--IT IS GOOD. ON THE WARNINGS OF THE ATLANTEAN MAGES, WE LEAVE TODAY.
THEY HAVE ADVISED US TO SEEK SHELTER IN THE DEEP CHASMS WEST OF HERE. FOR THE SAFETY OF ALL.
SAFETY? BUT THE YEARLY HARVEST, MY CHIEFTAIN! WE HAVE JUST BEGUN IT!
BAH! WE ARE NOT CITY-FOLK LIKE THE ATLANTEANS!
WE DO NOT FLEE! WE CAN STAND AND FIGHT!
YOUR COURAGE IS NOT IN QUESTION, MY FRIENDS.
THIS IS MERELY TEMPORARY. A TROOP OF GUARDS AND THREE EXPERIENCED SORCERERS WILL REMAIN.
ONCE THE DANGER IS PAST, YOU CAN--
HM?
WHAT--?

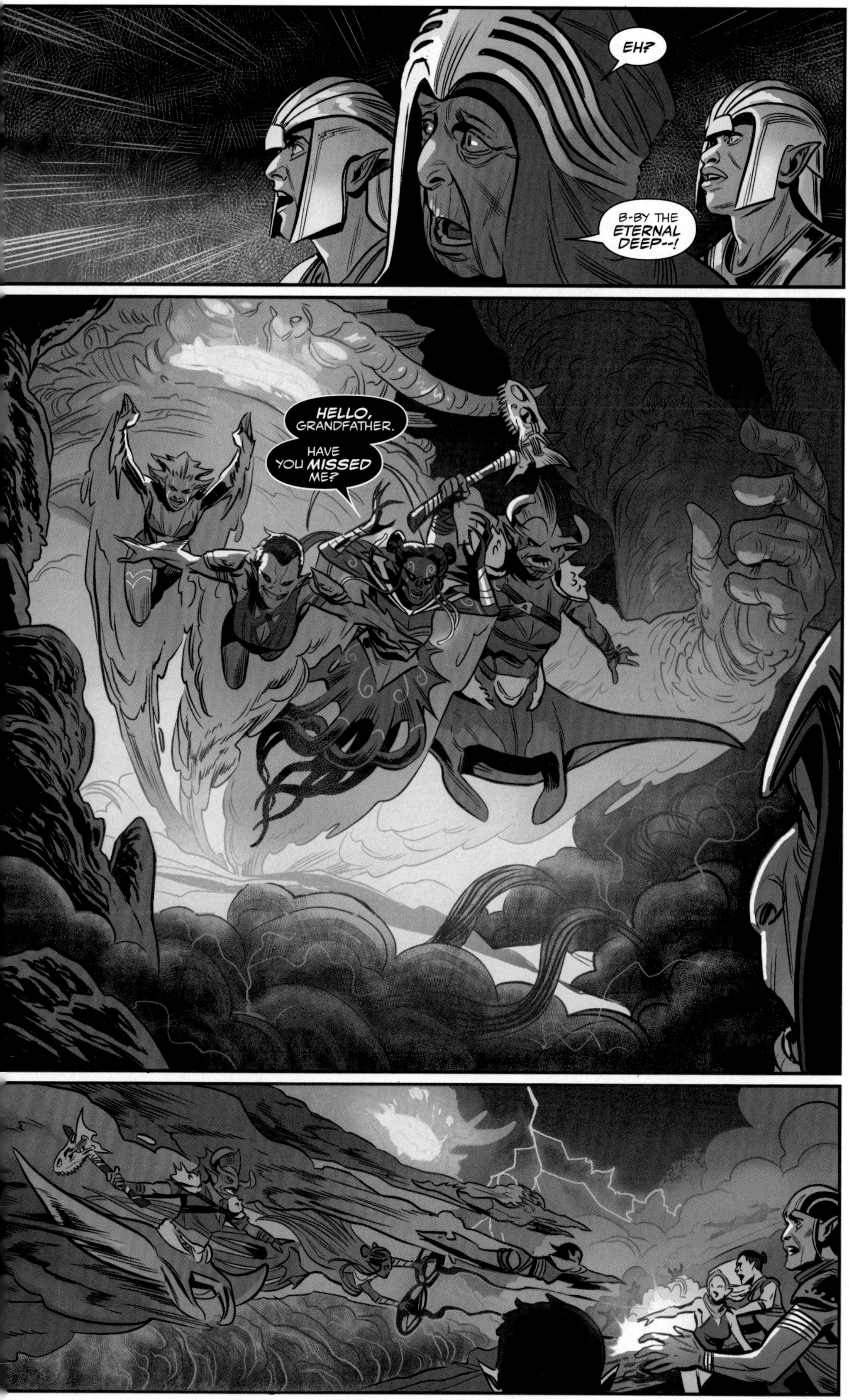
EH?
B-BY THE ETERNAL DEEP--!
HELLO, GRANDFATHER.
HAVE YOU MISSED ME?

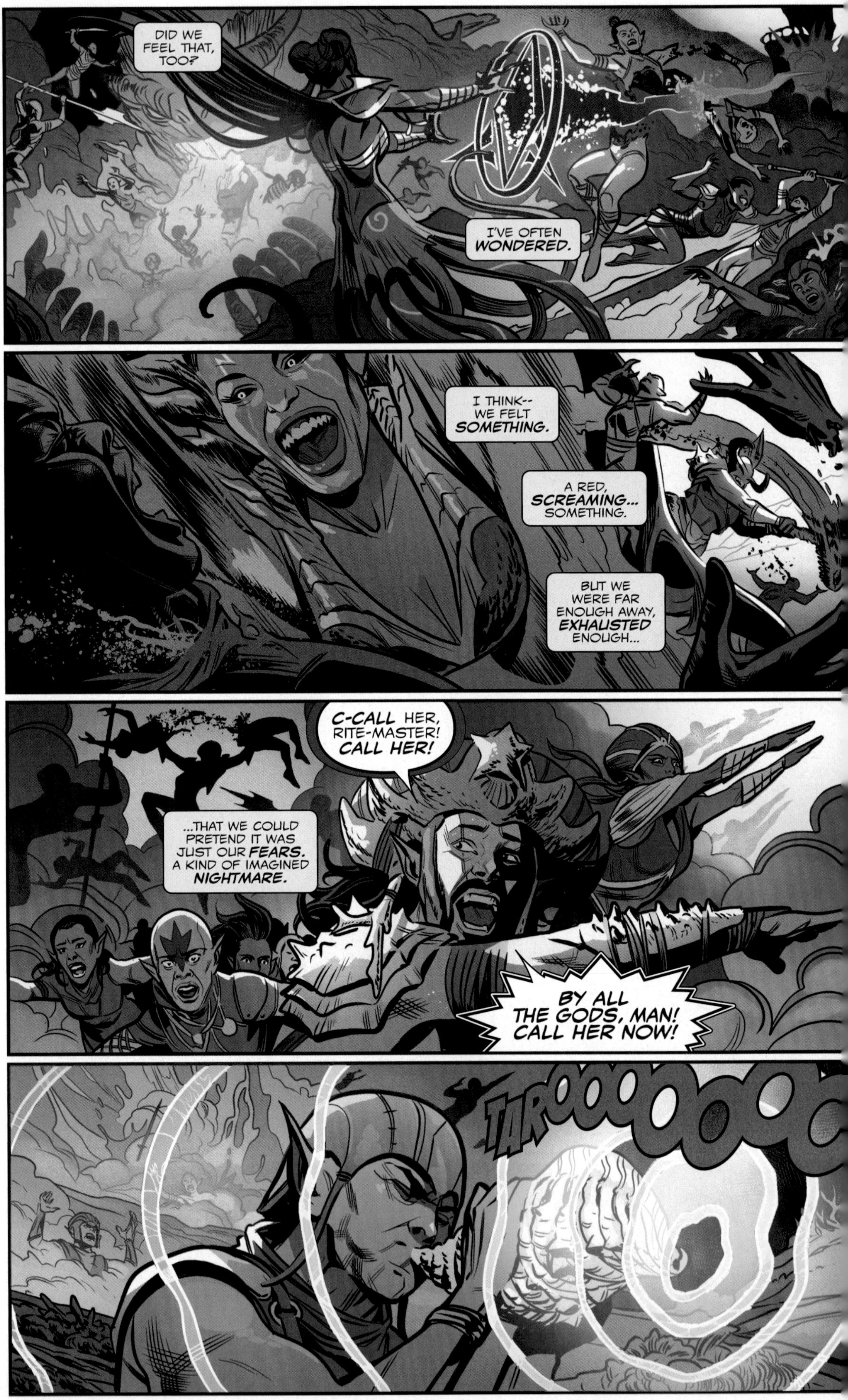
DID WE FEEL THAT, TOO?
I'VE OFTEN WONDERED.
I THINK-- WE FELT SOMETHING.
A RED, SCREAMING... SOMETHING.
BUT WE WERE FAR ENOUGH AWAY, EXHAUSTED ENOUGH...
C-CALL HER, RITE-MASTER! CALL HER!
...THAT WE COULD PRETEND IT WAS JUST OUR FEARS. A KIND OF IMAGINED NIGHTMARE.
BY ALL THE GODS, MAN! CALL HER NOW!
TAROOOOOOOO

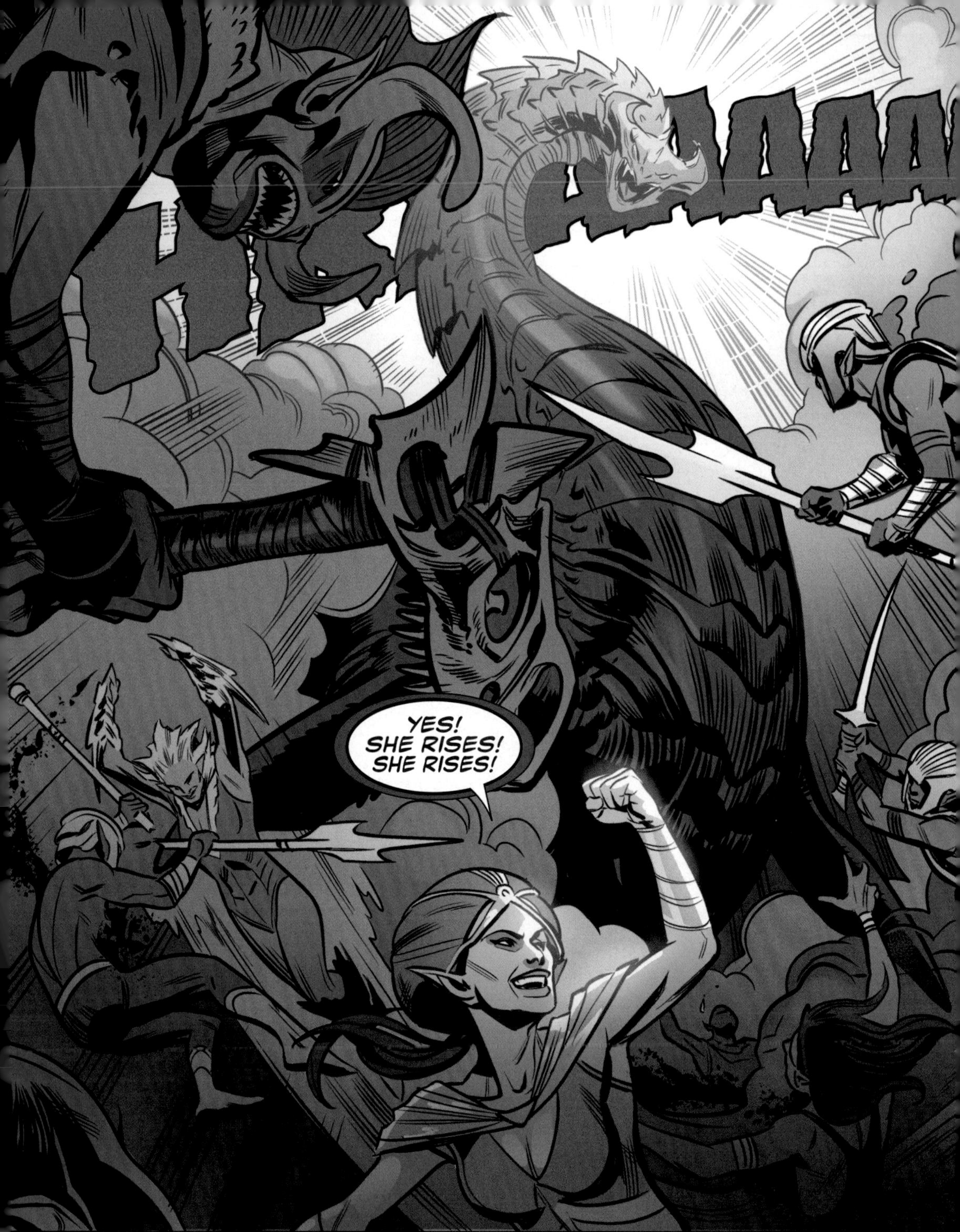
HHAAAAA
YES! SHE RISES! SHE RISES!
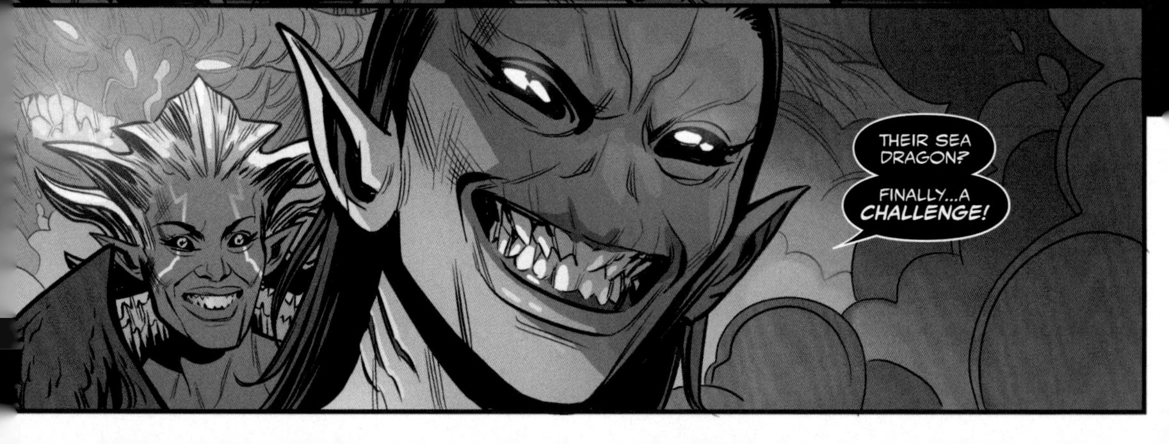
THEIR SEA DRAGON?
FINALLY...A CHALLENGE!

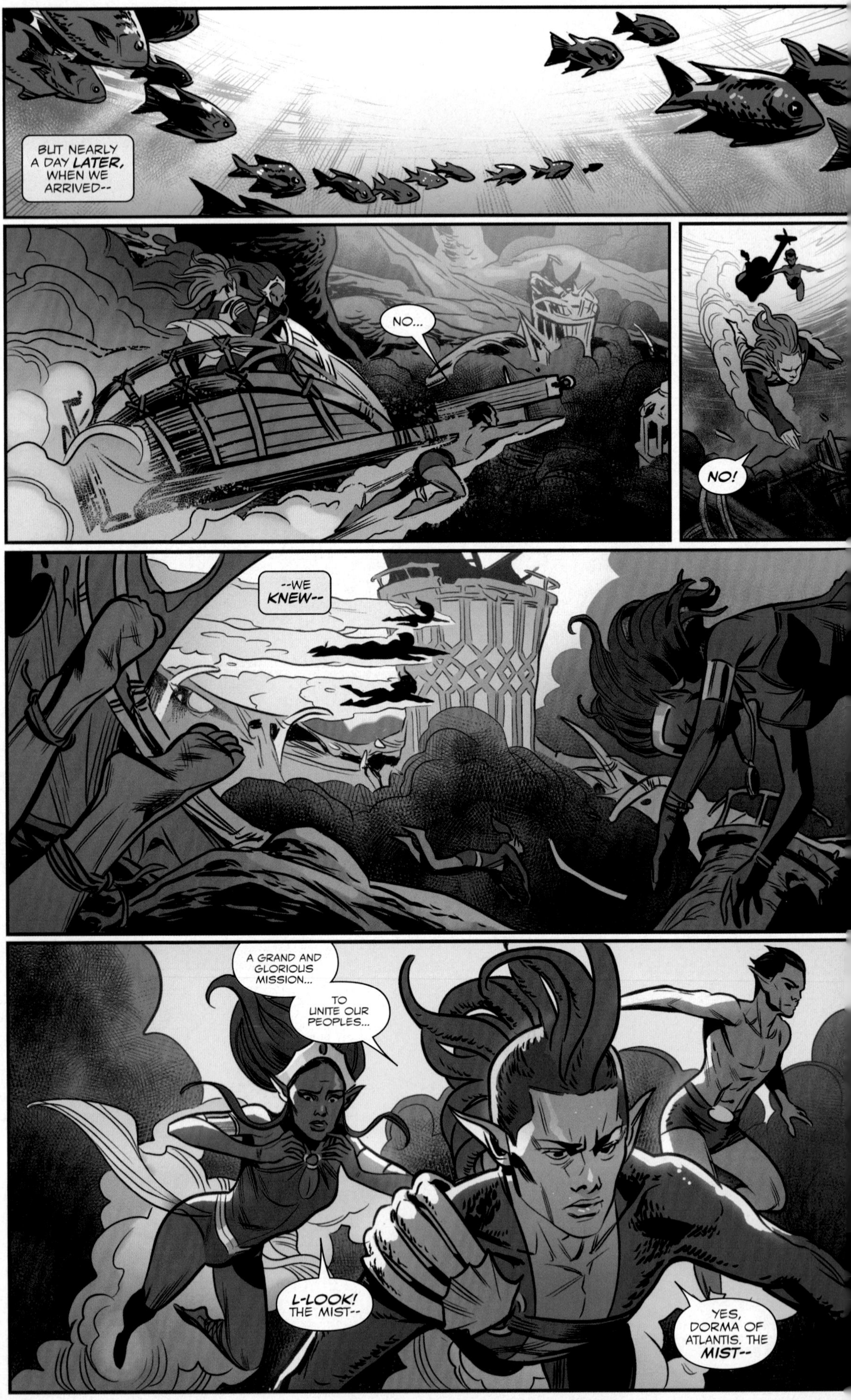
BUT NEARLY A DAY LATER, WHEN WE ARRIVED--
NO...
NO!
--WE KNEW--
A GRAND AND GLORIOUS MISSION...
TO UNITE OUR PEOPLES...
L-LOOK! THE MIST--
YES, DORMA OF ATLANTIS. THE MIST--

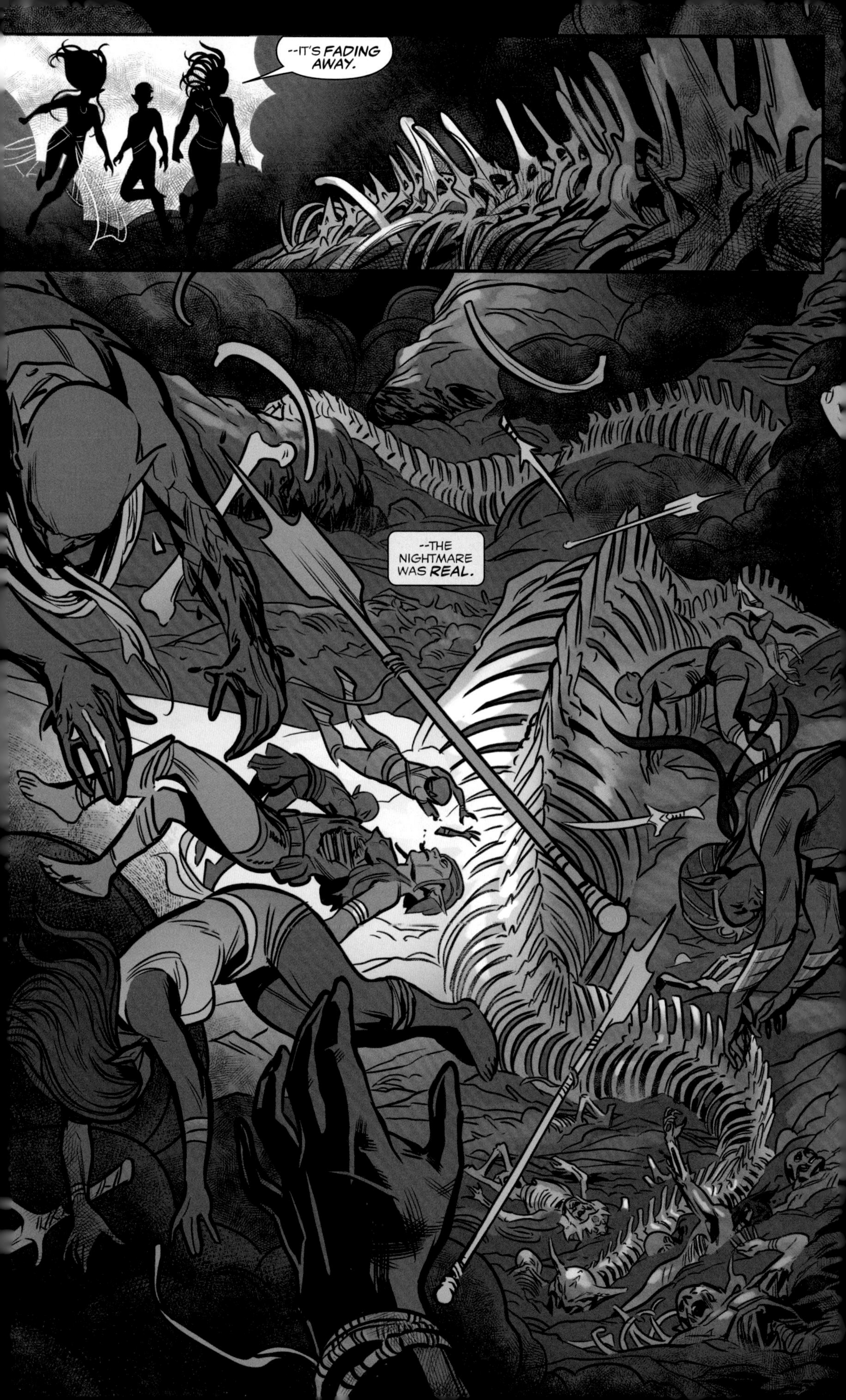
--IT'S FADING AWAY.
--THE NIGHTMARE WAS REAL.

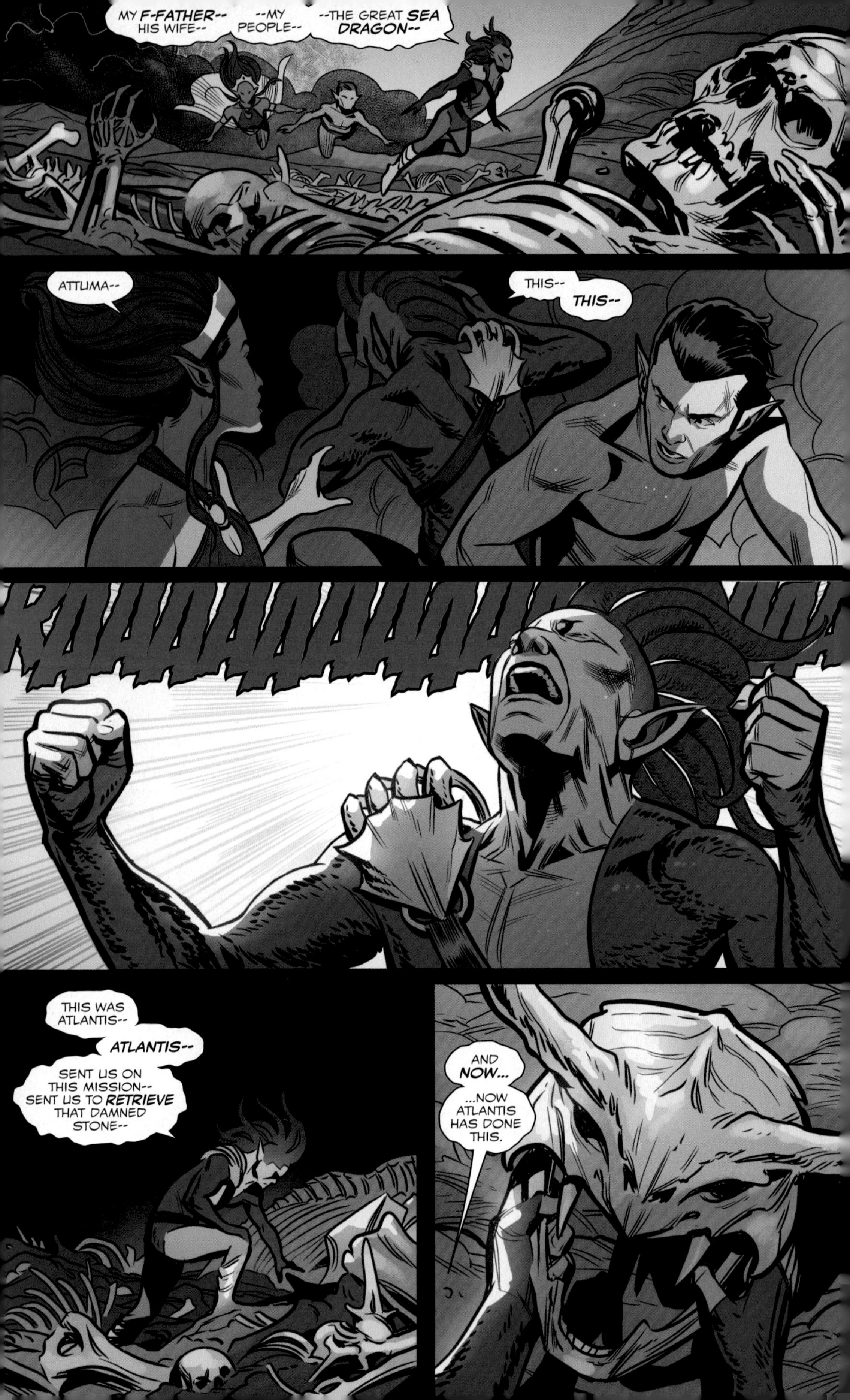
MY F-FATHER-- HIS WIFE--
--MY PEOPLE--
--THE GREAT SEA DRAGON--
ATTUMA--
THIS--
THIS--
RAAAAAAAAAA
THIS WAS ATLANTIS--
ATLANTIS--
SENT US ON THIS MISSION-- SENT US TO RETRIEVE THAT DAMNED STONE--
AND NOW...
...NOW ATLANTIS HAS DONE THIS.

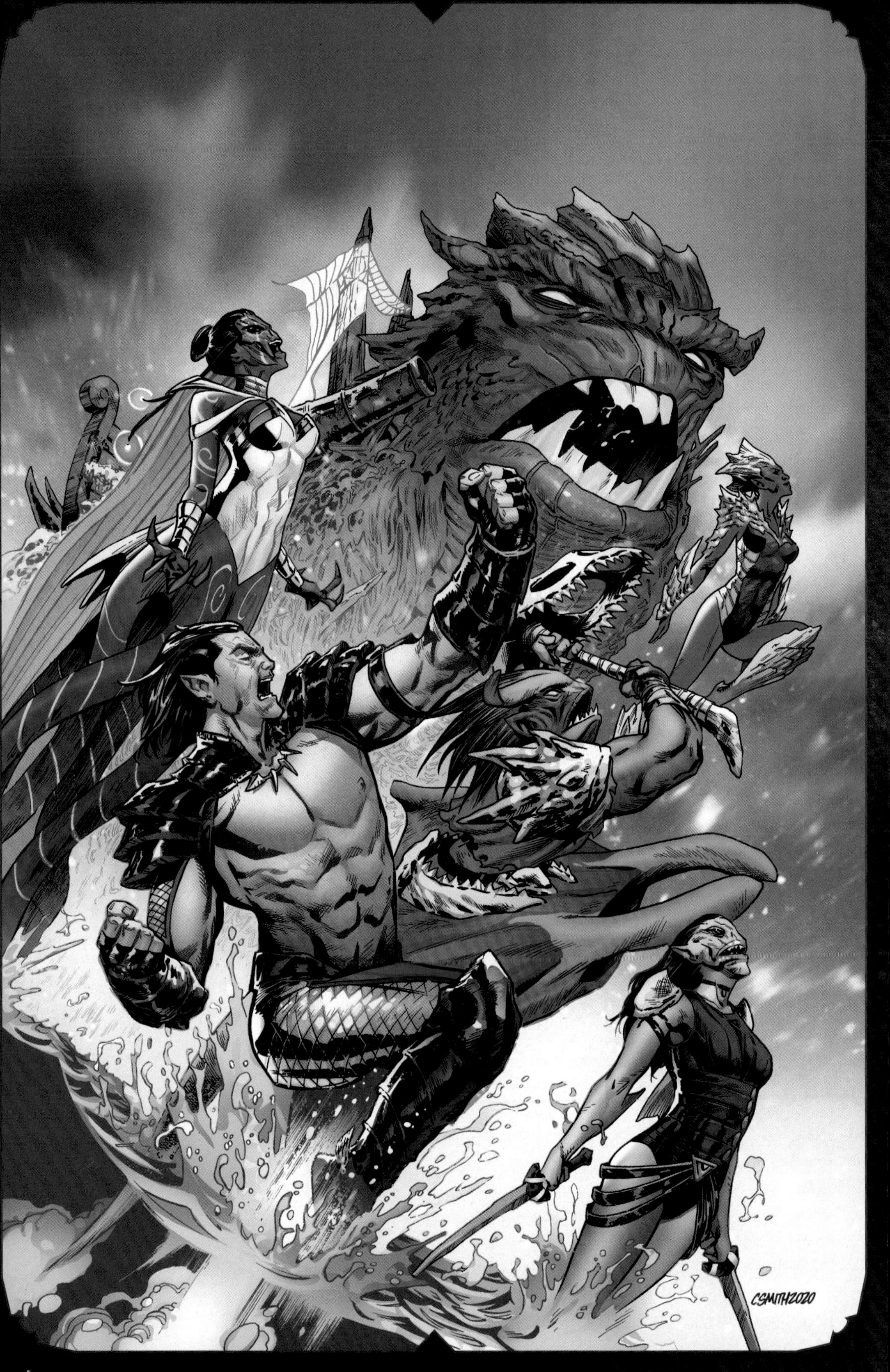
CSMITH2020

#1 VARIANT BY **CORY SMITH**

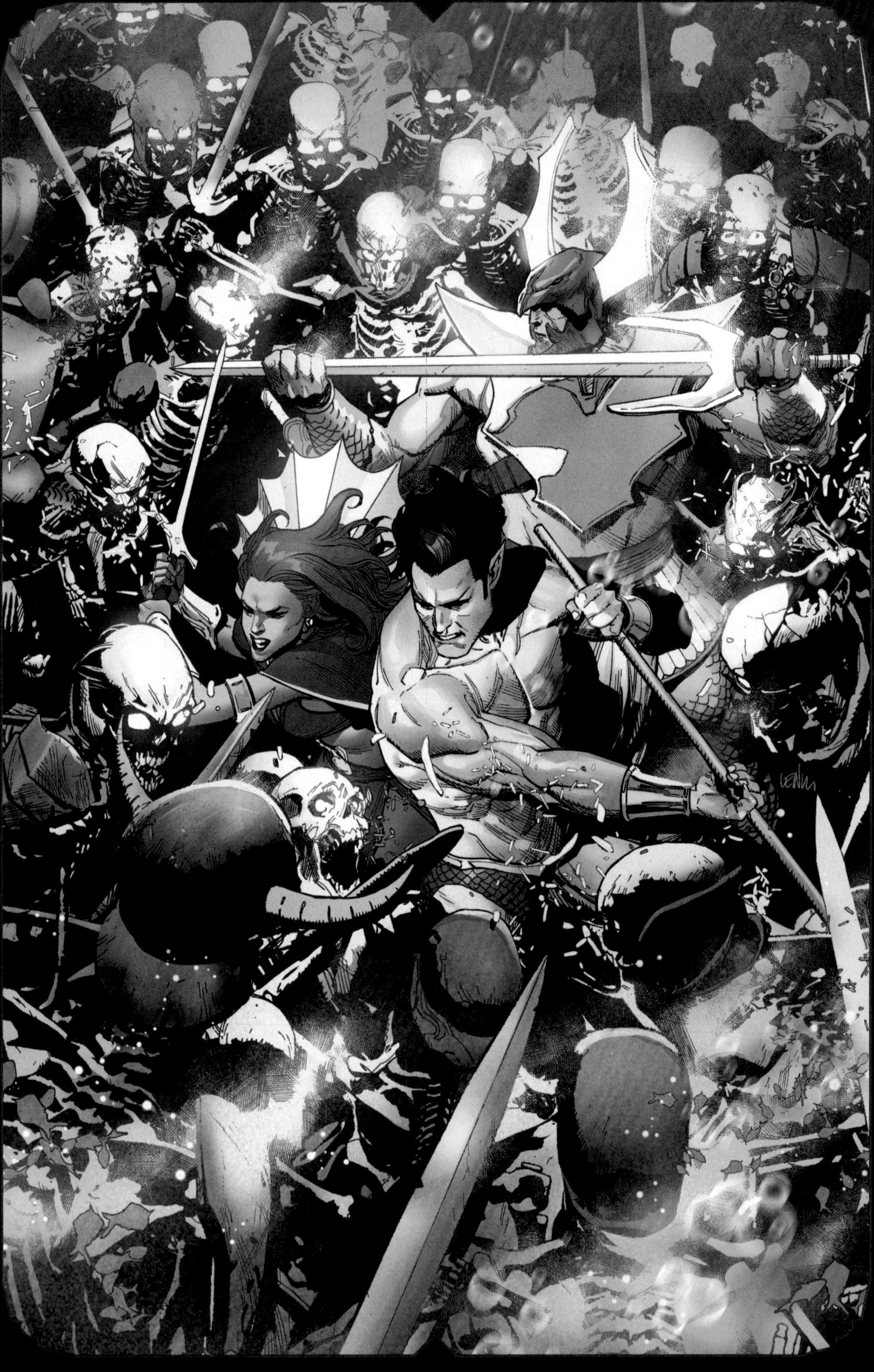

COLD CURRENTS
4

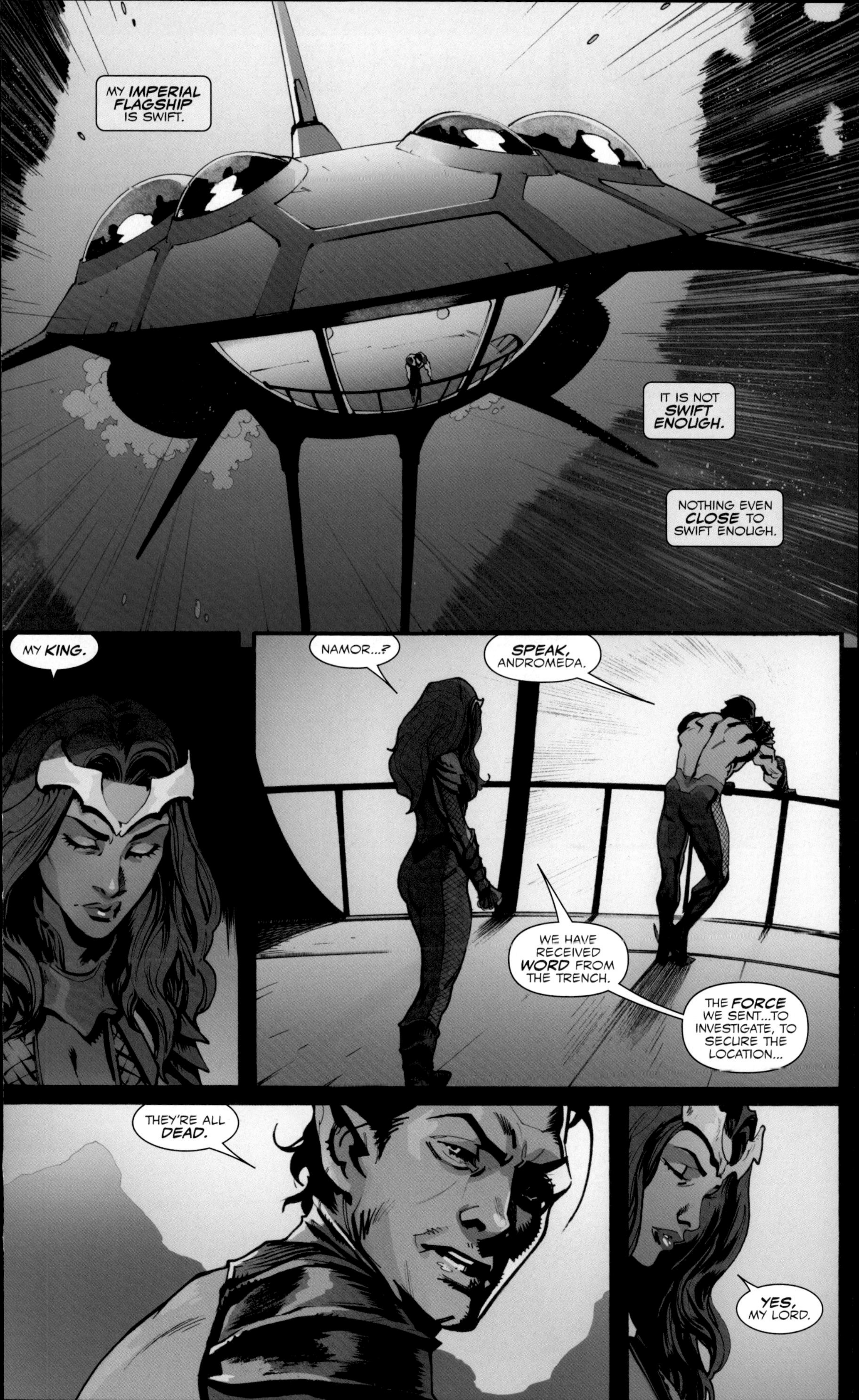
MY IMPERIAL FLAGSHIP IS SWIFT.
IT IS NOT SWIFT ENOUGH.
NOTHING EVEN CLOSE TO SWIFT ENOUGH.
MY KING.
NAMOR...?
SPEAK, ANDROMEDA.
WE HAVE RECEIVED WORD FROM THE TRENCH.
THE FORCE WE SENT...TO INVESTIGATE, TO SECURE THE LOCATION...
THEY'RE ALL DEAD.
YES, MY LORD.

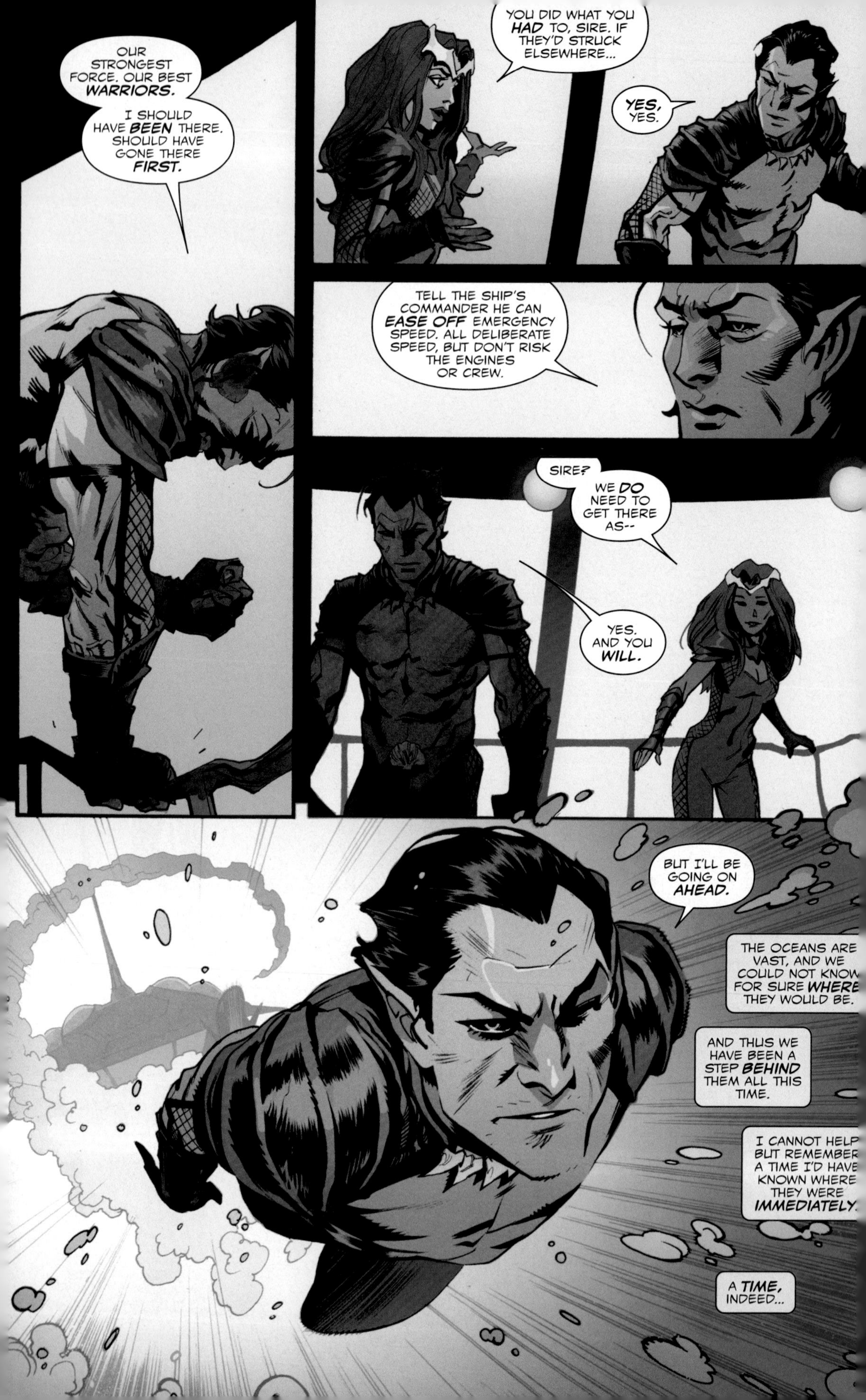
OUR STRONGEST FORCE. OUR BEST WARRIORS.
I SHOULD HAVE BEEN THERE. SHOULD HAVE GONE THERE FIRST.
YOU DID WHAT YOU HAD TO, SIRE. IF THEY'D STRUCK ELSEWHERE...
YES, YES.
TELL THE SHIP'S COMMANDER HE CAN EASE OFF EMERGENCY SPEED. ALL DELIBERATE SPEED, BUT DON'T RISK THE ENGINES OR CREW.
SIRE?
WE DO NEED TO GET THERE AS--
YES. AND YOU WILL.
BUT I'LL BE GOING ON AHEAD.
THE OCEANS ARE VAST, AND WE COULD NOT KNOW FOR SURE WHERE THEY WOULD BE.
AND THUS WE HAVE BEEN A STEP BEHIND THEM ALL THIS TIME.
I CANNOT HELP BUT REMEMBER A TIME I'D HAVE KNOWN WHERE THEY WERE IMMEDIATELY.
A TIME, INDEED...

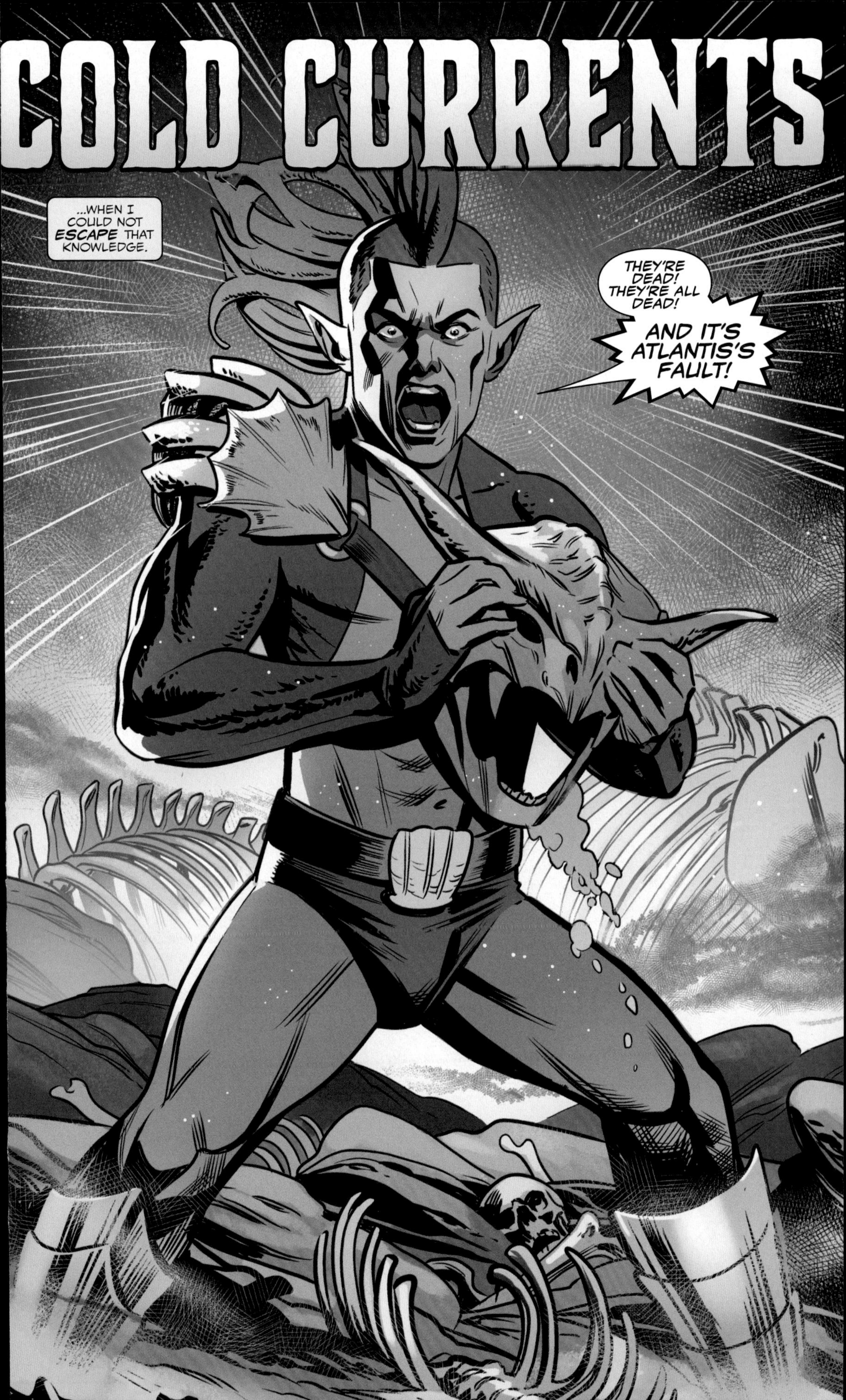
COLD CURRENTS
...WHEN I COULD NOT ESCAPE THAT KNOWLEDGE.
THEY'RE DEAD! THEY'RE ALL DEAD!
AND IT'S ATLANTIS'S FAULT!

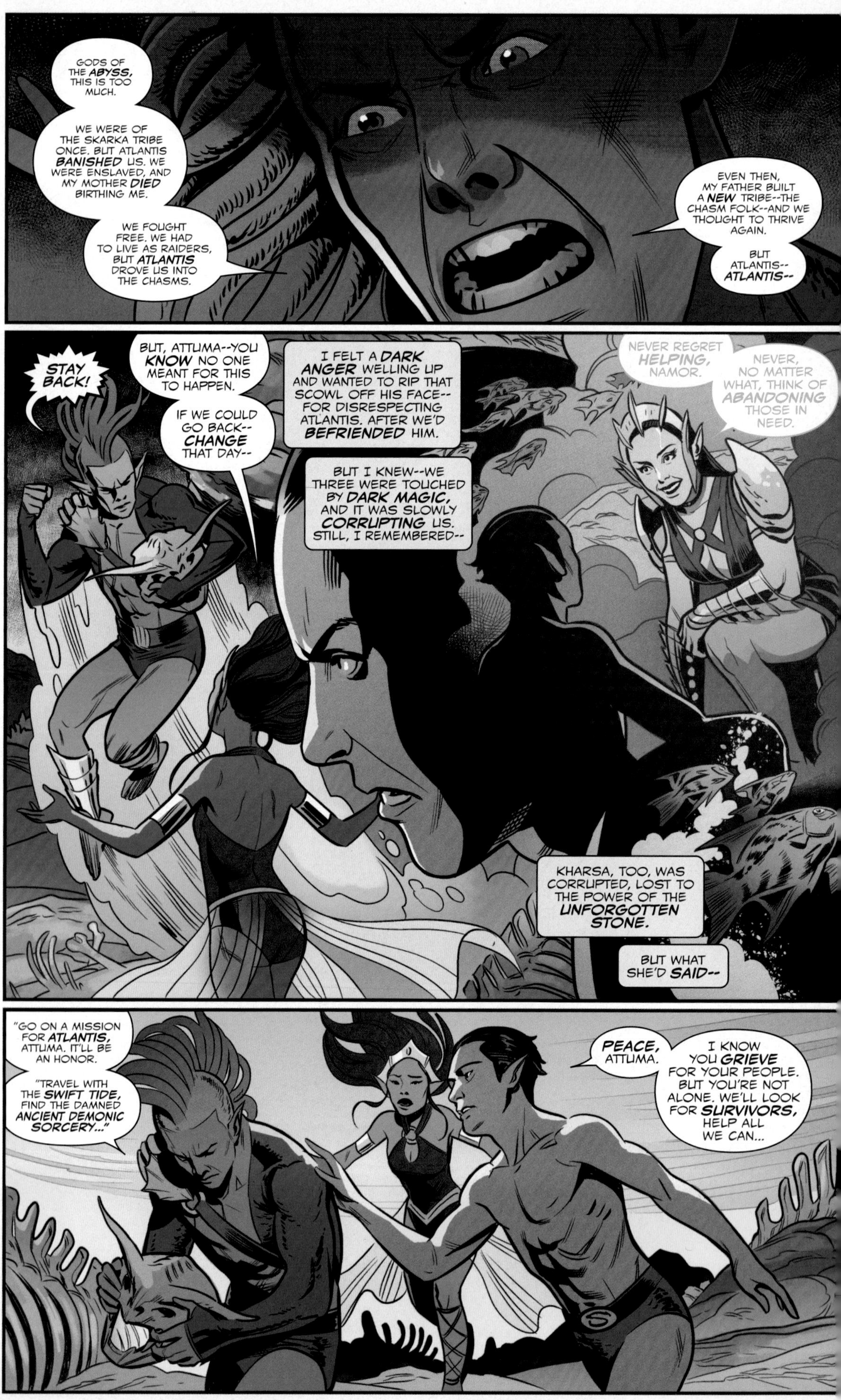
GODS OF THE ABYSS, THIS IS TOO MUCH.
WE WERE OF THE SKARKA TRIBE ONCE. BUT ATLANTIS BANISHED US. WE WERE ENSLAVED, AND MY MOTHER DIED BIRTHING ME.
WE FOUGHT FREE. WE HAD TO LIVE AS RAIDERS, BUT ATLANTIS DROVE US INTO THE CHASMS.
EVEN THEN, MY FATHER BUILT A NEW TRIBE--THE CHASM FOLK--AND WE THOUGHT TO THRIVE AGAIN.
BUT ATLANTIS-- ATLANTIS--
STAY BACK!
BUT, ATTUMA--YOU KNOW NO ONE MEANT FOR THIS TO HAPPEN.
IF WE COULD GO BACK-- CHANGE THAT DAY--
I FELT A DARK ANGER WELLING UP AND WANTED TO RIP THAT SCOWL OFF HIS FACE-- FOR DISRESPECTING ATLANTIS. AFTER WE'D BEFRIENDED HIM.
BUT I KNEW--WE THREE WERE TOUCHED BY DARK MAGIC, AND IT WAS SLOWLY CORRUPTING US. STILL, I REMEMBERED--
NEVER REGRET HELPING, NAMOR.
NEVER, NO MATTER WHAT, THINK OF ABANDONING THOSE IN NEED.
KHARSA, TOO, WAS CORRUPTED, LOST TO THE POWER OF THE UNFORGOTTEN STONE.
BUT WHAT SHE'D SAID--
"GO ON A MISSION FOR ATLANTIS, ATTUMA. IT'LL BE AN HONOR.
"TRAVEL WITH THE SWIFT TIDE, FIND THE DAMNED ANCIENT DEMONIC SORCERY..."
PEACE, ATTUMA.
I KNOW YOU GRIEVE FOR YOUR PEOPLE. BUT YOU'RE NOT ALONE. WE'LL LOOK FOR SURVIVORS, HELP ALL WE CAN...

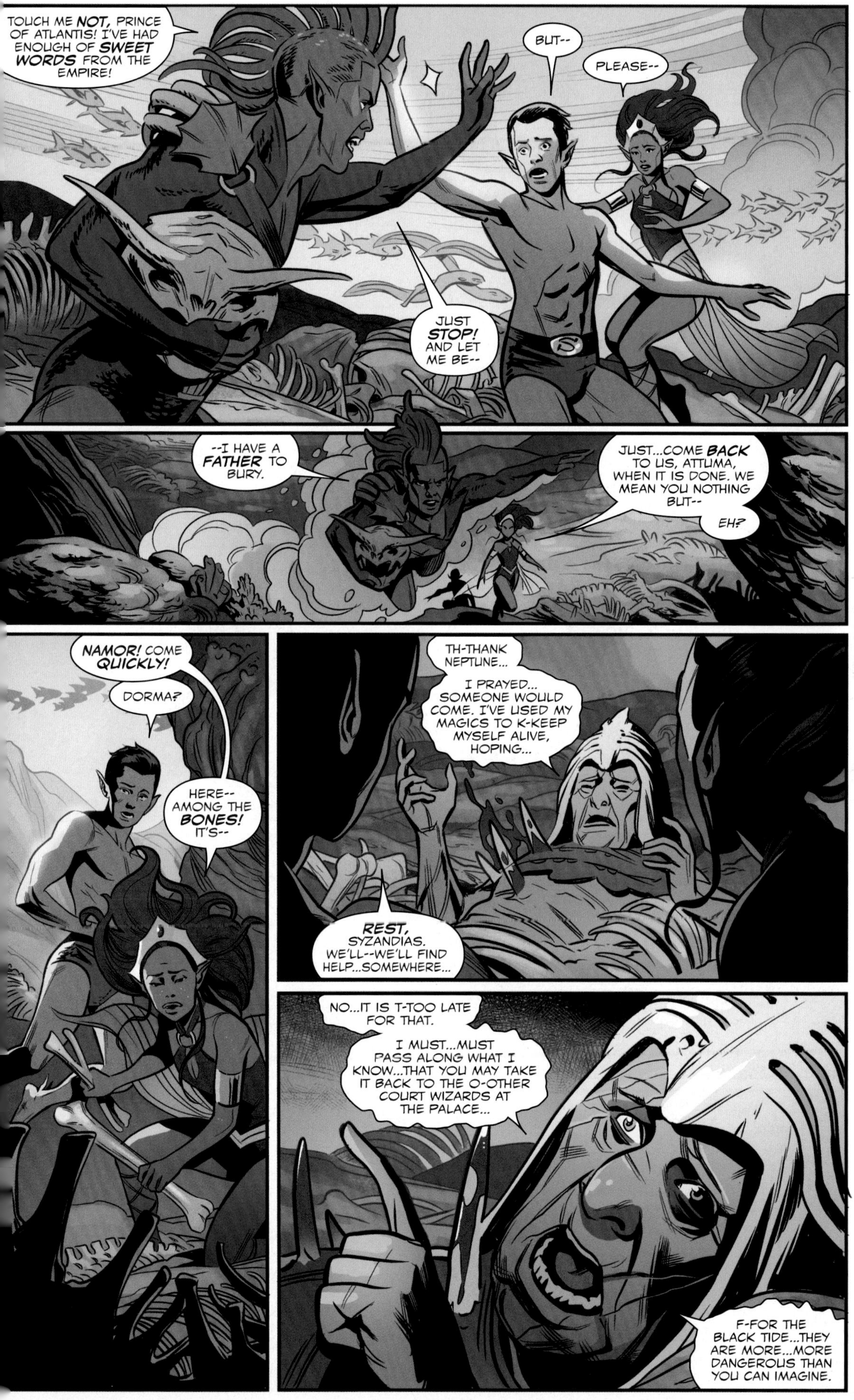
TOUCH ME NOT, PRINCE OF ATLANTIS! I'VE HAD ENOUGH OF SWEET WORDS FROM THE EMPIRE!
BUT--
PLEASE--
JUST STOP! AND LET ME BE--
--I HAVE A FATHER TO BURY.
JUST...COME BACK TO US, ATTUMA, WHEN IT IS DONE. WE MEAN YOU NOTHING BUT--
EH?
NAMOR! COME QUICKLY!
DORMA?
HERE-- AMONG THE BONES! IT'S--
TH-THANK NEPTUNE...
I PRAYED... SOMEONE WOULD COME. I'VE USED MY MAGICS TO K-KEEP MYSELF ALIVE, HOPING...
REST, SYZANDIAS. WE'LL--WE'LL FIND HELP...SOMEWHERE...
NO...IT IS T-TOO LATE FOR THAT.
I MUST...MUST PASS ALONG WHAT I KNOW...THAT YOU MAY TAKE IT BACK TO THE O-OTHER COURT WIZARDS AT THE PALACE...
F-FOR THE BLACK TIDE...THEY ARE MORE...MORE DANGEROUS THAN YOU CAN IMAGINE.

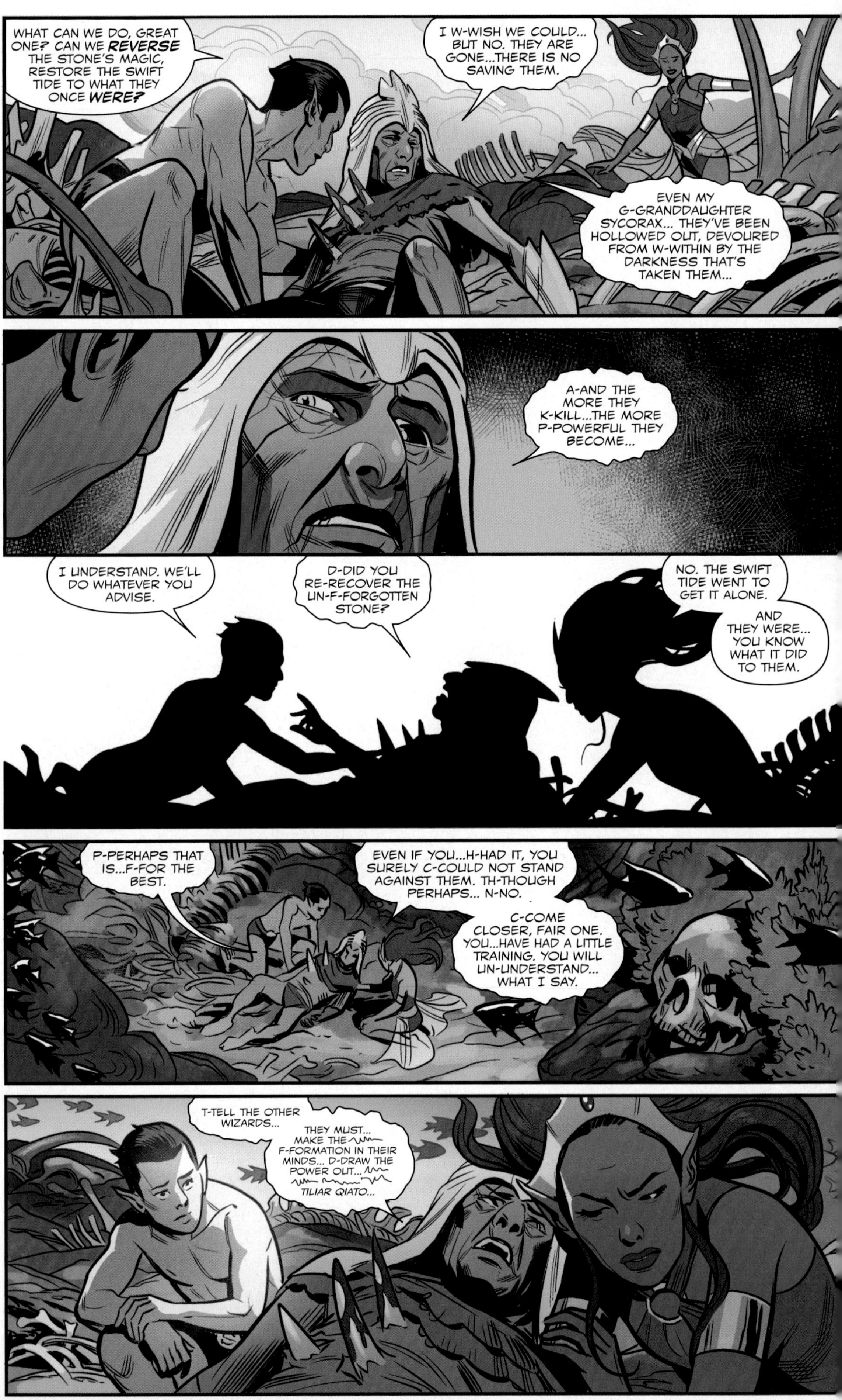
WHAT CAN WE DO, GREAT ONE? CAN WE REVERSE THE STONE'S MAGIC, RESTORE THE SWIFT TIDE TO WHAT THEY ONCE WERE?
I W-WISH WE COULD... BUT NO. THEY ARE GONE...THERE IS NO SAVING THEM.
EVEN MY G-GRANDDAUGHTER SYCORAX... THEY'VE BEEN HOLLOWED OUT, DEVOURED FROM W-WITHIN BY THE DARKNESS THAT'S TAKEN THEM...
A-AND THE MORE THEY K-KILL...THE MORE P-POWERFUL THEY BECOME...
I UNDERSTAND. WE'LL DO WHATEVER YOU ADVISE.
D-DID YOU RE-RECOVER THE UN-F-FORGOTTEN STONE?
NO. THE SWIFT TIDE WENT TO GET IT ALONE.
AND THEY WERE... YOU KNOW WHAT IT DID TO THEM.
P-PERHAPS THAT IS...F-FOR THE BEST.
EVEN IF YOU...H-HAD IT, YOU SURELY C-COULD NOT STAND AGAINST THEM. TH-THOUGH PERHAPS... N-NO.
C-COME CLOSER, FAIR ONE. YOU...HAVE HAD A LITTLE TRAINING. YOU WILL UN-UNDERSTAND... WHAT I SAY.
T-TELL THE OTHER WIZARDS...
THEY MUST... MAKE THE F-FORMATION IN THEIR MINDS... D-DRAW THE POWER OUT...
TILIAR QIATO...

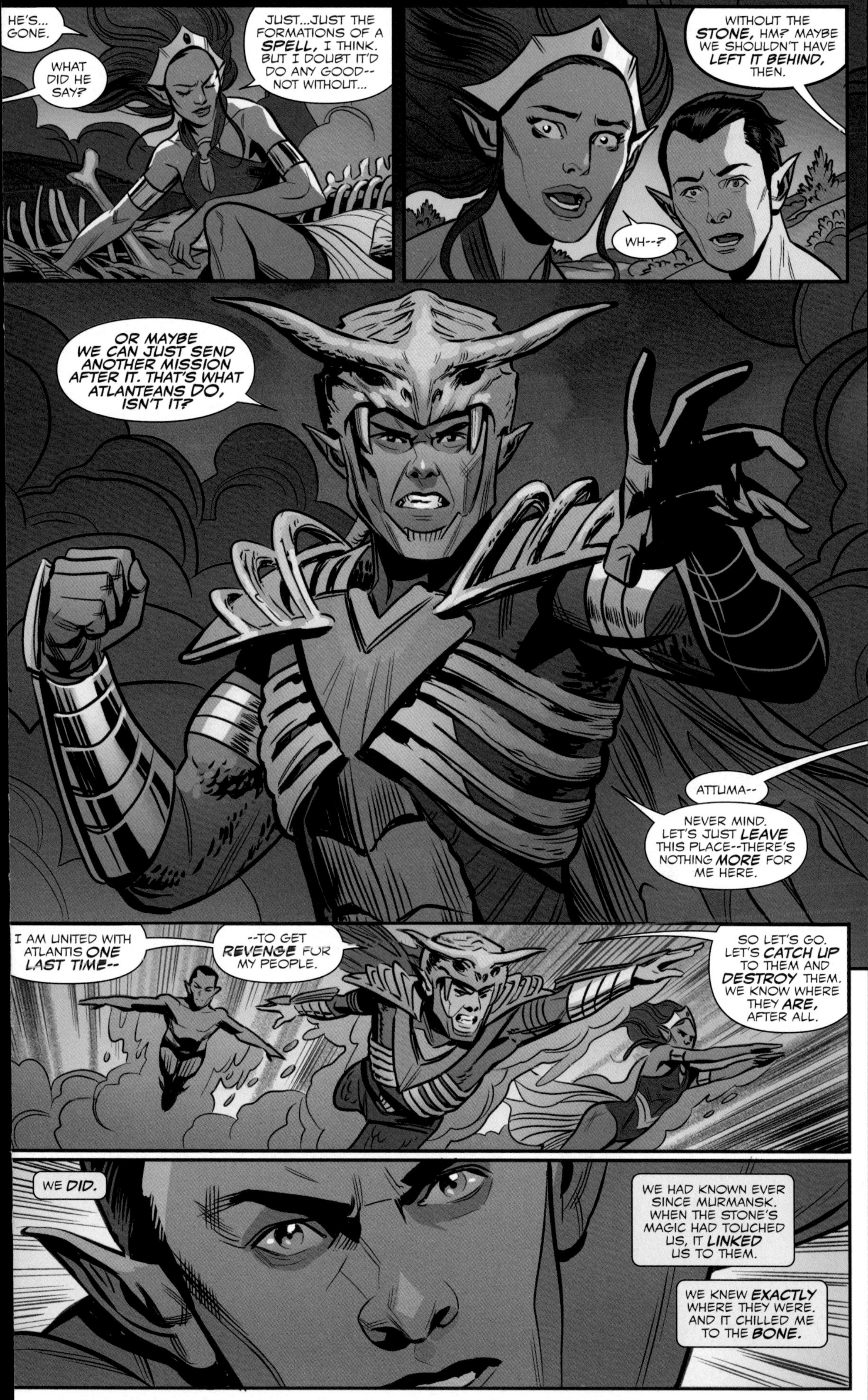
HE'S... GONE.
WHAT DID HE SAY?
JUST...JUST THE FORMATIONS OF A SPELL, I THINK. BUT I DOUBT IT'D DO ANY GOOD-- NOT WITHOUT...
WITHOUT THE STONE, HM? MAYBE WE SHOULDN'T HAVE LEFT IT BEHIND, THEN.
WH--?
OR MAYBE WE CAN JUST SEND ANOTHER MISSION AFTER IT. THAT'S WHAT ATLANTEANS DO, ISN'T IT?
ATTUMA--
NEVER MIND. LET'S JUST LEAVE THIS PLACE--THERE'S NOTHING MORE FOR ME HERE.
I AM UNITED WITH ATLANTIS ONE LAST TIME--
--TO GET REVENGE FOR MY PEOPLE.
SO LET'S GO. LET'S CATCH UP TO THEM AND DESTROY THEM. WE KNOW WHERE THEY ARE, AFTER ALL.
WE DID.
WE HAD KNOWN EVER SINCE MURMANSK. WHEN THE STONE'S MAGIC HAD TOUCHED US, IT LINKED US TO THEM.
WE KNEW EXACTLY WHERE THEY WERE. AND IT CHILLED ME TO THE BONE.

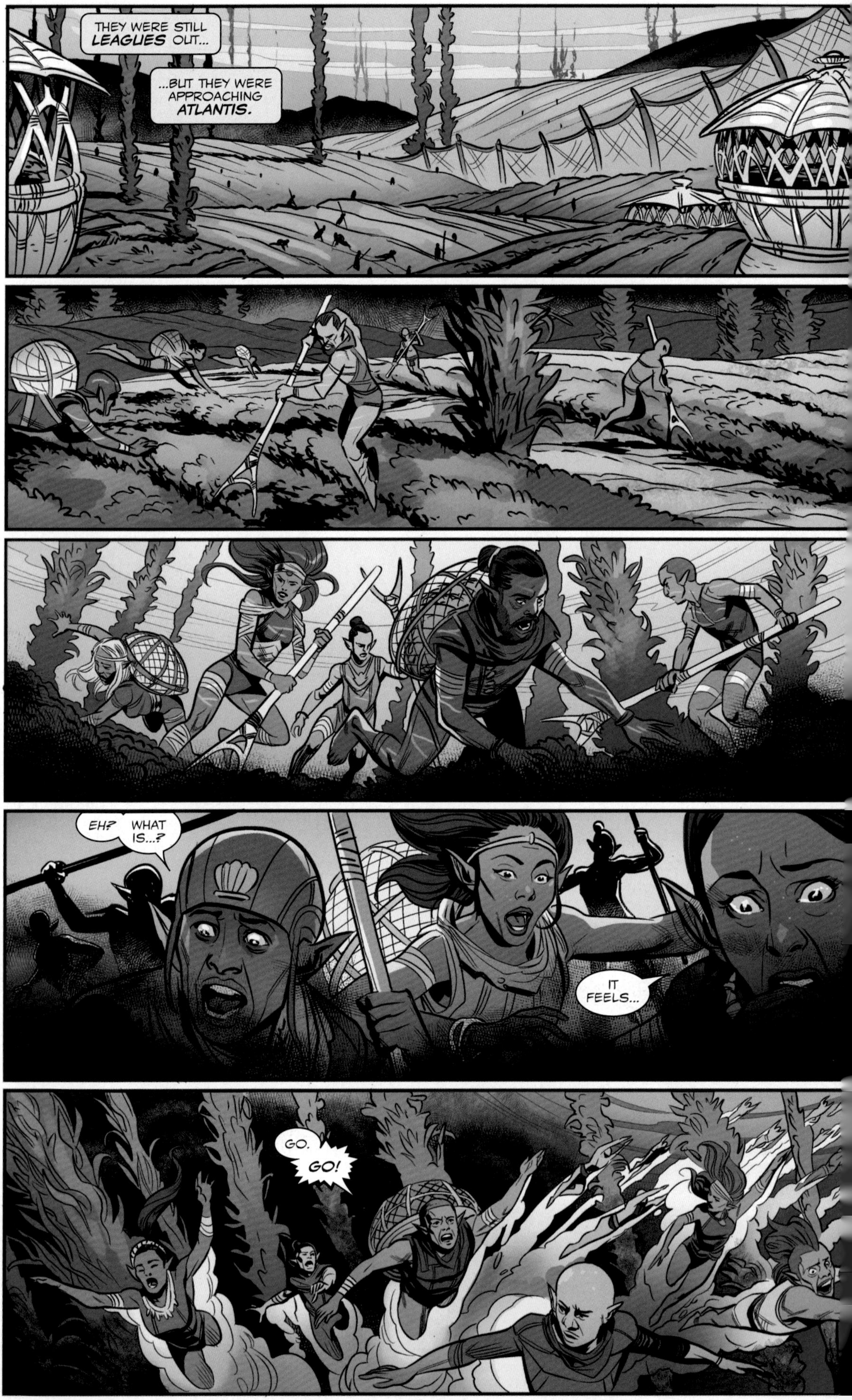
THEY WERE STILL LEAGUES OUT...
...BUT THEY WERE APPROACHING ATLANTIS.
EH? WHAT IS...?
IT FEELS...
GO. GO!

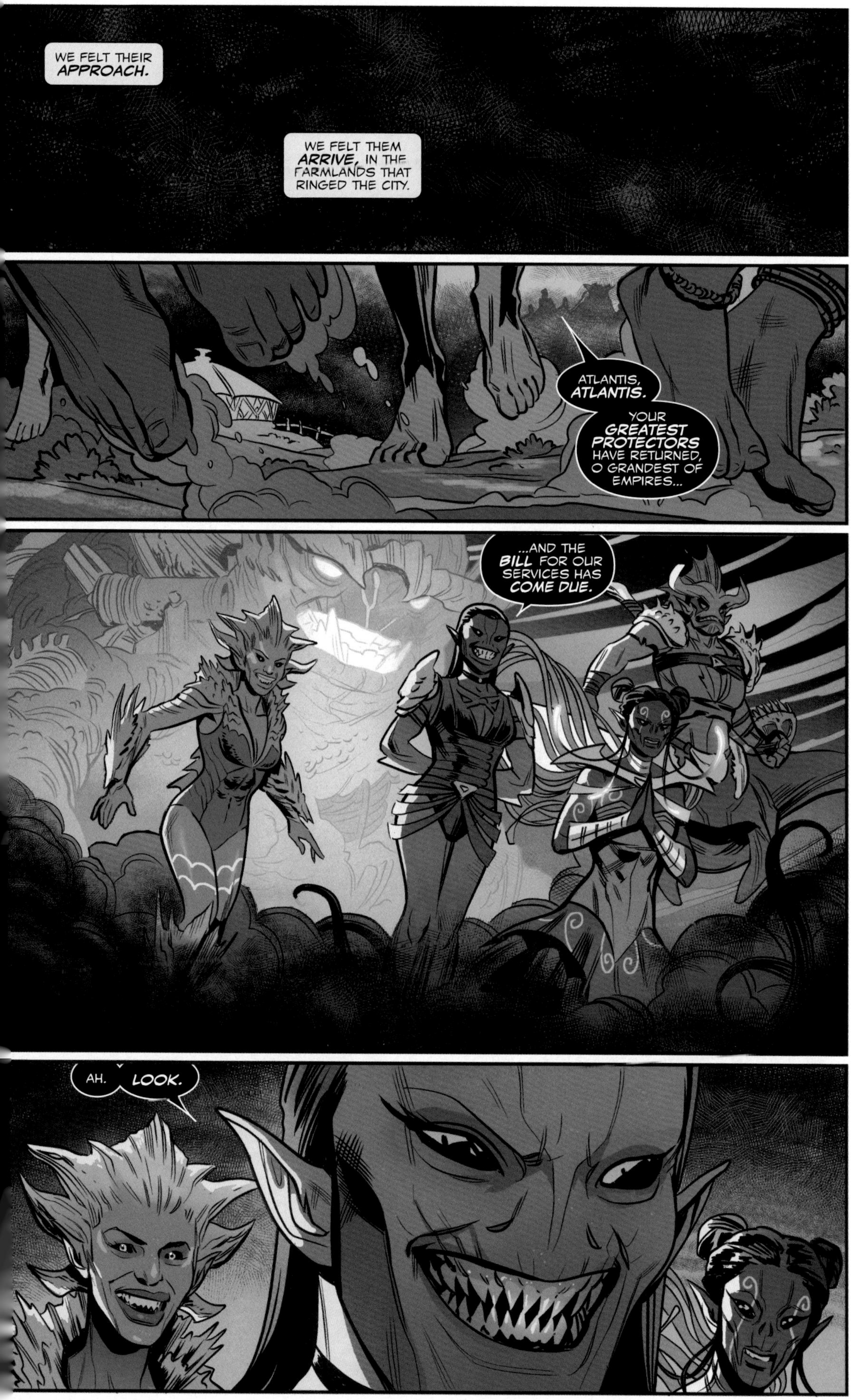
WE FELT THEIR APPROACH.
WE FELT THEM ARRIVE, IN THE FARMLANDS THAT RINGED THE CITY.
ATLANTIS, ATLANTIS.
YOUR GREATEST PROTECTORS HAVE RETURNED, O GRANDEST OF EMPIRES...
...AND THE BILL FOR OUR SERVICES HAS COME DUE.
AH.
LOOK.

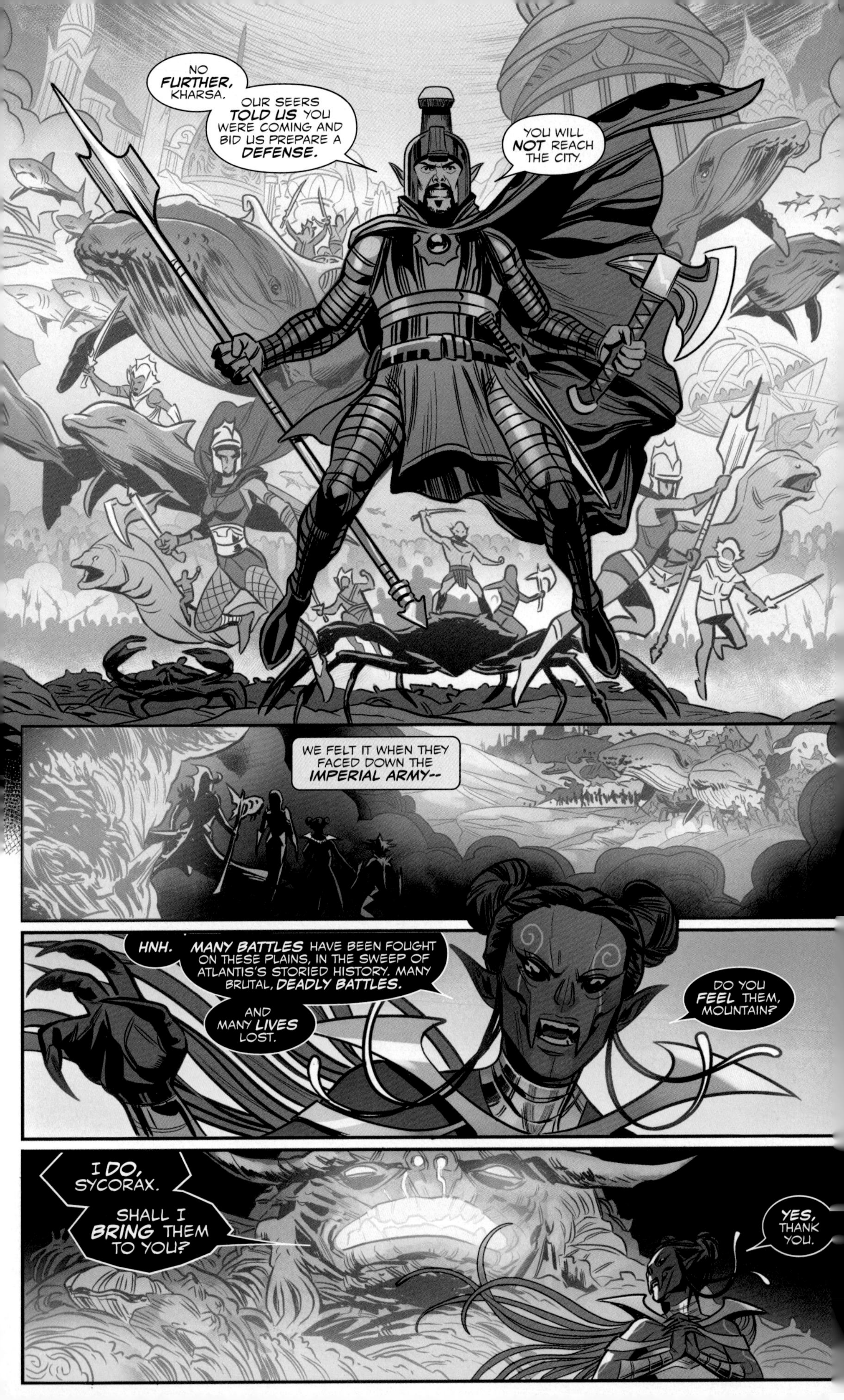

NO FURTHER, KHARSA.
OUR SEERS TOLD US YOU WERE COMING AND BID US PREPARE A DEFENSE.
YOU WILL NOT REACH THE CITY.
WE FELT IT WHEN THEY FACED DOWN THE IMPERIAL ARMY--
HNH.
MANY BATTLES HAVE BEEN FOUGHT ON THESE PLAINS, IN THE SWEEP OF ATLANTIS'S STORIED HISTORY. MANY BRUTAL, DEADLY BATTLES.
AND MANY LIVES LOST.
DO YOU FEEL THEM, MOUNTAIN?
I DO, SYCORAX.
SHALL I BRING THEM TO YOU?
YES, THANK YOU.

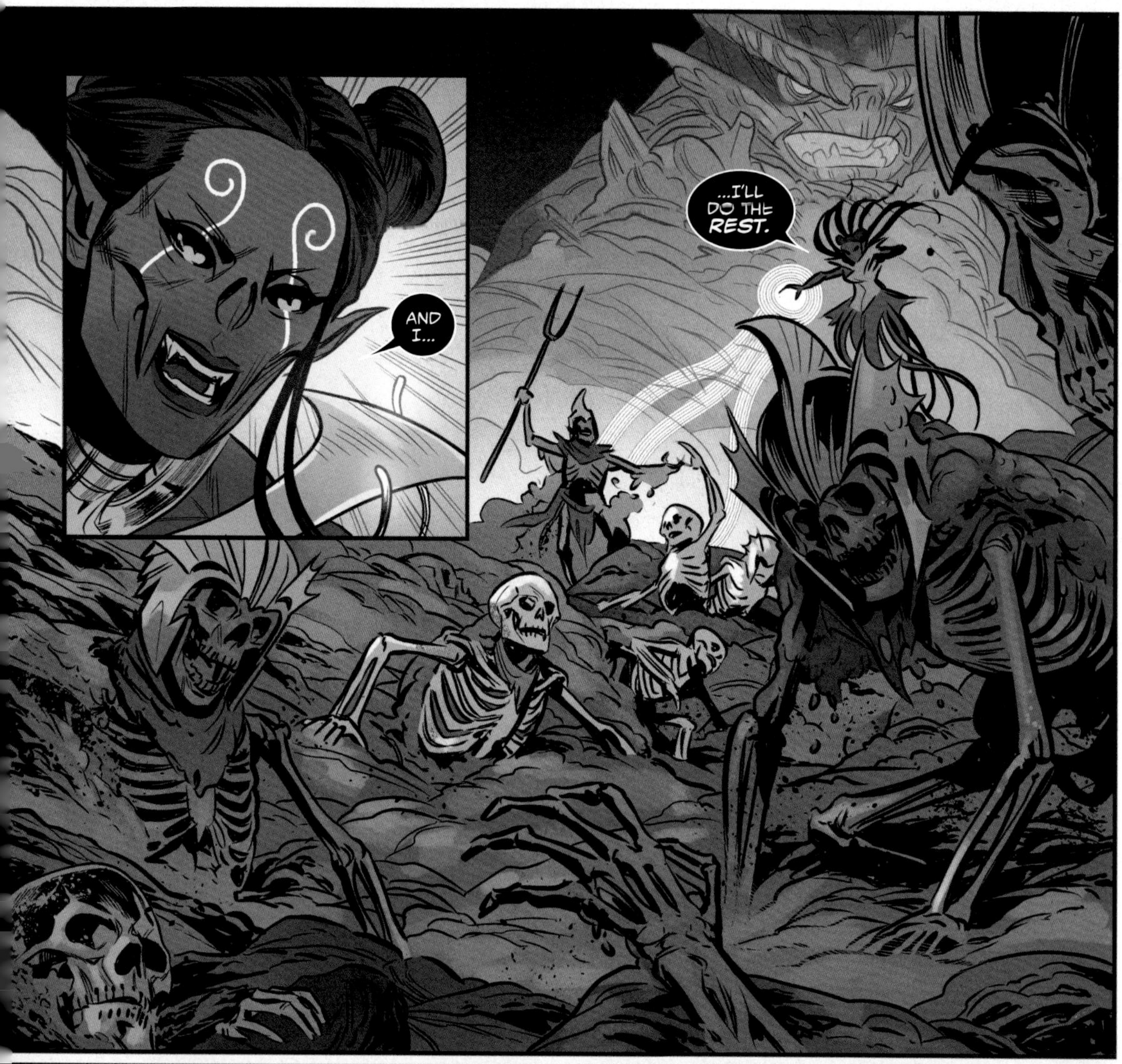
AND I...
...I'LL DO THE REST.

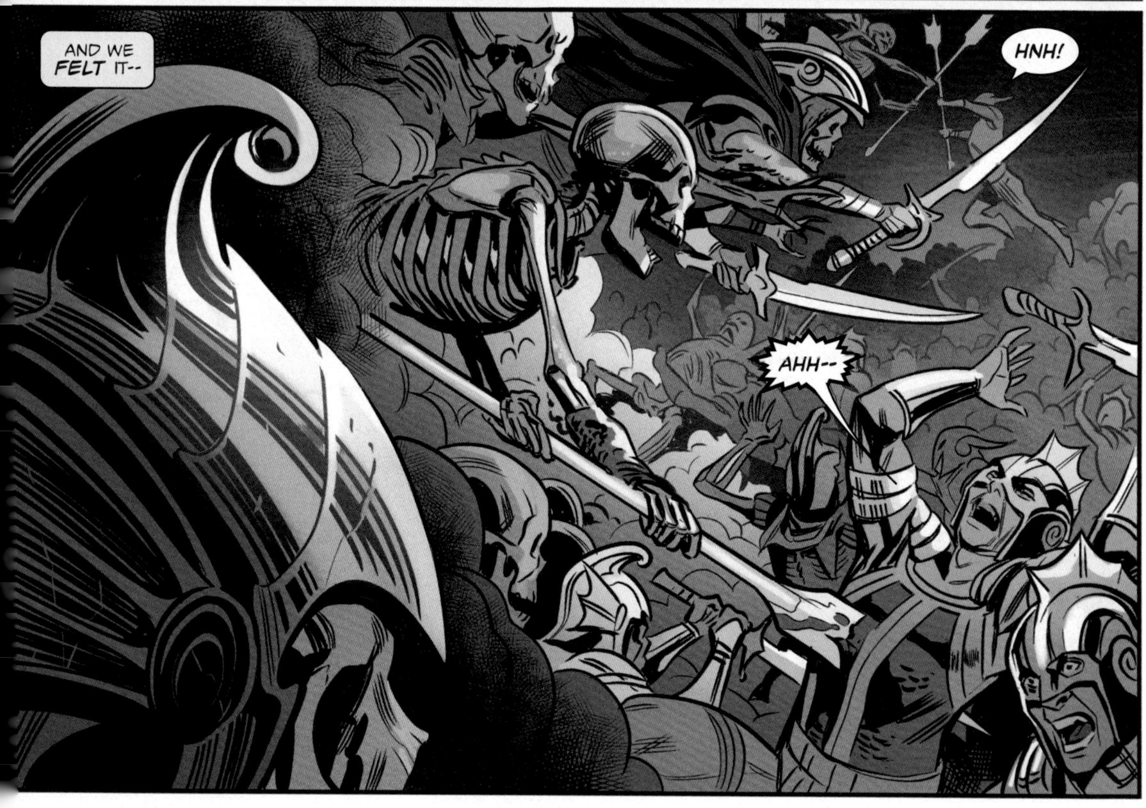
AND WE FELT IT--
HNH!
AHH--

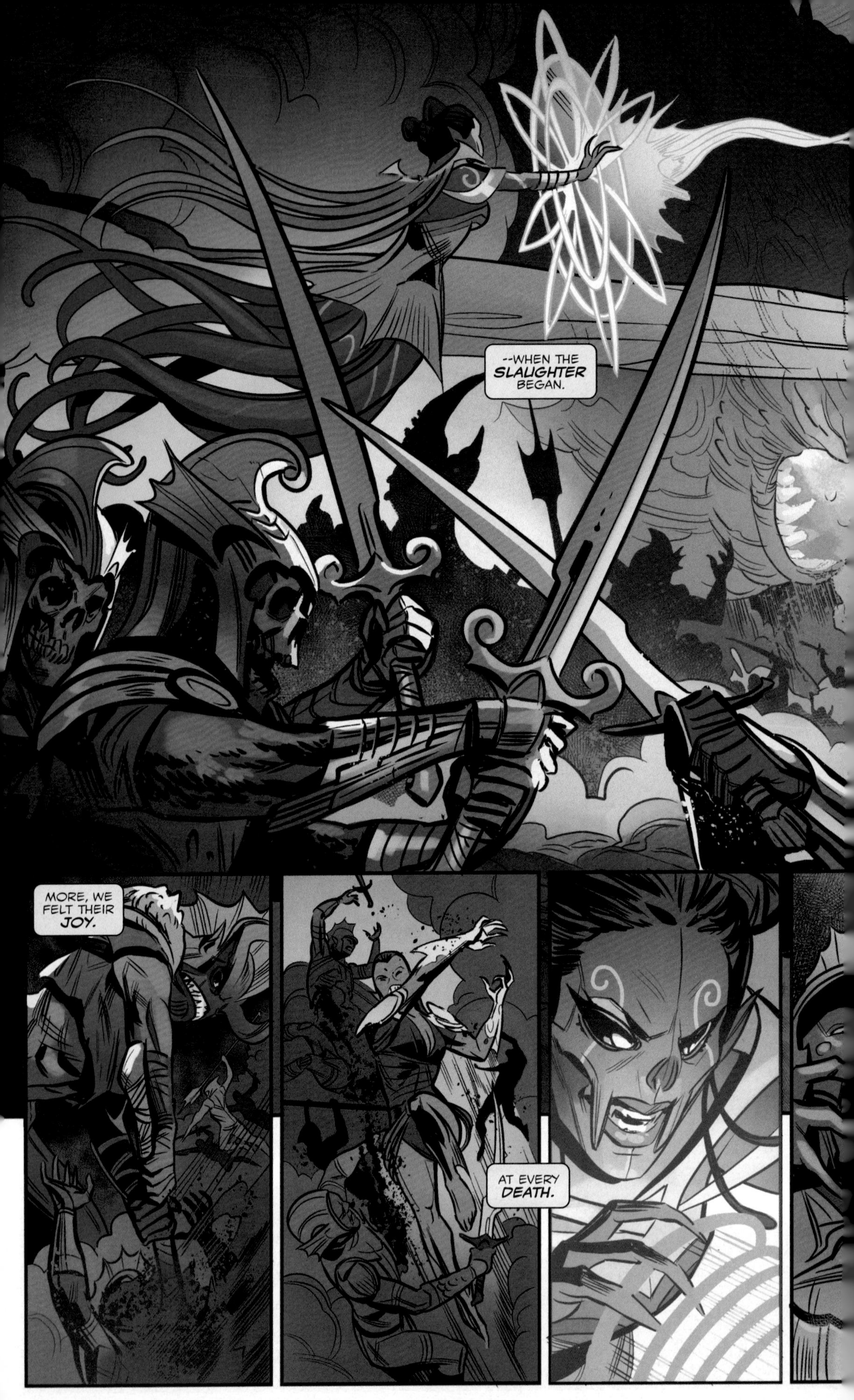
--WHEN THE SLAUGHTER BEGAN.
MORE, WE FELT THEIR JOY.
AT EVERY DEATH.

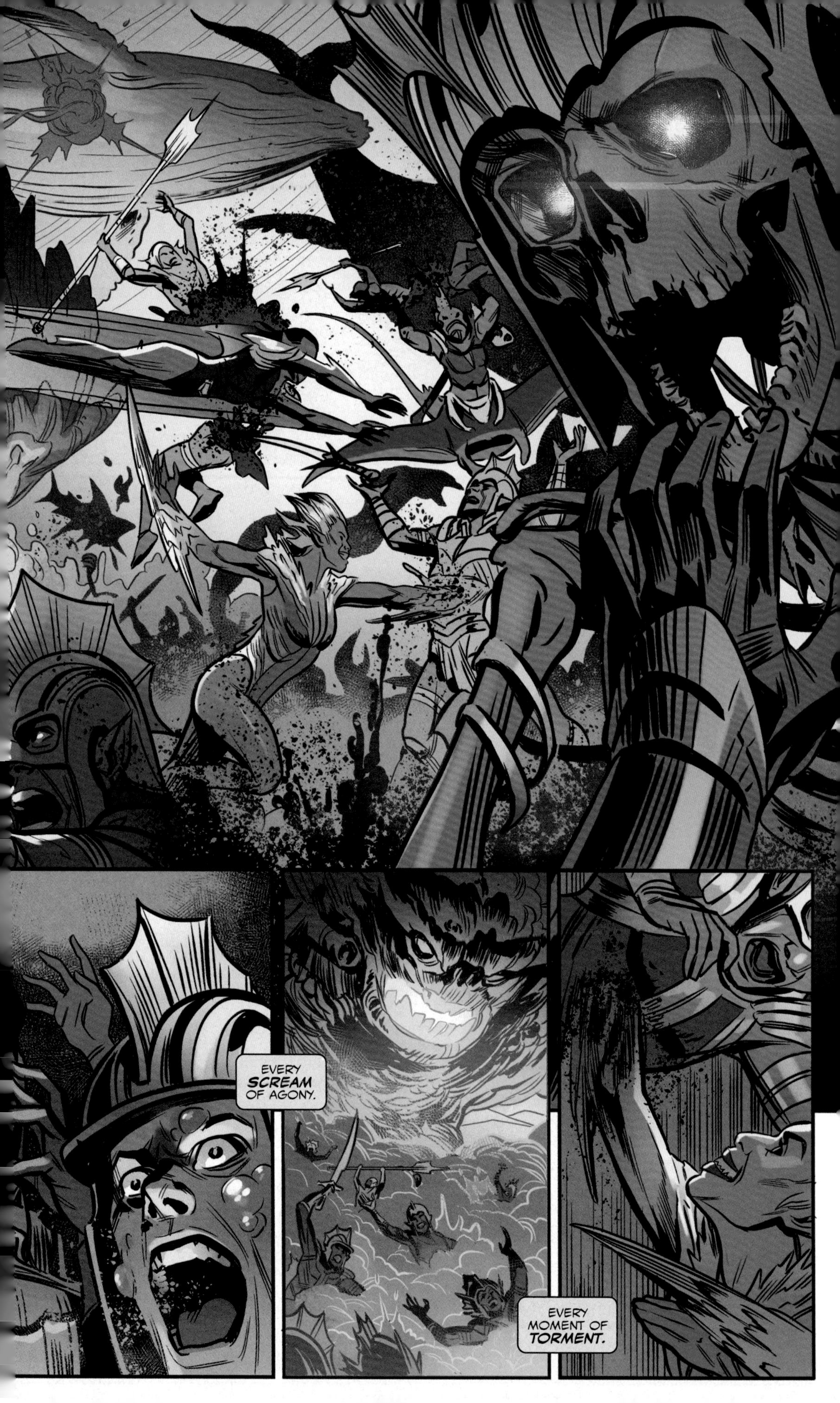
EVERY SCREAM OF AGONY.
EVERY MOMENT OF TORMENT.

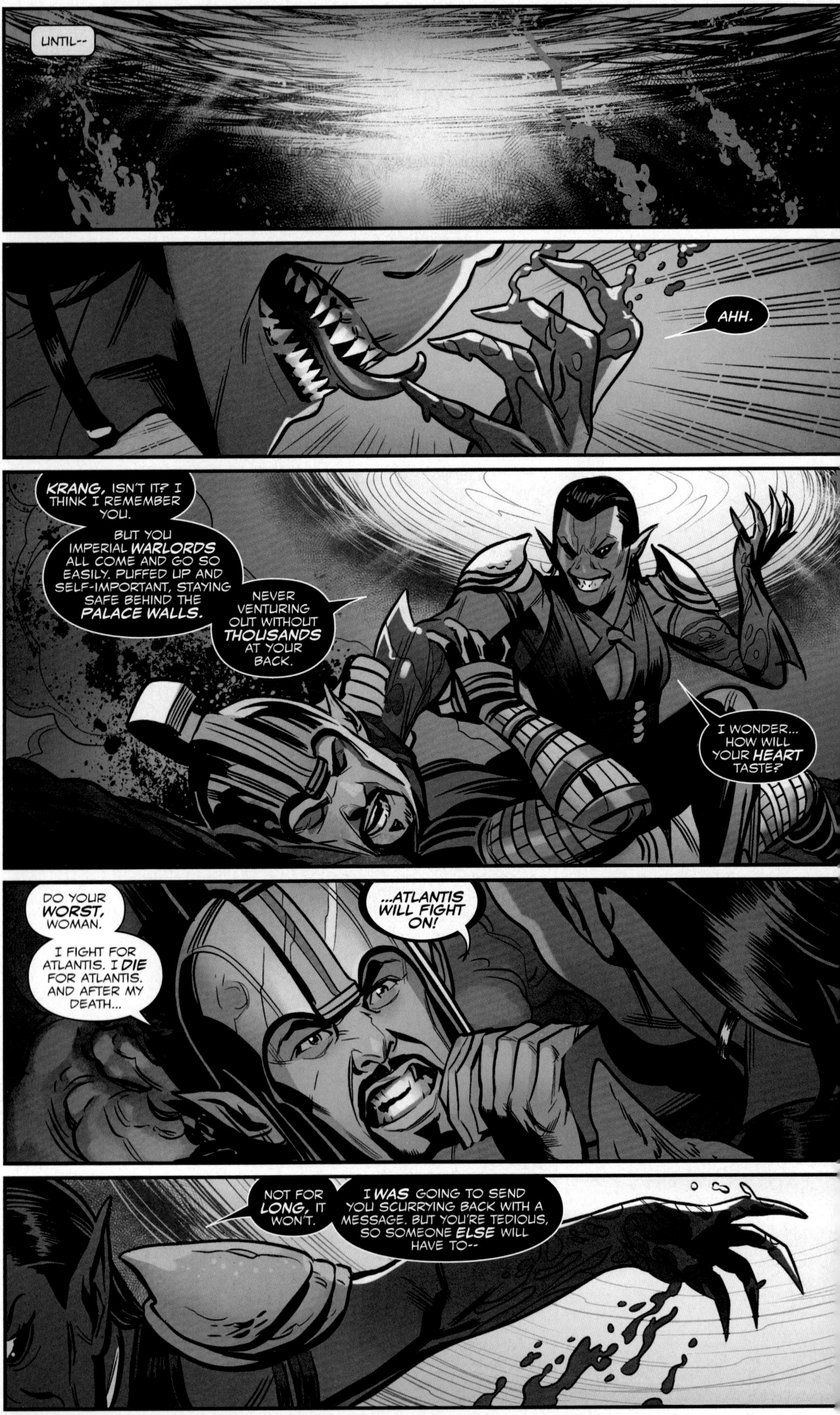

UNTIL--
AHH.
KRANG, ISN'T IT? I THINK I REMEMBER YOU.
BUT YOU IMPERIAL WARLORDS ALL COME AND GO SO EASILY. PUFFED UP AND SELF-IMPORTANT, STAYING SAFE BEHIND THE PALACE WALLS.
NEVER VENTURING OUT WITHOUT THOUSANDS AT YOUR BACK.
I WONDER... HOW WILL YOUR HEART TASTE?
DO YOUR WORST, WOMAN.
I FIGHT FOR ATLANTIS. I DIE FOR ATLANTIS. AND AFTER MY DEATH...
...ATLANTIS WILL FIGHT ON!
NOT FOR LONG, IT WON'T.
I WAS GOING TO SEND YOU SCURRYING BACK WITH A MESSAGE. BUT YOU'RE TEDIOUS, SO SOMEONE ELSE WILL HAVE TO--

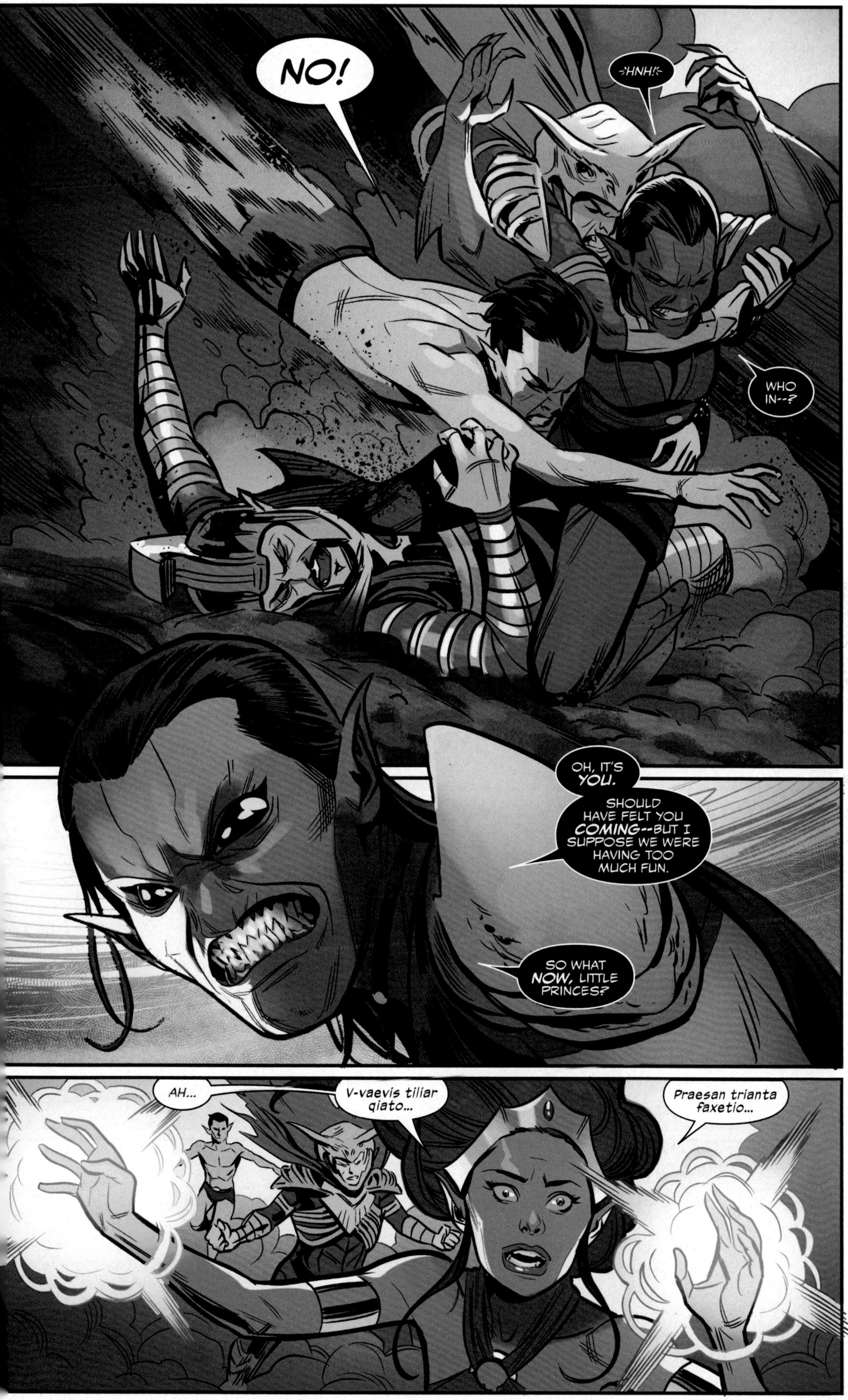
NO!
-HNH!-
WHO IN--?
OH, IT'S YOU.
SHOULD HAVE FELT YOU COMING--BUT I SUPPOSE WE WERE HAVING TOO MUCH FUN.
SO WHAT NOW, LITTLE PRINCES?
AH...
V-vaevis tiliar qiato...
Praesan trianta faxetio...

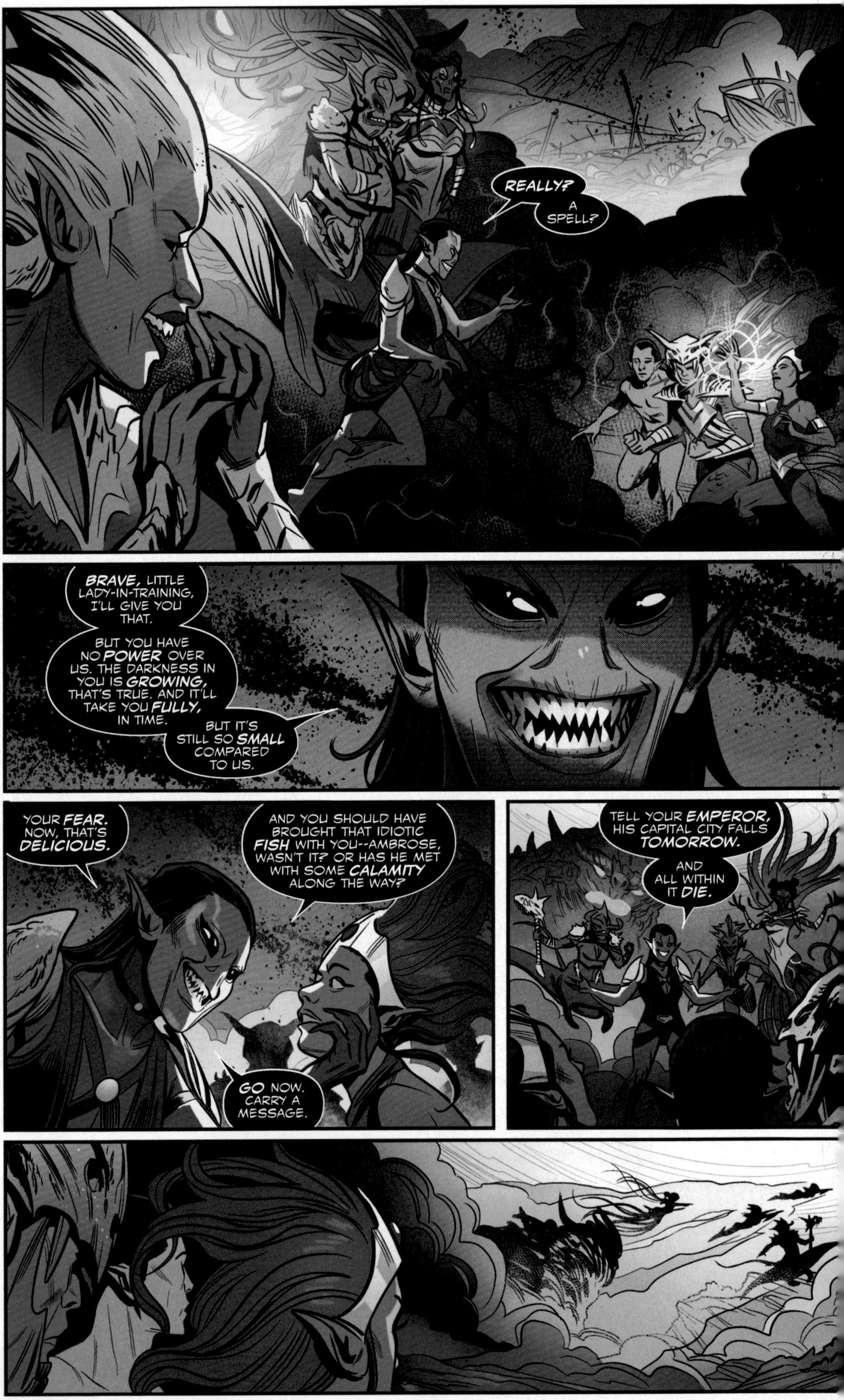
REALLY? A SPELL?
BRAVE, LITTLE LADY-IN-TRAINING, I'LL GIVE YOU THAT.
BUT YOU HAVE NO POWER OVER US. THE DARKNESS IN YOU IS GROWING, THAT'S TRUE. AND IT'LL TAKE YOU FULLY, IN TIME.
BUT IT'S STILL SO SMALL COMPARED TO US.
YOUR FEAR. NOW, THAT'S DELICIOUS.
AND YOU SHOULD HAVE BROUGHT THAT IDIOTIC FISH WITH YOU--AMBROSE, WASN'T IT? OR HAS HE MET WITH SOME CALAMITY ALONG THE WAY?
GO NOW. CARRY A MESSAGE.
TELL YOUR EMPEROR, HIS CAPITAL CITY FALLS TOMORROW.
AND ALL WITHIN IT DIE.

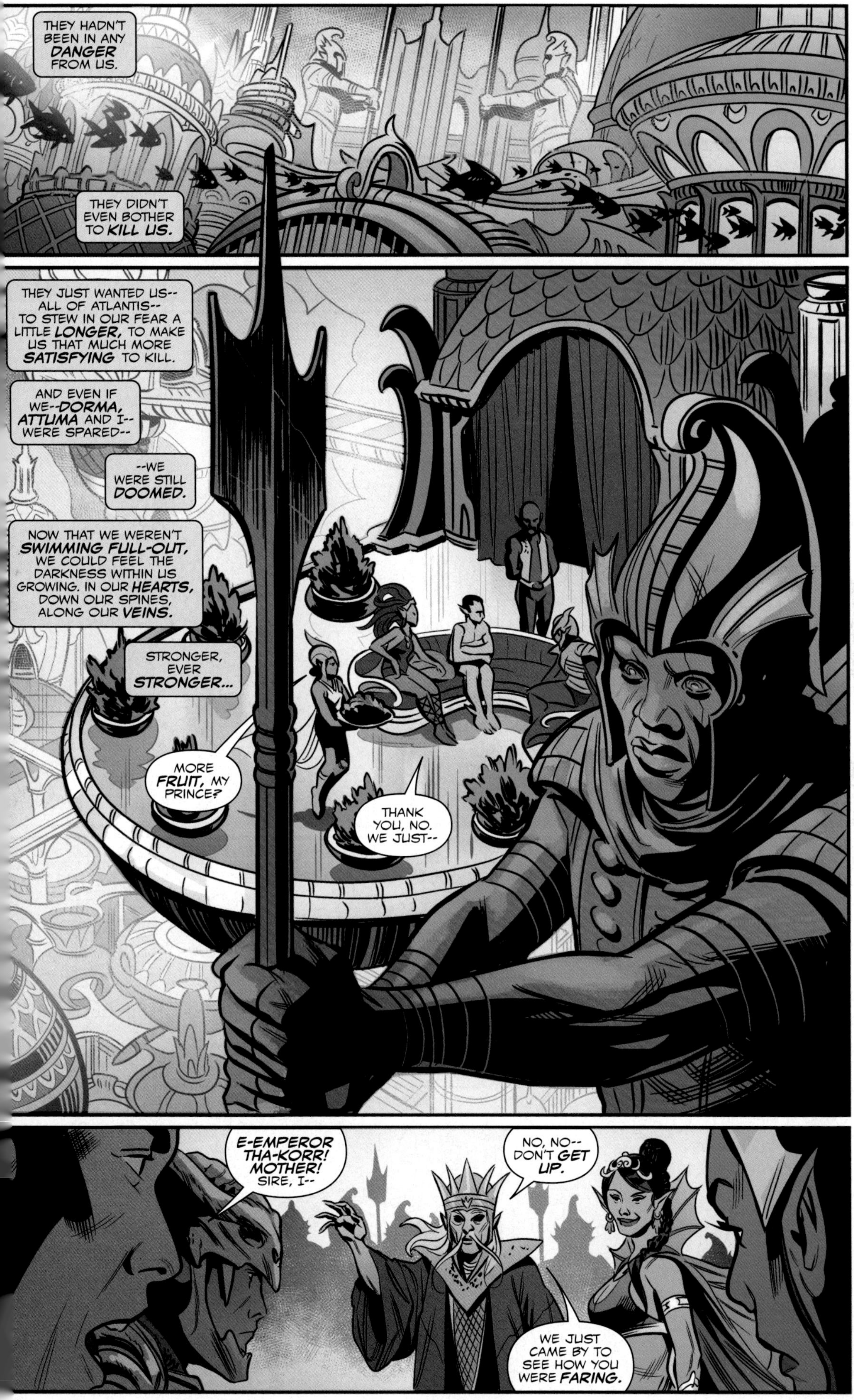
THEY HADN'T BEEN IN ANY DANGER FROM US.
THEY DIDN'T EVEN BOTHER TO KILL US.
THEY JUST WANTED US-- ALL OF ATLANTIS-- TO STEW IN OUR FEAR A LITTLE LONGER, TO MAKE US THAT MUCH MORE SATISFYING TO KILL.
AND EVEN IF WE--DORMA, ATTUMA AND I-- WERE SPARED--
--WE WERE STILL DOOMED.
NOW THAT WE WEREN'T SWIMMING FULL-OUT, WE COULD FEEL THE DARKNESS WITHIN US GROWING. IN OUR HEARTS, DOWN OUR SPINES, ALONG OUR VEINS.
STRONGER, EVER STRONGER...
MORE FRUIT, MY PRINCE?
THANK YOU, NO. WE JUST--
E-EMPEROR THA-KORR! MOTHER! SIRE, I--
NO, NO-- DON'T GET UP.
WE JUST CAME BY TO SEE HOW YOU WERE FARING.

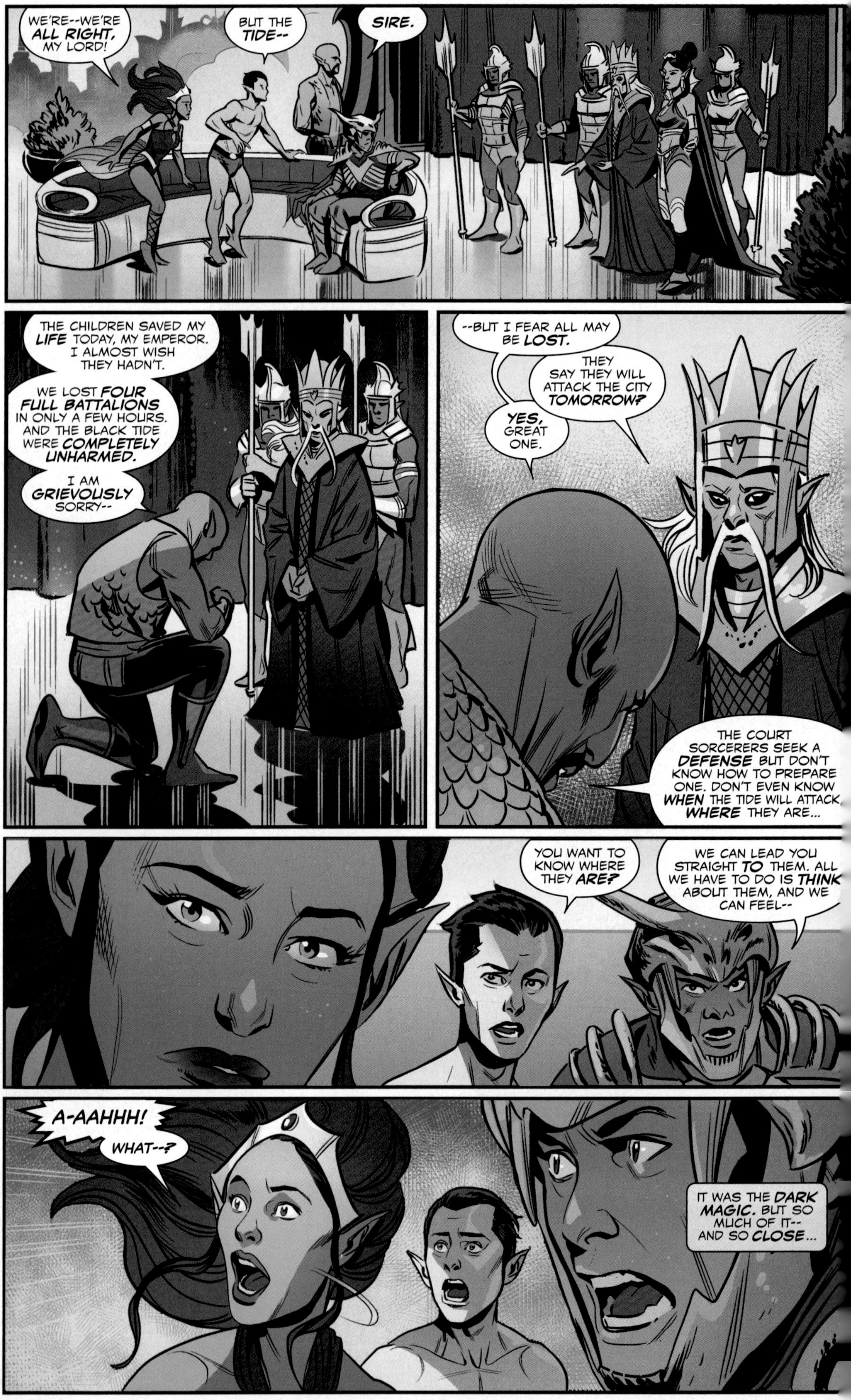
WE'RE--WE'RE ALL RIGHT, MY LORD!
BUT THE TIDE--
SIRE.
THE CHILDREN SAVED MY LIFE TODAY, MY EMPEROR. I ALMOST WISH THEY HADN'T.
WE LOST FOUR FULL BATTALIONS IN ONLY A FEW HOURS. AND THE BLACK TIDE WERE COMPLETELY UNHARMED.
I AM GRIEVOUSLY SORRY--
--BUT I FEAR ALL MAY BE LOST.
THEY SAY THEY WILL ATTACK THE CITY TOMORROW?
YES, GREAT ONE.
THE COURT SORCERERS SEEK A DEFENSE BUT DON'T KNOW HOW TO PREPARE ONE. DON'T EVEN KNOW WHEN THE TIDE WILL ATTACK, WHERE THEY ARE...
YOU WANT TO KNOW WHERE THEY ARE?
WE CAN LEAD YOU STRAIGHT TO THEM. ALL WE HAVE TO DO IS THINK ABOUT THEM, AND WE CAN FEEL--
A-AAHHH!
WHAT--?
IT WAS THE DARK MAGIC. BUT SO MUCH OF IT-- AND SO CLOSE...

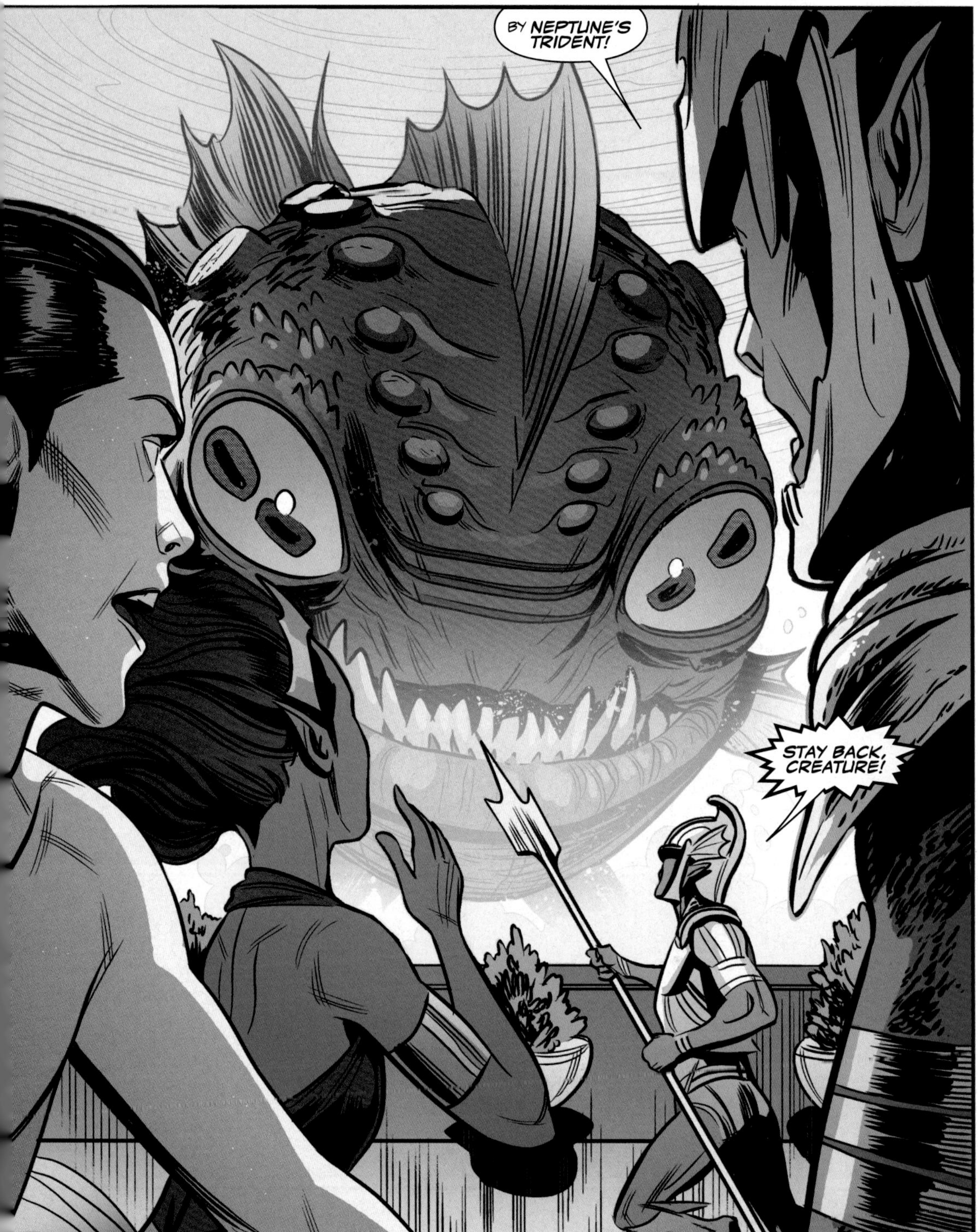
BY NEPTUNE'S TRIDENT!
STAY BACK, CREATURE!

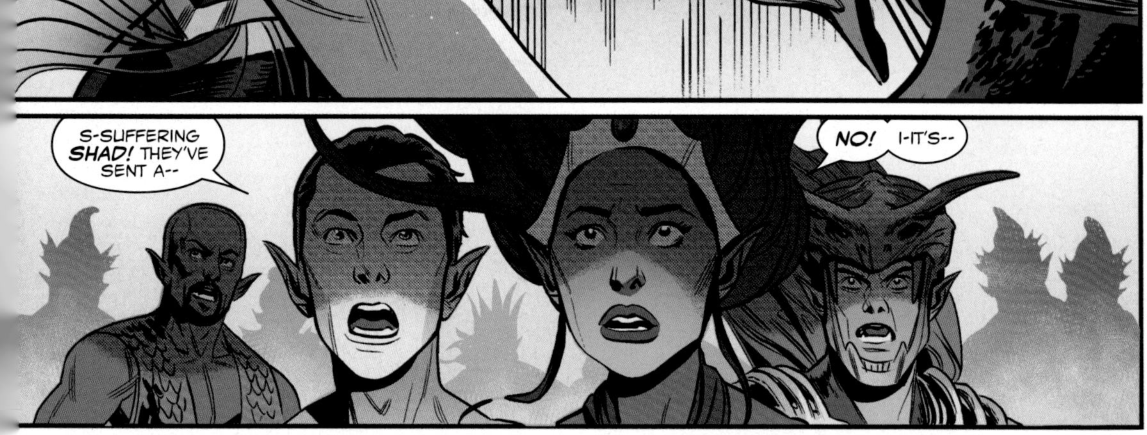
S-SUFFERING SHAD! THEY'VE SENT A--
NO! I-IT'S--

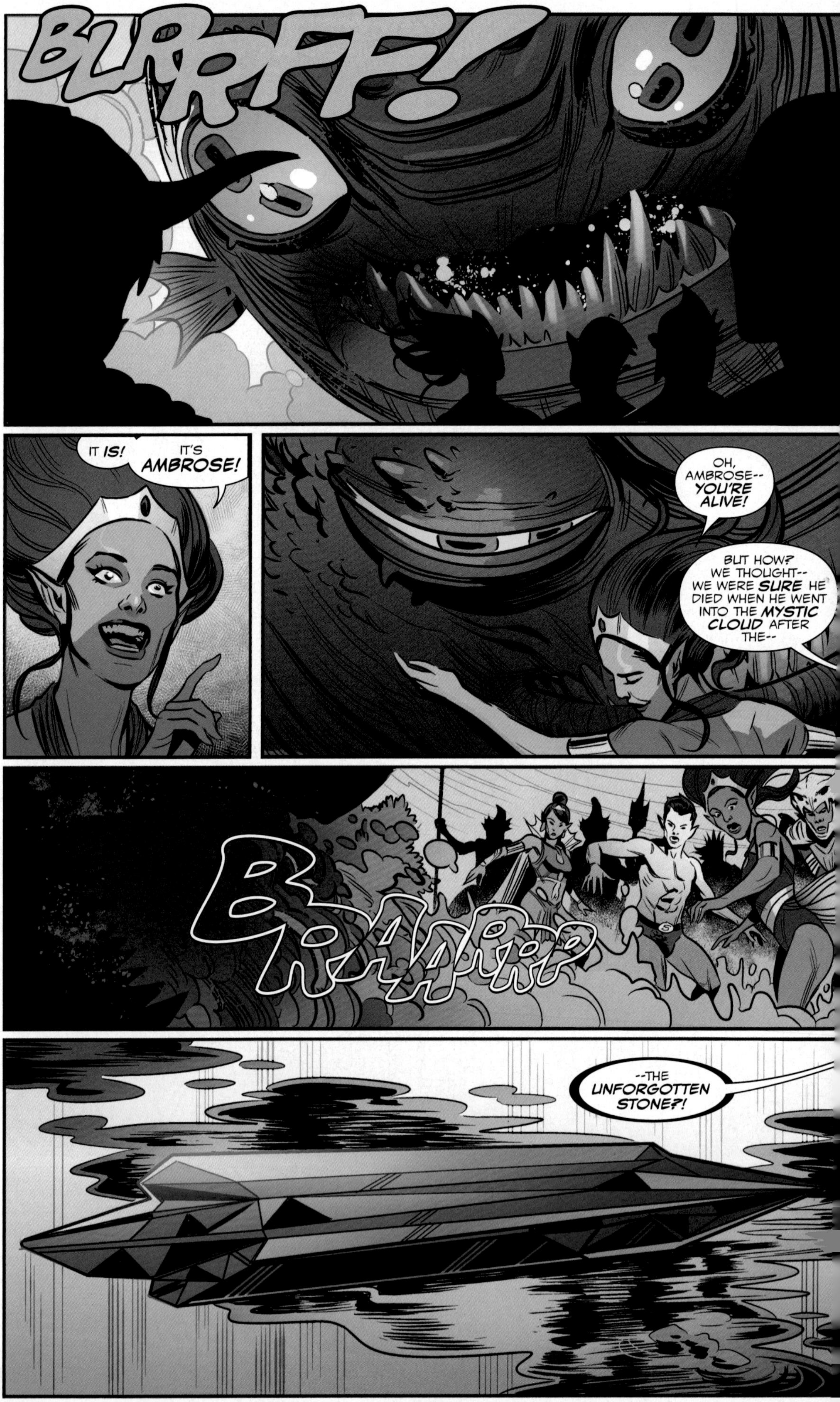
BLRRFF!
IT IS!
IT'S AMBROSE!
OH, AMBROSE-- YOU'RE ALIVE!
BUT HOW? WE THOUGHT-- WE WERE SURE HE DIED WHEN HE WENT INTO THE MYSTIC CLOUD AFTER THE--
BRAAARP
--THE UNFORGOTTEN STONE?!

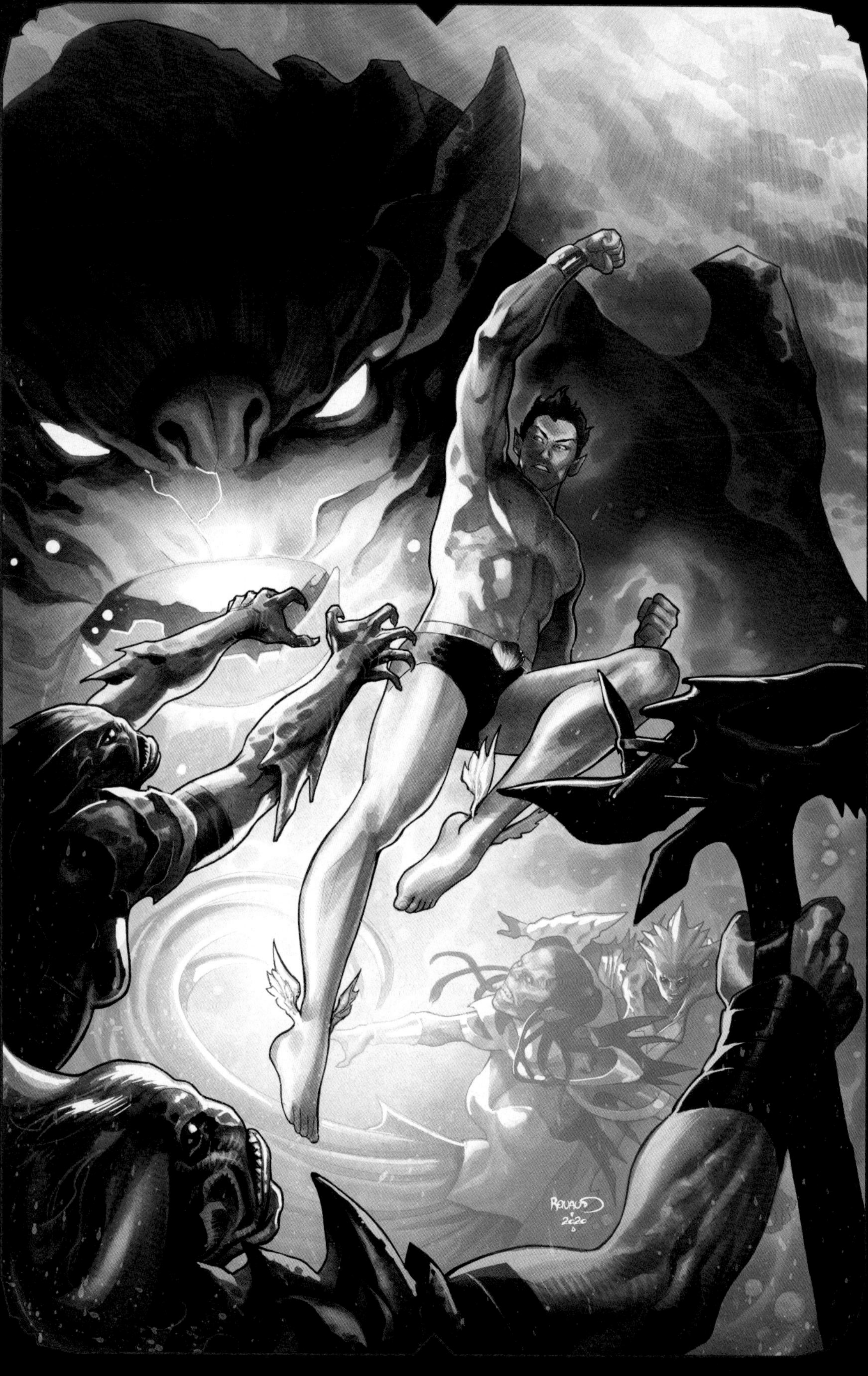

#3 VARIANT BY **PAUL RENAUD**

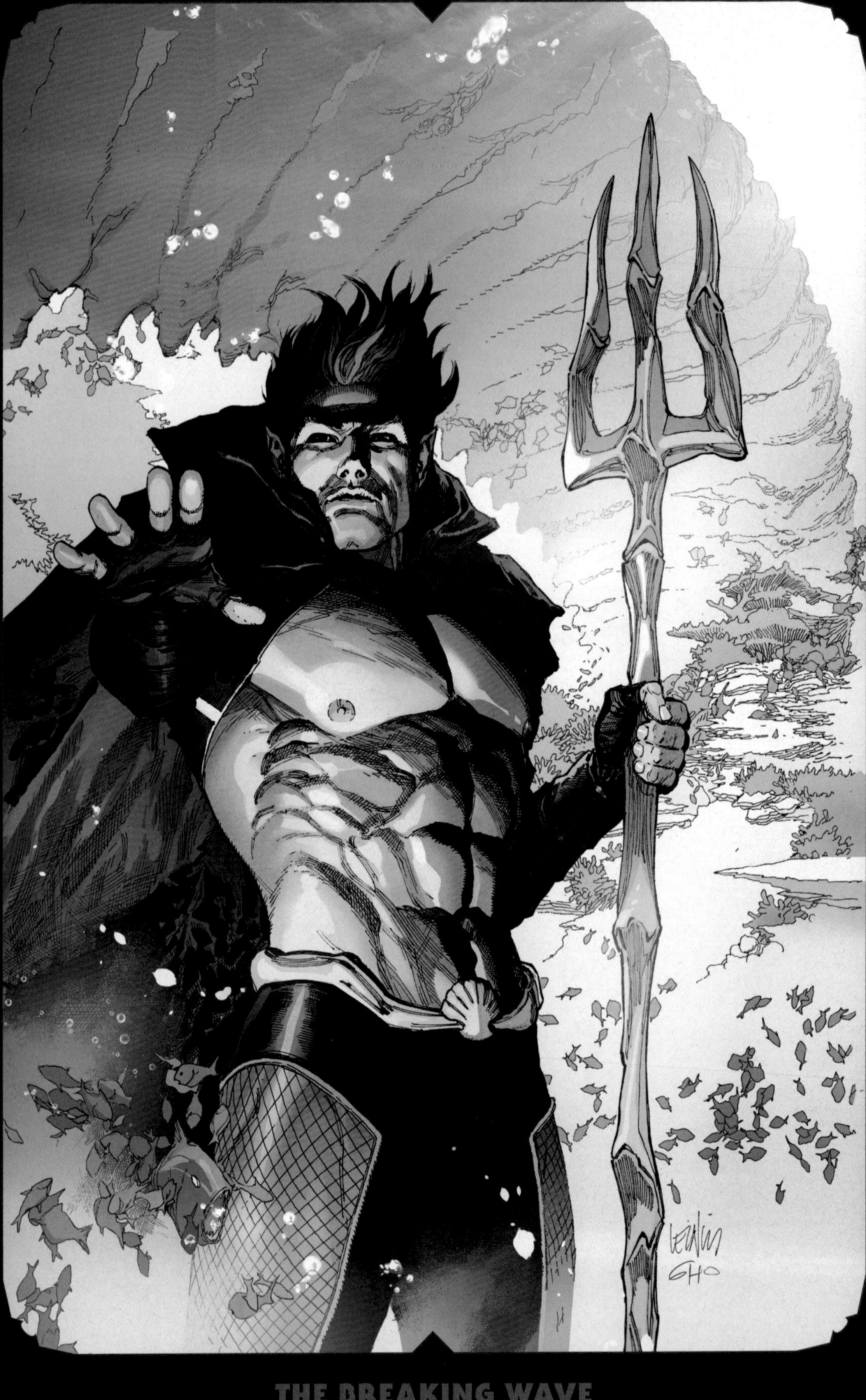

THE BREAKING WAVE

5

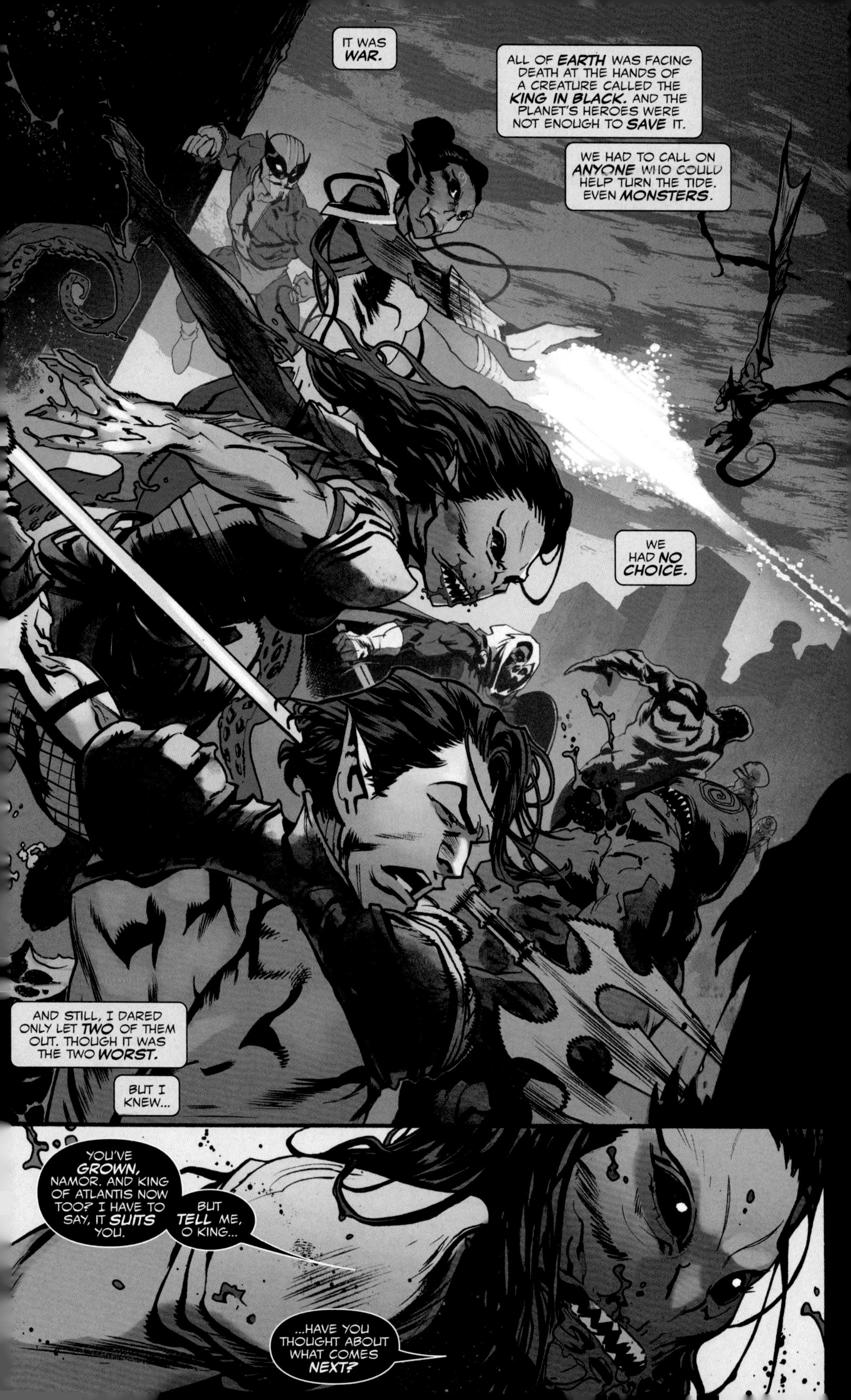
IT WAS WAR.
ALL OF EARTH WAS FACING DEATH AT THE HANDS OF A CREATURE CALLED THE KING IN BLACK. AND THE PLANET'S HEROES WERE NOT ENOUGH TO SAVE IT.
WE HAD TO CALL ON ANYONE WHO COULD HELP TURN THE TIDE. EVEN MONSTERS.
WE HAD NO CHOICE.
AND STILL, I DARED ONLY LET TWO OF THEM OUT. THOUGH IT WAS THE TWO WORST.
BUT I KNEW...
YOU'VE GROWN, NAMOR. AND KING OF ATLANTIS NOW TOO? I HAVE TO SAY, IT SUITS YOU.
BUT TELL ME, O KING...
...HAVE YOU THOUGHT ABOUT WHAT COMES NEXT?

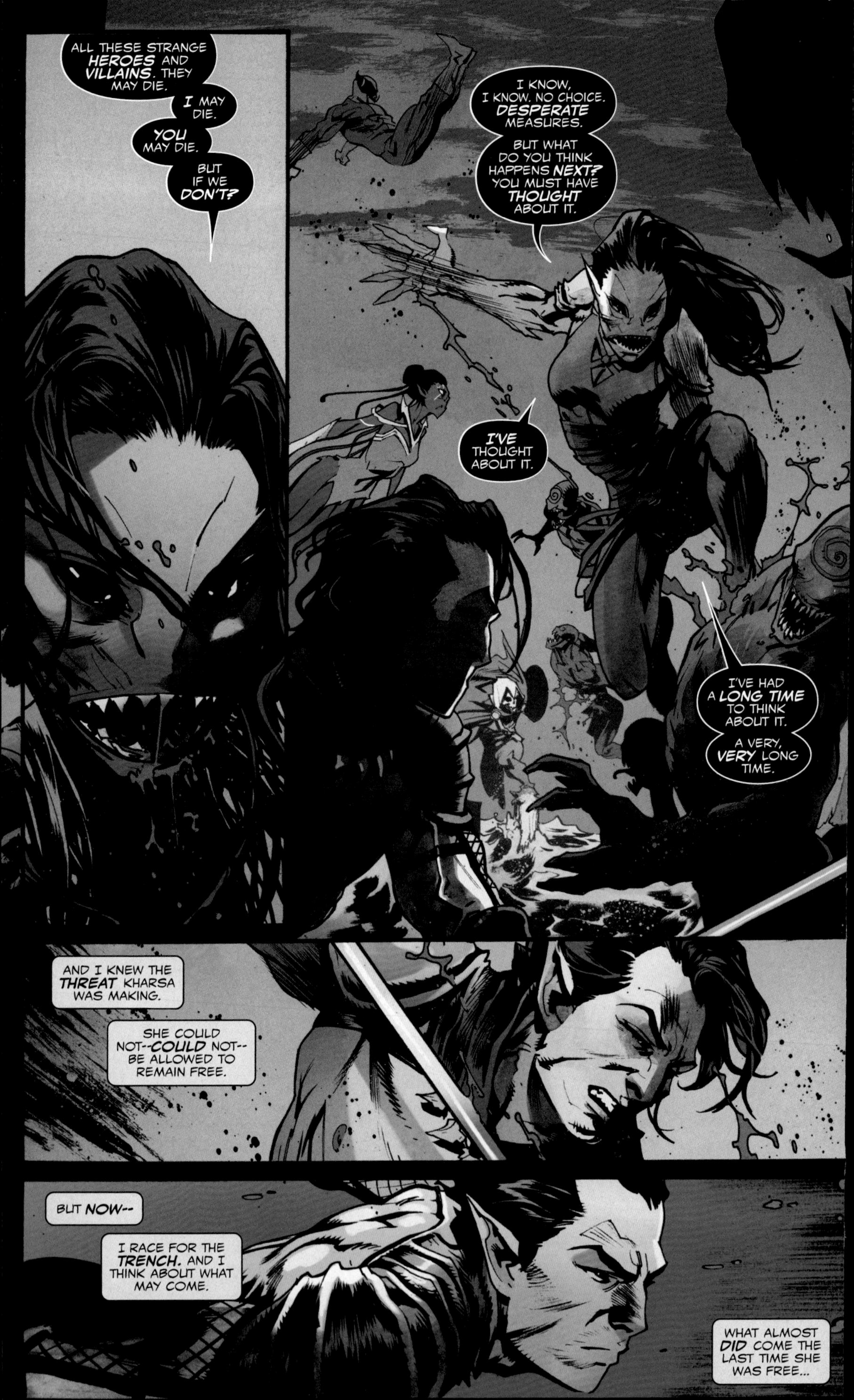
ALL THESE STRANGE HEROES AND VILLAINS. THEY MAY DIE.
I MAY DIE.
YOU MAY DIE.
BUT IF WE DON'T?
I KNOW, I KNOW. NO CHOICE. DESPERATE MEASURES.
BUT WHAT DO YOU THINK HAPPENS NEXT? YOU MUST HAVE THOUGHT ABOUT IT.
I'VE THOUGHT ABOUT IT.
I'VE HAD A LONG TIME TO THINK ABOUT IT.
A VERY, VERY LONG TIME.
AND I KNEW THE THREAT KHARSA WAS MAKING.
SHE COULD NOT--COULD NOT--BE ALLOWED TO REMAIN FREE.
BUT NOW--
I RACE FOR THE TRENCH. AND I THINK ABOUT WHAT MAY COME.
WHAT ALMOST DID COME THE LAST TIME SHE WAS FREE...

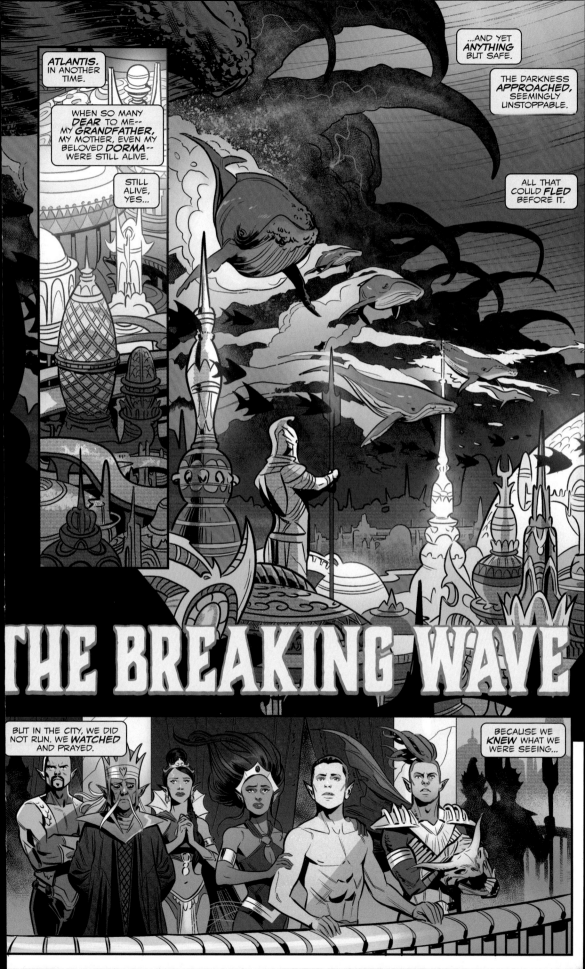

ATLANTIS. IN ANOTHER TIME.

WHEN SO MANY *DEAR* TO ME-- MY *GRANDFATHER,* MY MOTHER, EVEN MY BELOVED *DORMA*-- WERE STILL ALIVE.

STILL ALIVE, YES...

...AND YET *ANYTHING* BUT SAFE.

THE DARKNESS *APPROACHED,* SEEMINGLY UNSTOPPABLE.

ALL THAT COULD *FLED* BEFORE IT.

THE BREAKING WAVE

BUT IN THE CITY, WE DID NOT RUN. WE *WATCHED* AND PRAYED.

BECAUSE WE *KNEW* WHAT WE WERE SEEING...

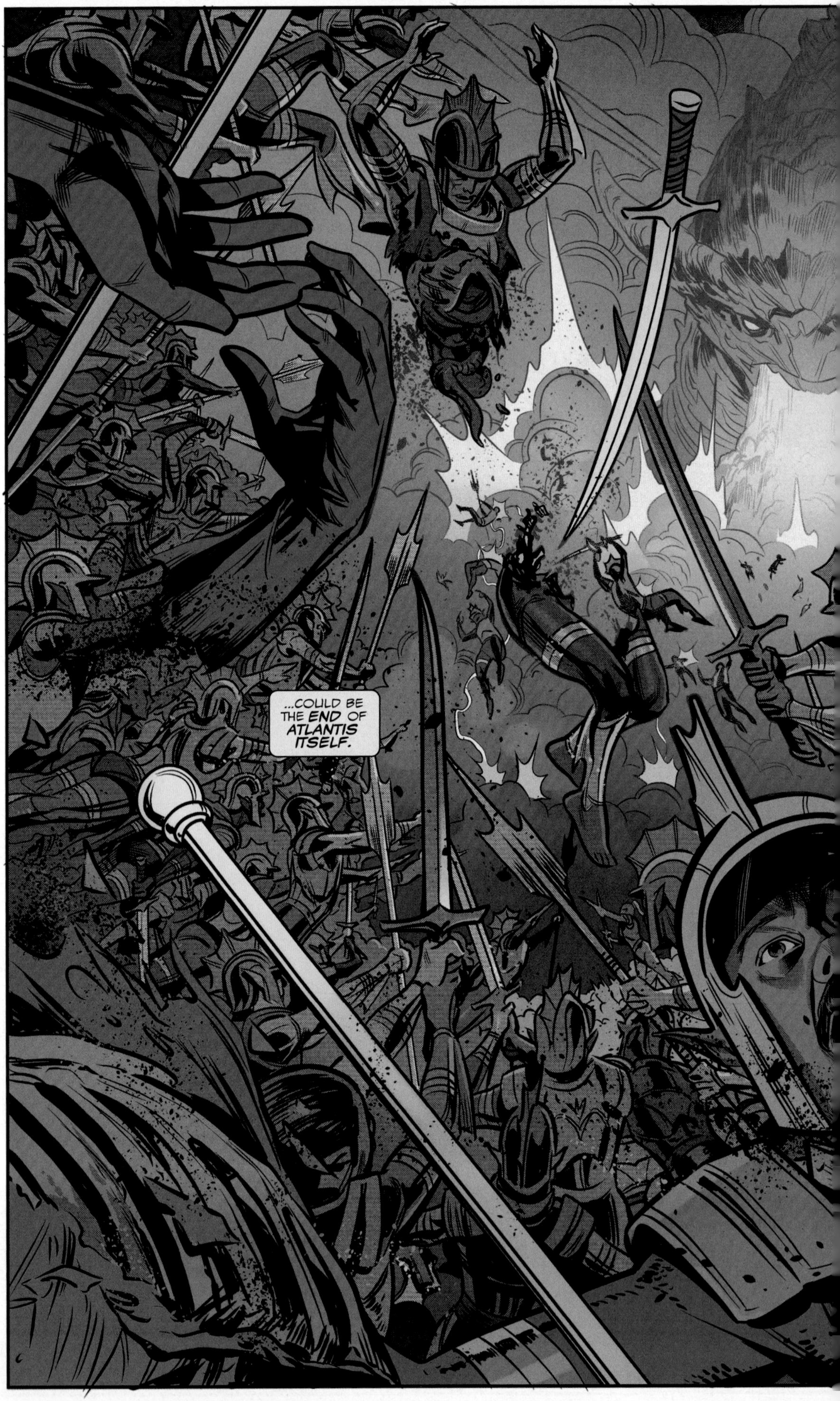
...COULD BE THE END OF ATLANTIS ITSELF.

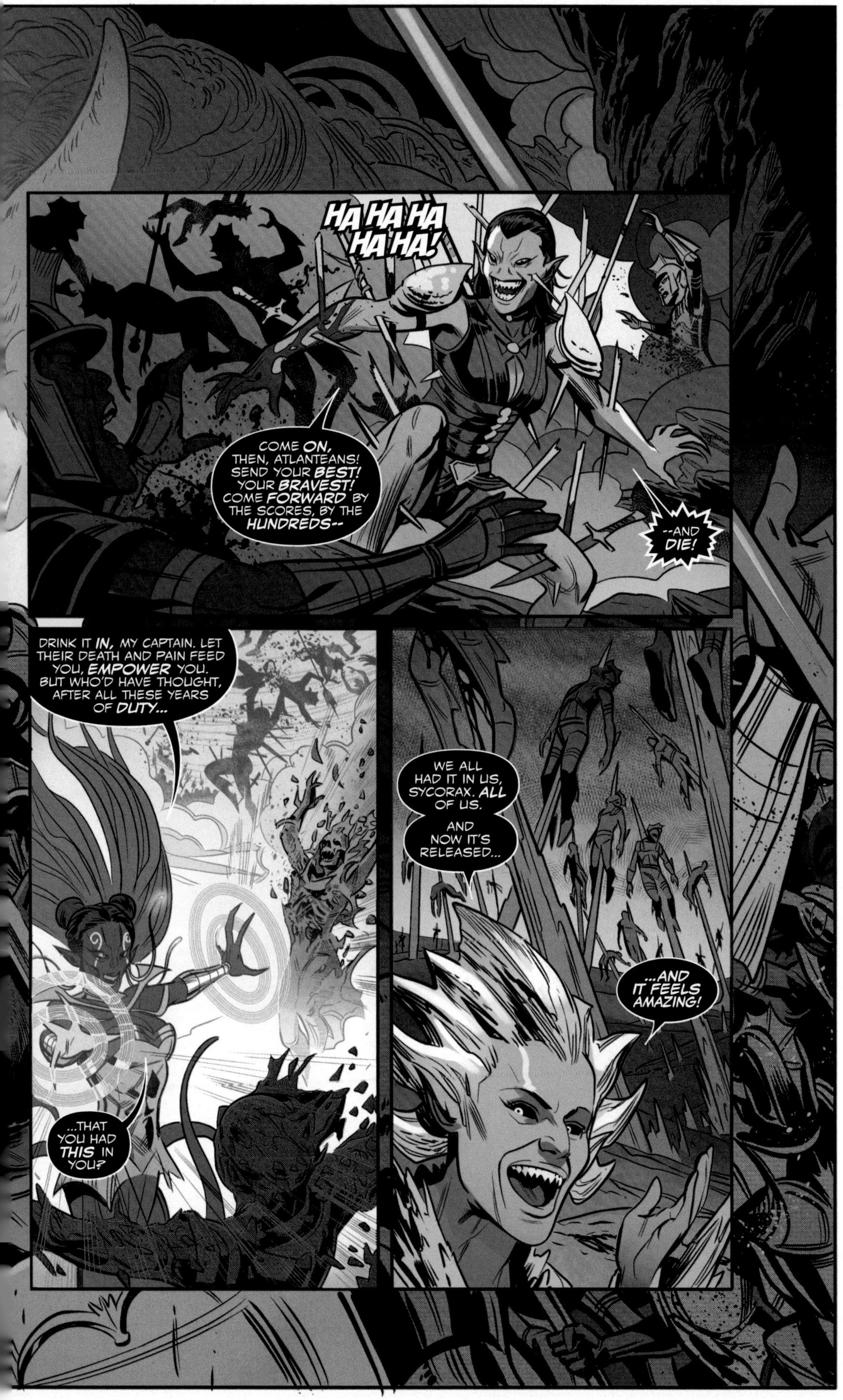
HA HA HA HA HA!
COME ON, THEN, ATLANTEANS! SEND YOUR BEST! YOUR BRAVEST! COME FORWARD BY THE SCORES, BY THE HUNDREDS--
--AND DIE!
DRINK IT IN, MY CAPTAIN. LET THEIR DEATH AND PAIN FEED YOU, EMPOWER YOU. BUT WHO'D HAVE THOUGHT, AFTER ALL THESE YEARS OF DUTY...
...THAT YOU HAD THIS IN YOU?
WE ALL HAD IT IN US, SYCORAX. ALL OF US.
AND NOW IT'S RELEASED...
...AND IT FEELS AMAZING!

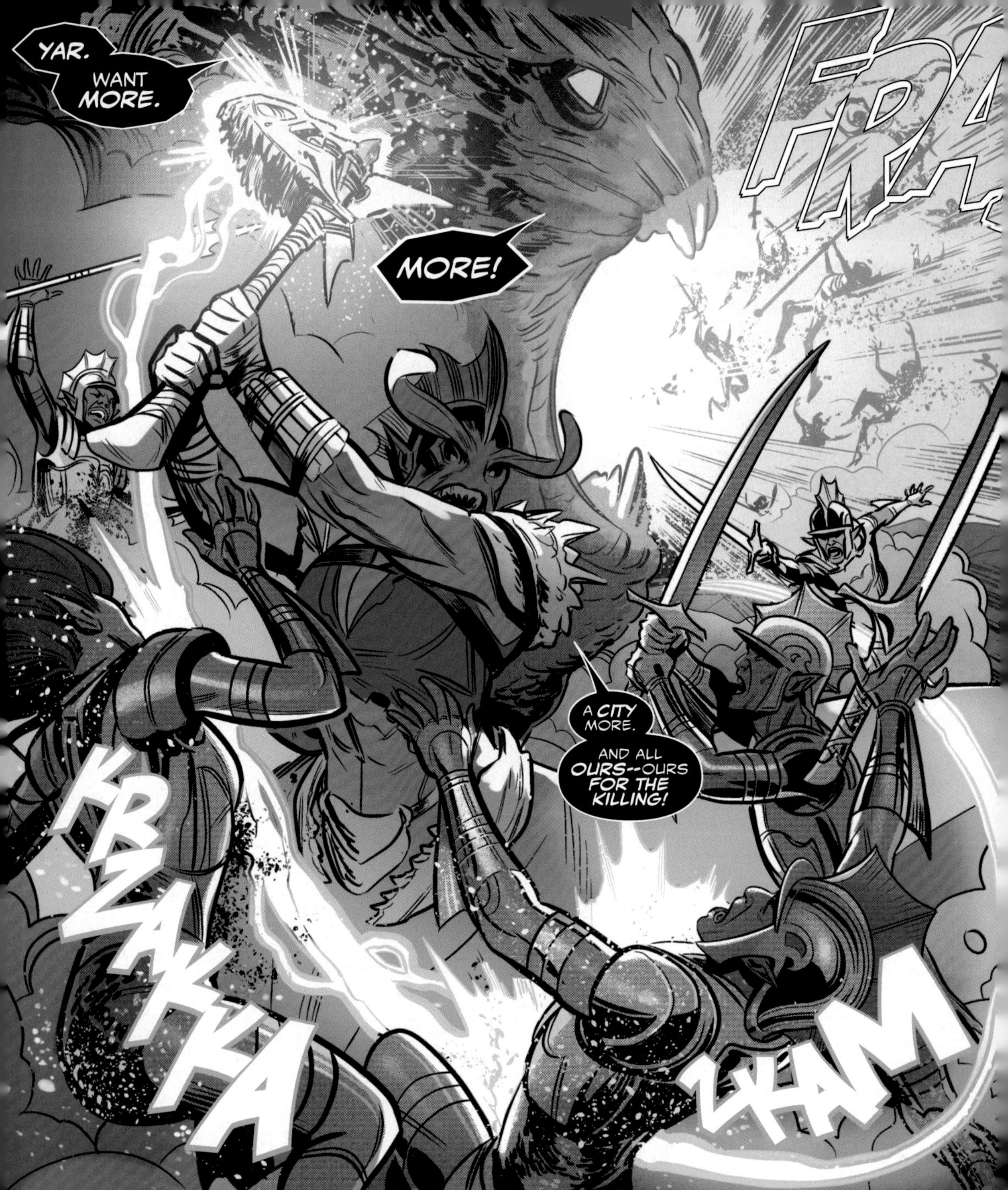
YAR. WANT MORE.
MORE!
KRZAKKA
A CITY MORE.
AND ALL OURS--OURS FOR THE KILLING!
ZKAM

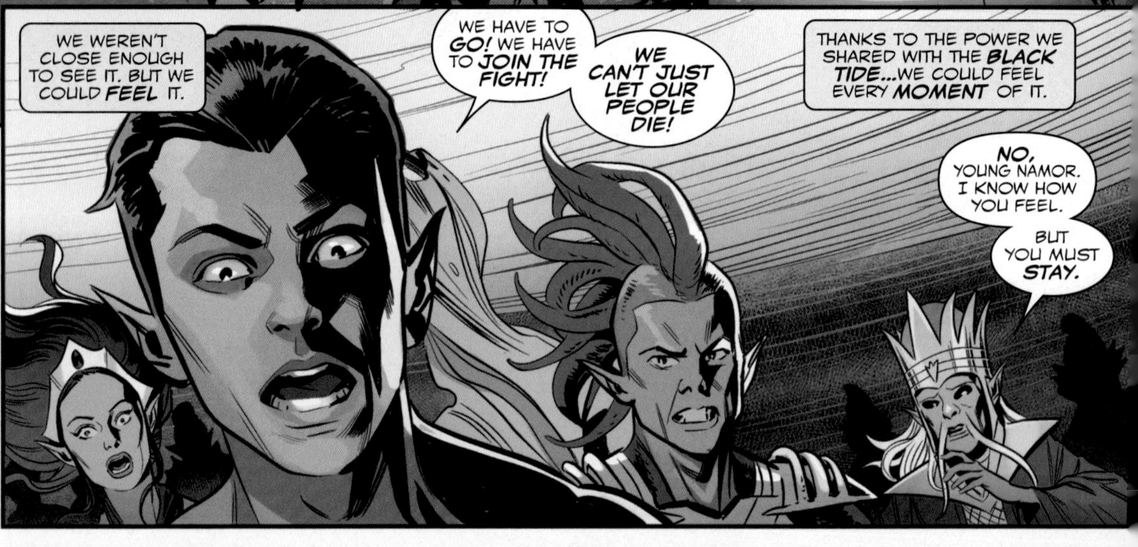
WE WEREN'T CLOSE ENOUGH TO SEE IT. BUT WE COULD FEEL IT.
WE HAVE TO GO! WE HAVE TO JOIN THE FIGHT!
WE CAN'T JUST LET OUR PEOPLE DIE!
THANKS TO THE POWER WE SHARED WITH THE BLACK TIDE...WE COULD FEEL EVERY MOMENT OF IT.
NO, YOUNG NAMOR. I KNOW HOW YOU FEEL.
BUT YOU MUST STAY.

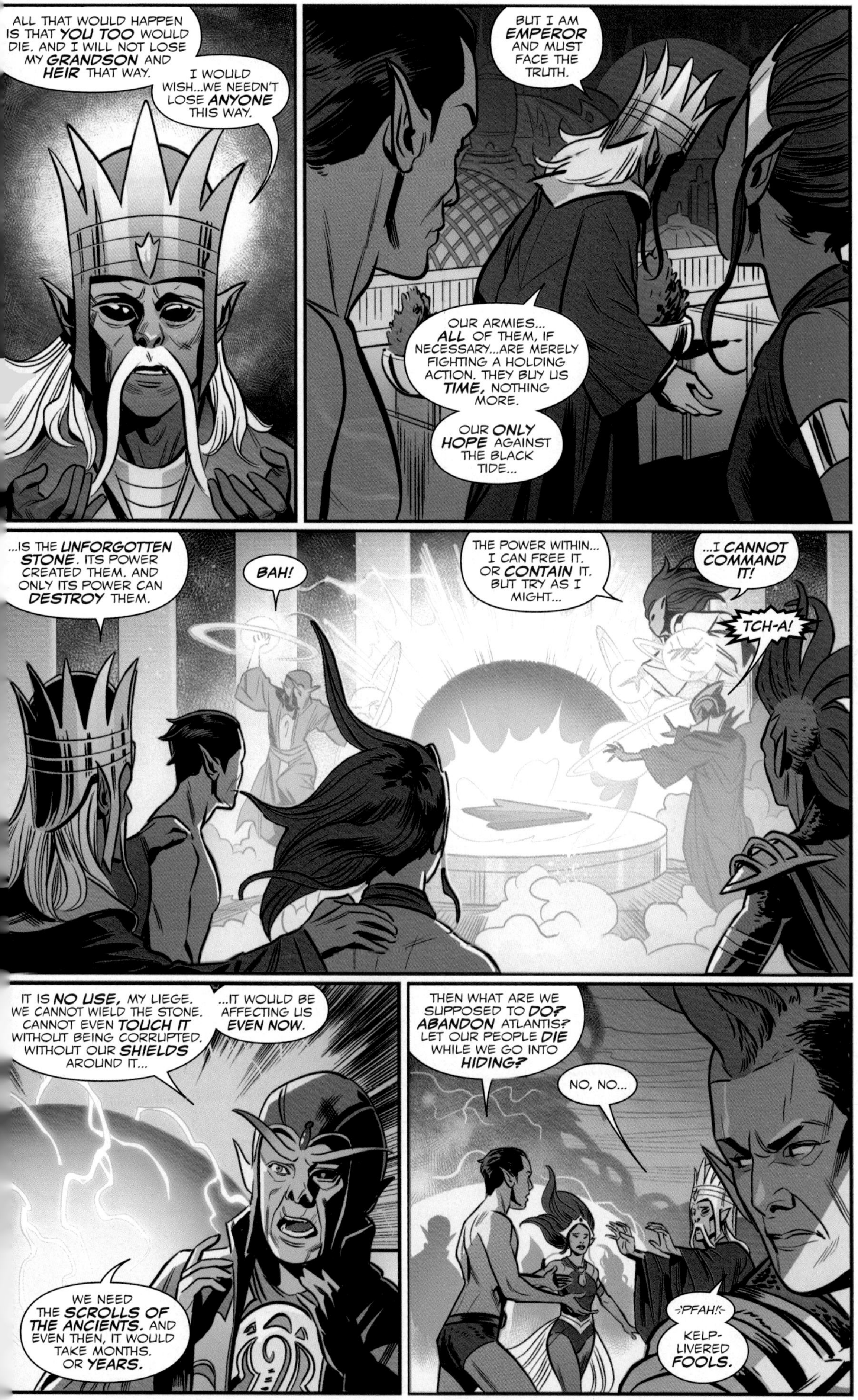

ALL THAT WOULD HAPPEN IS THAT YOU TOO WOULD DIE. AND I WILL NOT LOSE MY GRANDSON AND HEIR THAT WAY.
I WOULD WISH...WE NEEDN'T LOSE ANYONE THIS WAY.
BUT I AM EMPEROR AND MUST FACE THE TRUTH.
OUR ARMIES... ALL OF THEM, IF NECESSARY...ARE MERELY FIGHTING A HOLDING ACTION. THEY BUY US TIME, NOTHING MORE.
OUR ONLY HOPE AGAINST THE BLACK TIDE...
...IS THE UNFORGOTTEN STONE. ITS POWER CREATED THEM. AND ONLY ITS POWER CAN DESTROY THEM.
BAH!
THE POWER WITHIN... I CAN FREE IT. OR CONTAIN IT. BUT TRY AS I MIGHT...
...I CANNOT COMMAND IT!
TCH-A!
IT IS NO USE, MY LIEGE. WE CANNOT WIELD THE STONE. CANNOT EVEN TOUCH IT WITHOUT BEING CORRUPTED. WITHOUT OUR SHIELDS AROUND IT...
...IT WOULD BE AFFECTING US EVEN NOW.
WE NEED THE SCROLLS OF THE ANCIENTS. AND EVEN THEN, IT WOULD TAKE MONTHS. OR YEARS.
THEN WHAT ARE WE SUPPOSED TO DO? ABANDON ATLANTIS? LET OUR PEOPLE DIE WHILE WE GO INTO HIDING?
NO, NO...
PFAH!
KELP-LIVERED FOOLS.

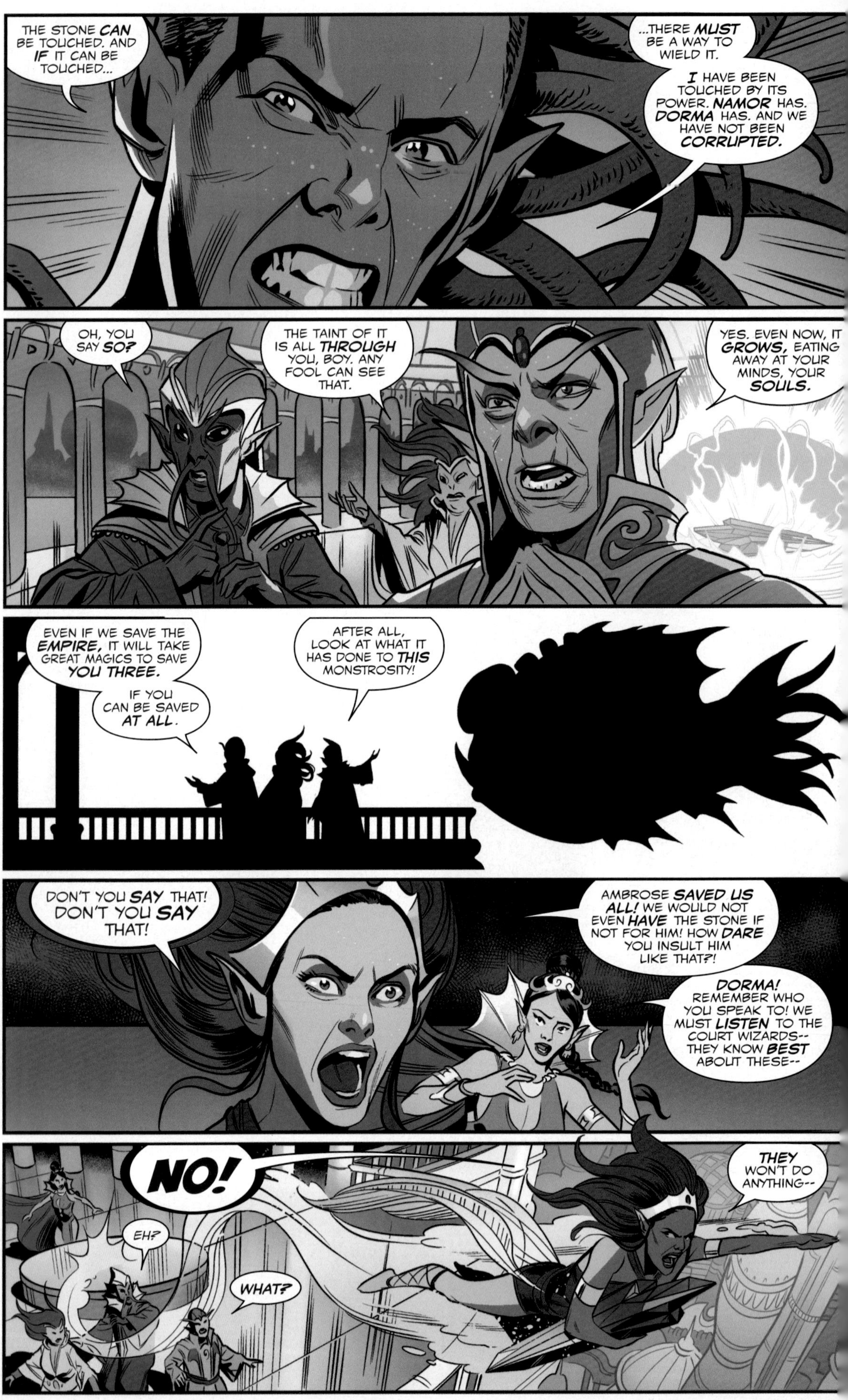
THE STONE CAN BE TOUCHED. AND IF IT CAN BE TOUCHED...
...THERE MUST BE A WAY TO WIELD IT.
I HAVE BEEN TOUCHED BY ITS POWER. NAMOR HAS. DORMA HAS. AND WE HAVE NOT BEEN CORRUPTED.
OH, YOU SAY SO?
THE TAINT OF IT IS ALL THROUGH YOU, BOY. ANY FOOL CAN SEE THAT.
YES. EVEN NOW, IT GROWS, EATING AWAY AT YOUR MINDS, YOUR SOULS.
EVEN IF WE SAVE THE EMPIRE, IT WILL TAKE GREAT MAGICS TO SAVE YOU THREE.
IF YOU CAN BE SAVED AT ALL.
AFTER ALL, LOOK AT WHAT IT HAS DONE TO THIS MONSTROSITY!
DON'T YOU SAY THAT! DON'T YOU SAY THAT!
AMBROSE SAVED US ALL! WE WOULD NOT EVEN HAVE THE STONE IF NOT FOR HIM! HOW DARE YOU INSULT HIM LIKE THAT?!
DORMA! REMEMBER WHO YOU SPEAK TO! WE MUST LISTEN TO THE COURT WIZARDS-- THEY KNOW BEST ABOUT THESE--
NO!
EH?
WHAT?
THEY WON'T DO ANYTHING--

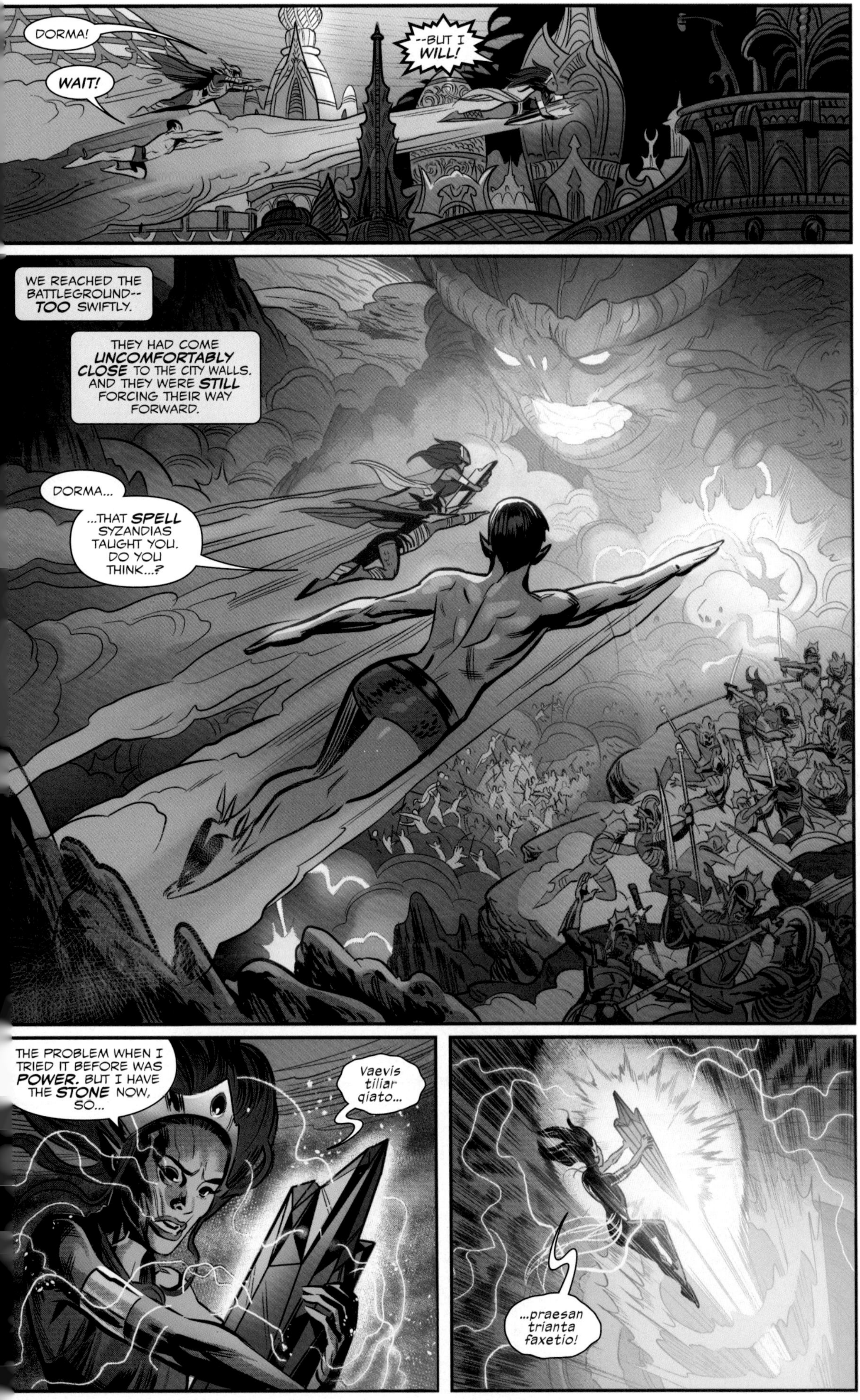
DORMA!
WAIT!
--BUT I WILL!
WE REACHED THE BATTLEGROUND-- TOO SWIFTLY.
THEY HAD COME UNCOMFORTABLY CLOSE TO THE CITY WALLS. AND THEY WERE STILL FORCING THEIR WAY FORWARD.
DORMA...
...THAT SPELL SYZANDIAS TAUGHT YOU. DO YOU THINK...?
THE PROBLEM WHEN I TRIED IT BEFORE WAS POWER. BUT I HAVE THE STONE NOW, SO...
Vaevis tiliar qiato...
...praesan trianta faxetio!

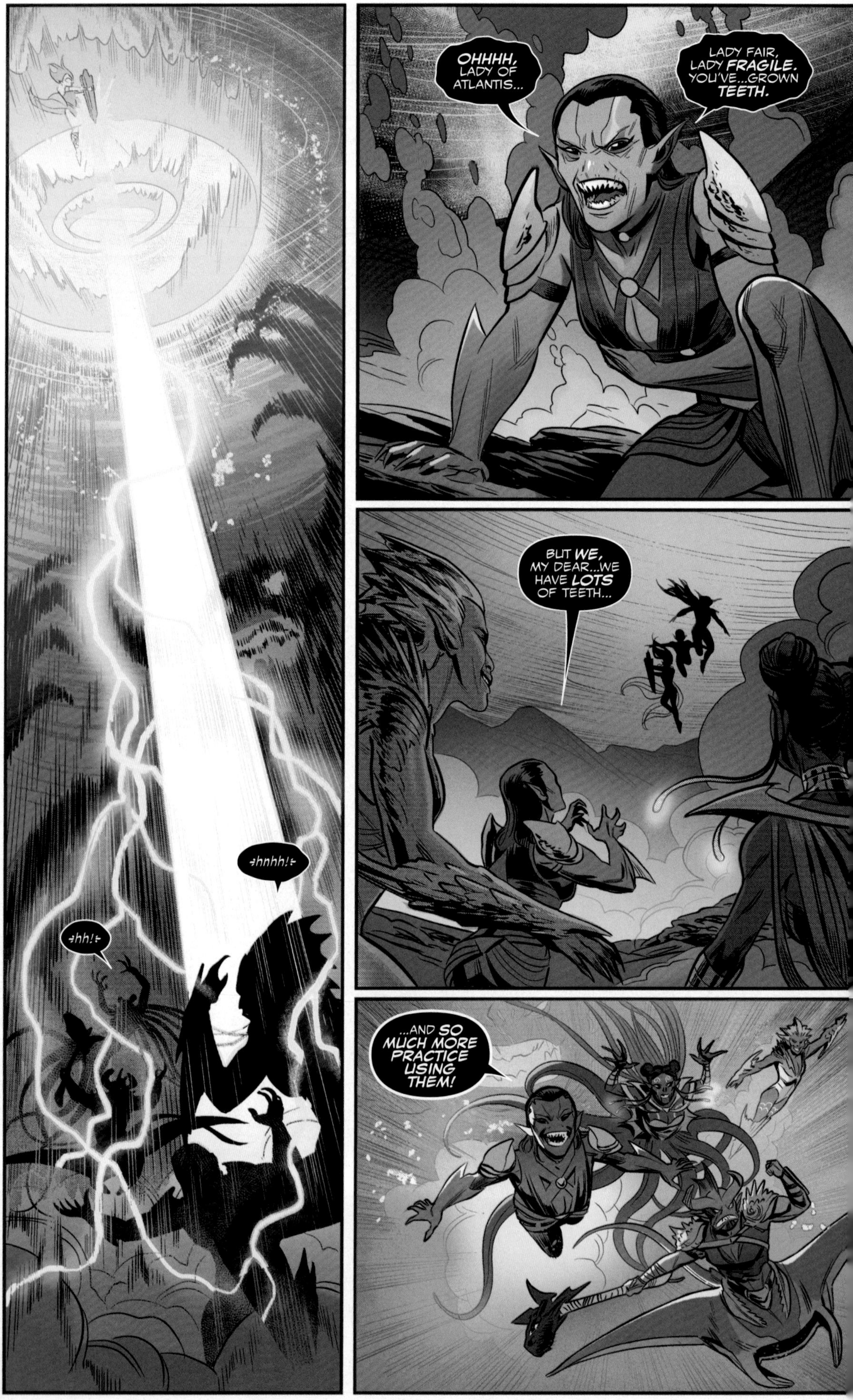

‑hnhh!‑
‑hh!‑
OHHHH, LADY OF ATLANTIS...
LADY FAIR, LADY FRAGILE. YOU'VE...GROWN TEETH.
BUT WE, MY DEAR...WE HAVE LOTS OF TEETH...
...AND SO MUCH MORE PRACTICE USING THEM!

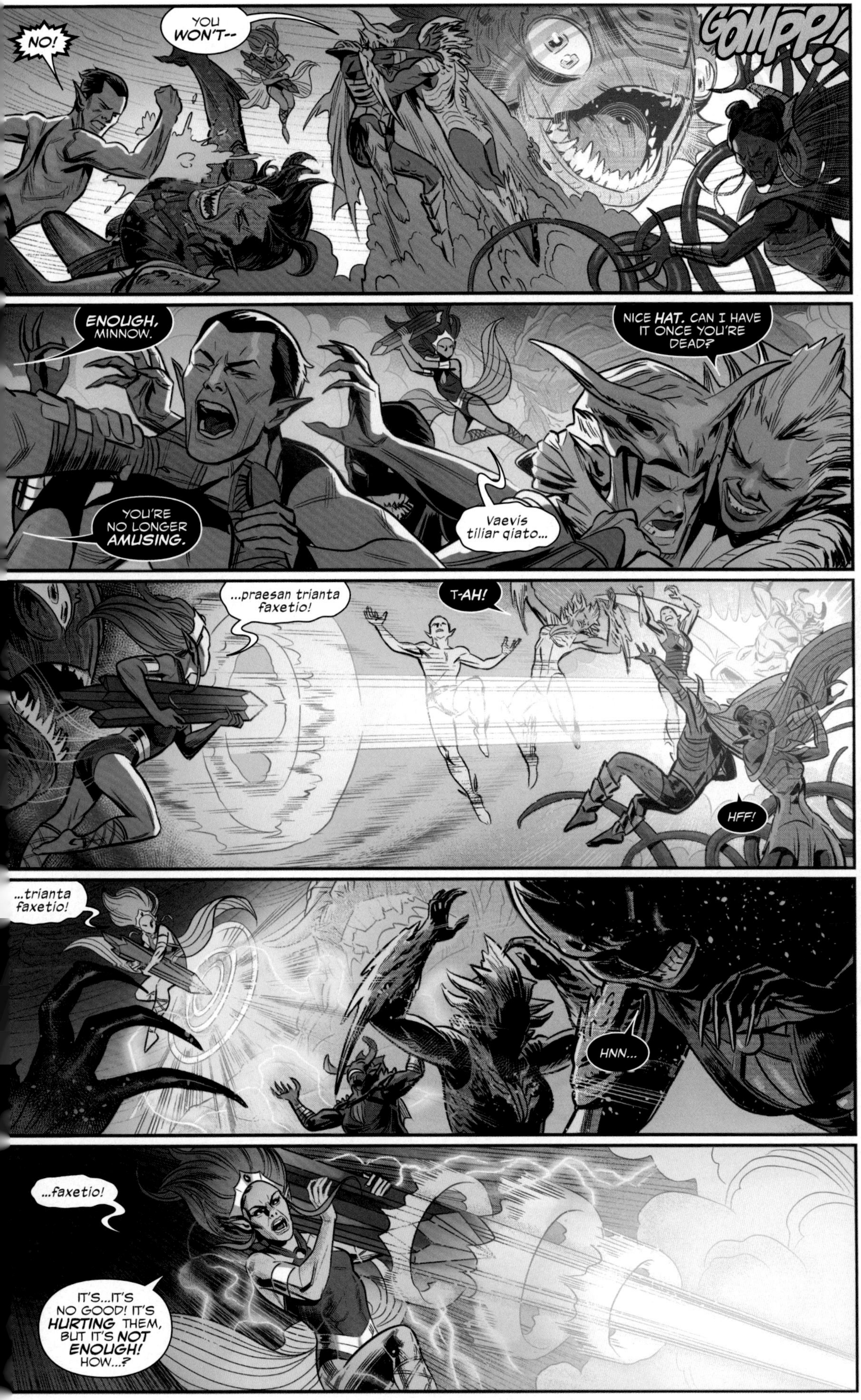
NO!
YOU WON'T--
GOMPP!
ENOUGH, MINNOW.
NICE HAT. CAN I HAVE IT ONCE YOU'RE DEAD?
YOU'RE NO LONGER AMUSING.
Vaevis tiliar qiato...
...praesan trianta faxetio!
T-AH!
HFF!
...trianta faxetio!
HNN...
...faxetio!
IT'S...IT'S NO GOOD! IT'S HURTING THEM, BUT IT'S NOT ENOUGH! HOW...?

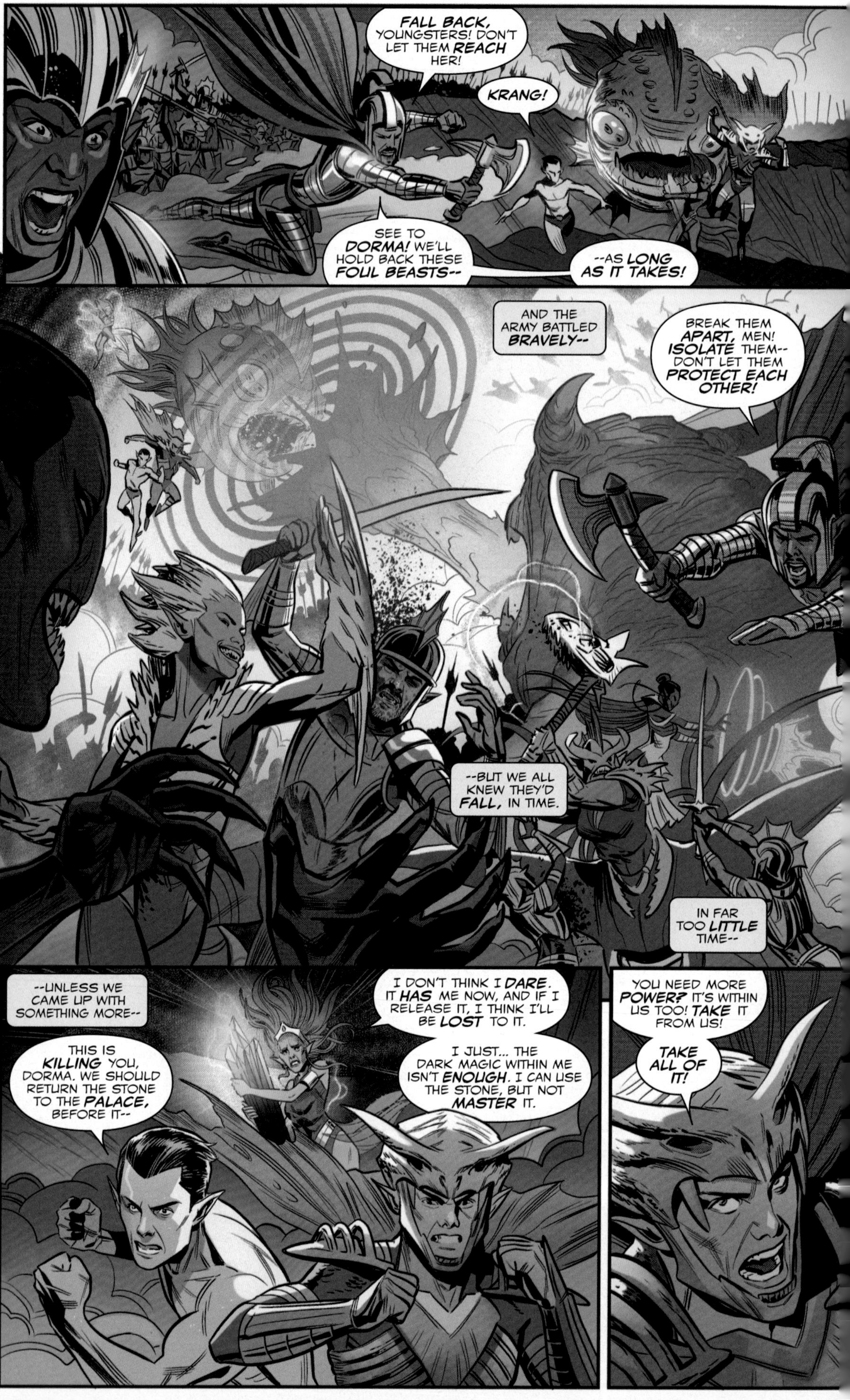
FALL BACK, YOUNGSTERS! DON'T LET THEM REACH HER!
KRANG!
SEE TO DORMA! WE'LL HOLD BACK THESE FOUL BEASTS--
--AS LONG AS IT TAKES!
AND THE ARMY BATTLED BRAVELY--
BREAK THEM APART, MEN! ISOLATE THEM-- DON'T LET THEM PROTECT EACH OTHER!
--BUT WE ALL KNEW THEY'D FALL, IN TIME.
IN FAR TOO LITTLE TIME--
--UNLESS WE CAME UP WITH SOMETHING MORE--
THIS IS KILLING YOU, DORMA. WE SHOULD RETURN THE STONE TO THE PALACE, BEFORE IT--
I DON'T THINK I DARE. IT HAS ME NOW, AND IF I RELEASE IT, I THINK I'LL BE LOST TO IT.
I JUST... THE DARK MAGIC WITHIN ME ISN'T ENOUGH. I CAN USE THE STONE, BUT NOT MASTER IT.
YOU NEED MORE POWER? IT'S WITHIN US TOO! TAKE IT FROM US!
TAKE ALL OF IT!

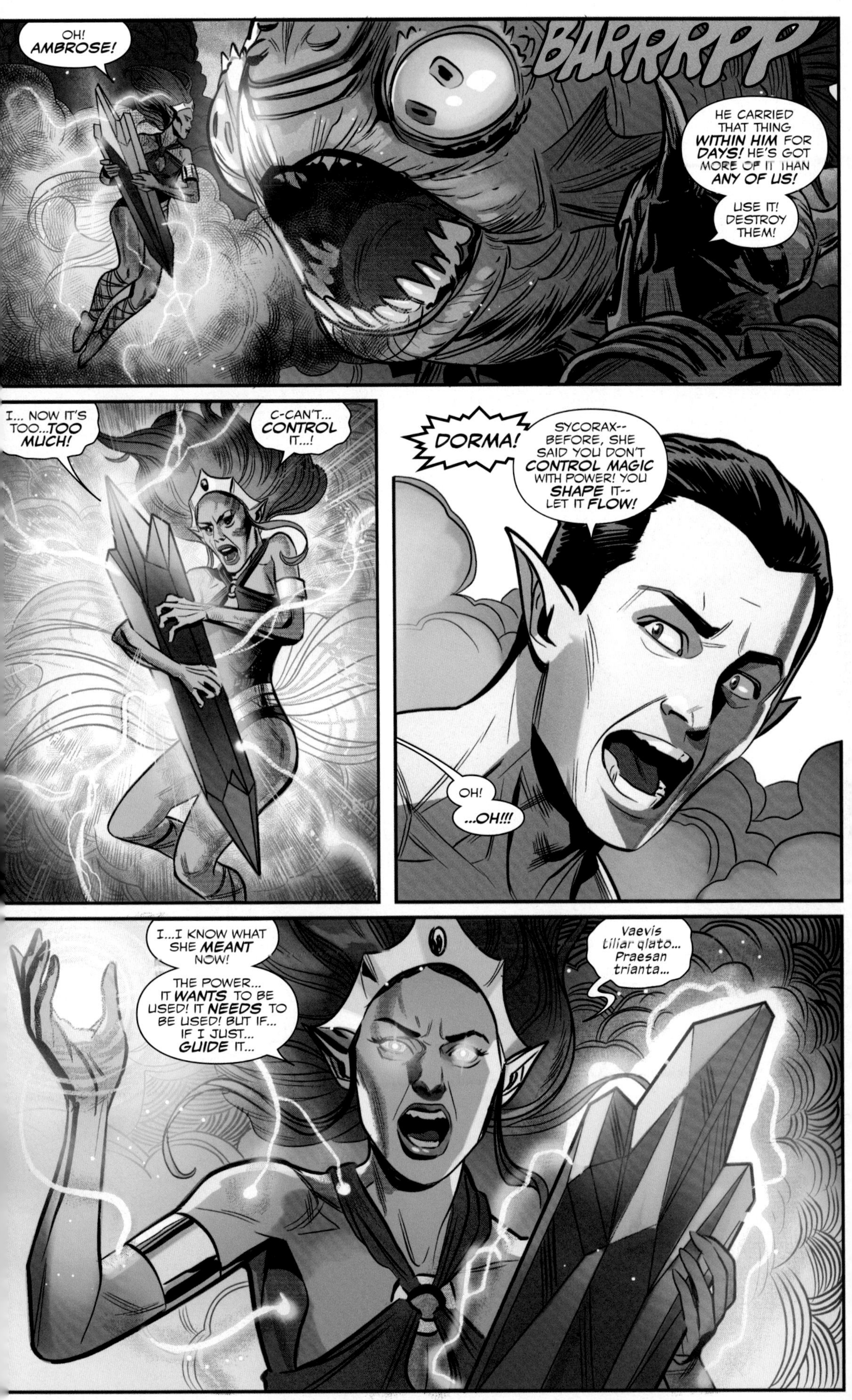
OH! AMBROSE!
BARRRPP
HE CARRIED THAT THING WITHIN HIM FOR DAYS! HE'S GOT MORE OF IT THAN ANY OF US!
USE IT! DESTROY THEM!
I... NOW IT'S TOO...TOO MUCH!
C-CAN'T... CONTROL IT...!
DORMA!
SYCORAX-- BEFORE, SHE SAID YOU DON'T CONTROL MAGIC WITH POWER! YOU SHAPE IT-- LET IT FLOW!
OH!
...OH!!!
I...I KNOW WHAT SHE MEANT NOW!
THE POWER... IT WANTS TO BE USED! IT NEEDS TO BE USED! BUT IF... IF I JUST... GUIDE IT...
Vaevis tiliar qlato... Praesan trianta...

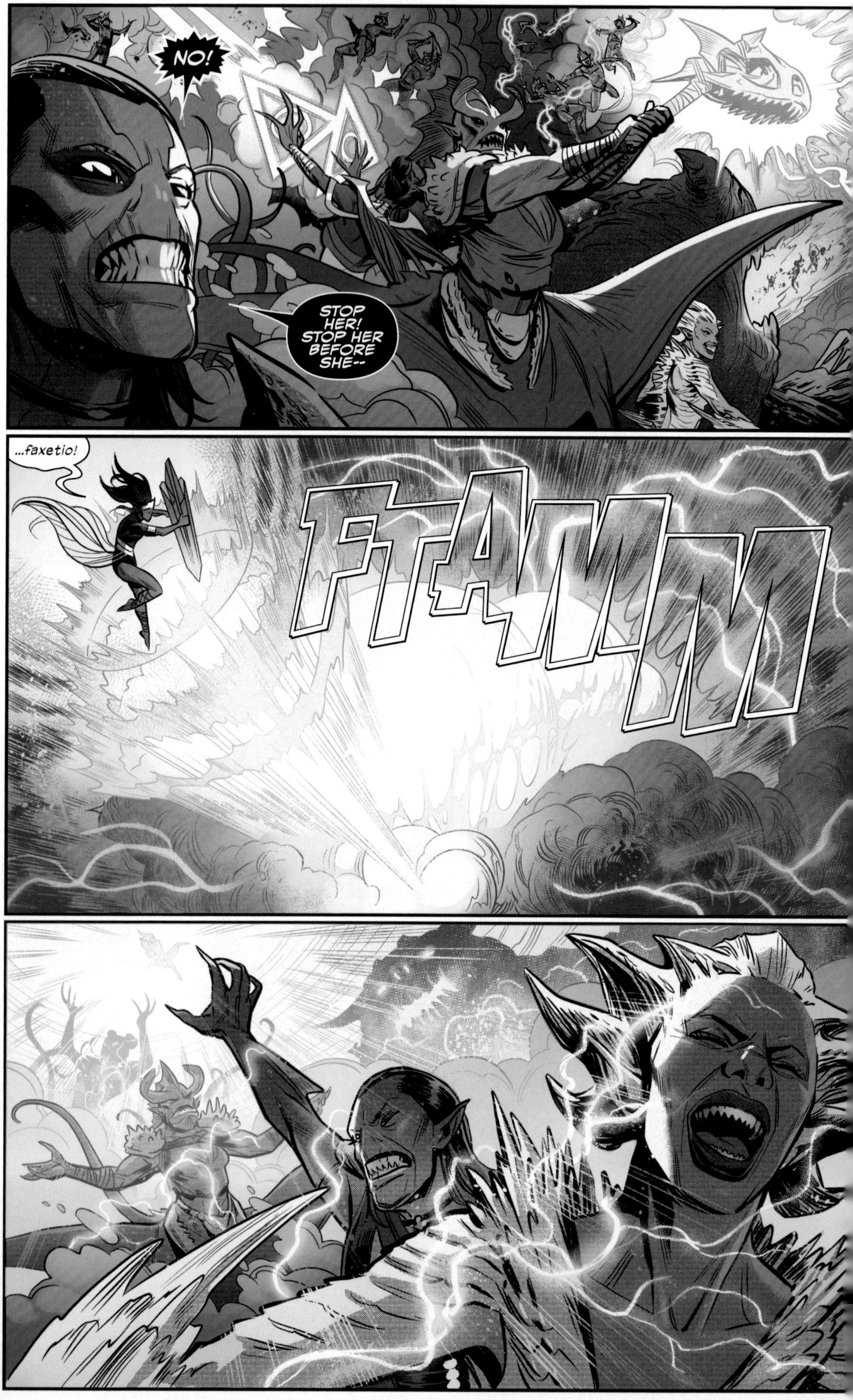
NO!
STOP HER! STOP HER BEFORE SHE--
...faxetio!
FTAMM

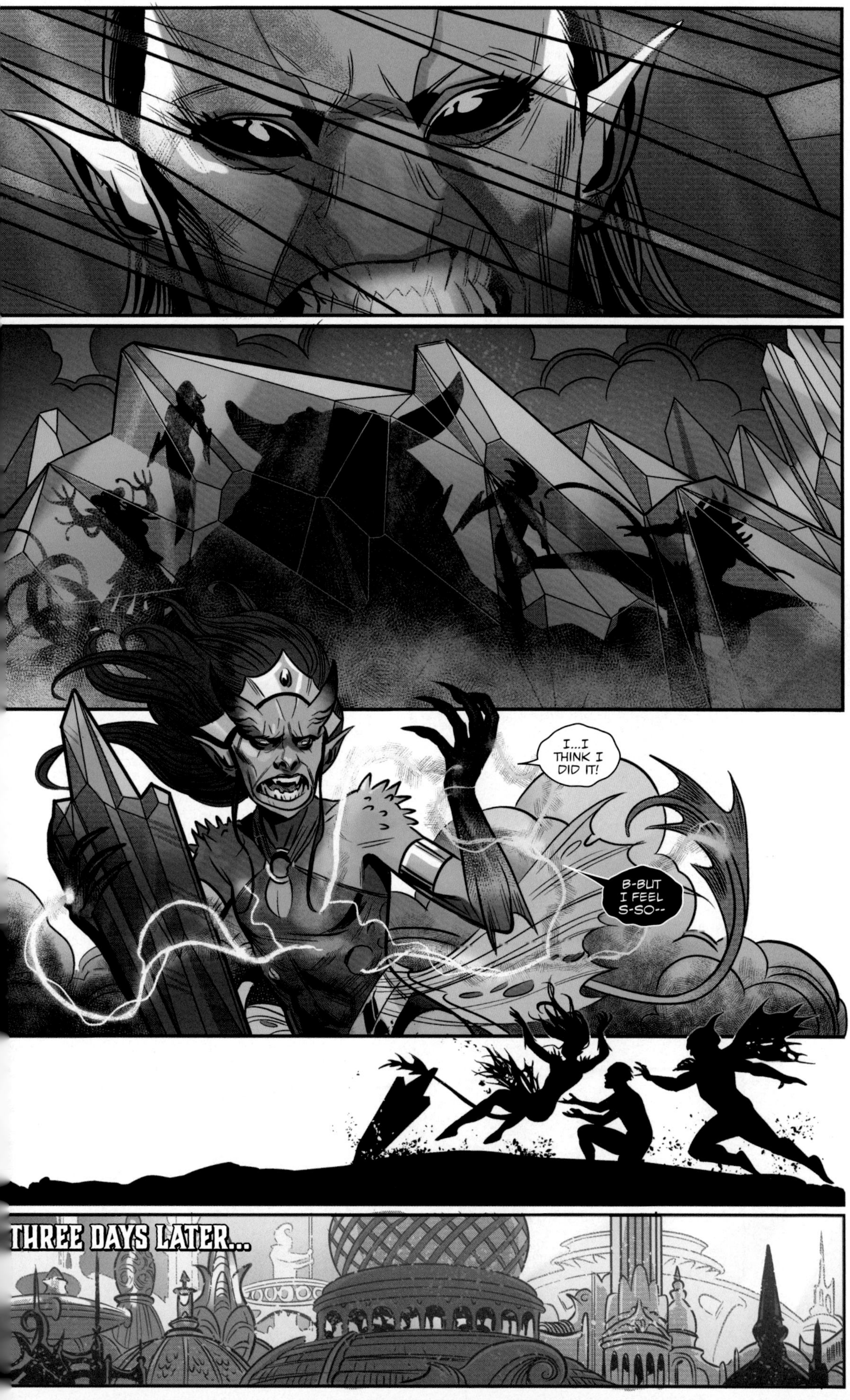
I...I THINK I DID IT!
B-BUT I FEEL S-SO--
THREE DAYS LATER...

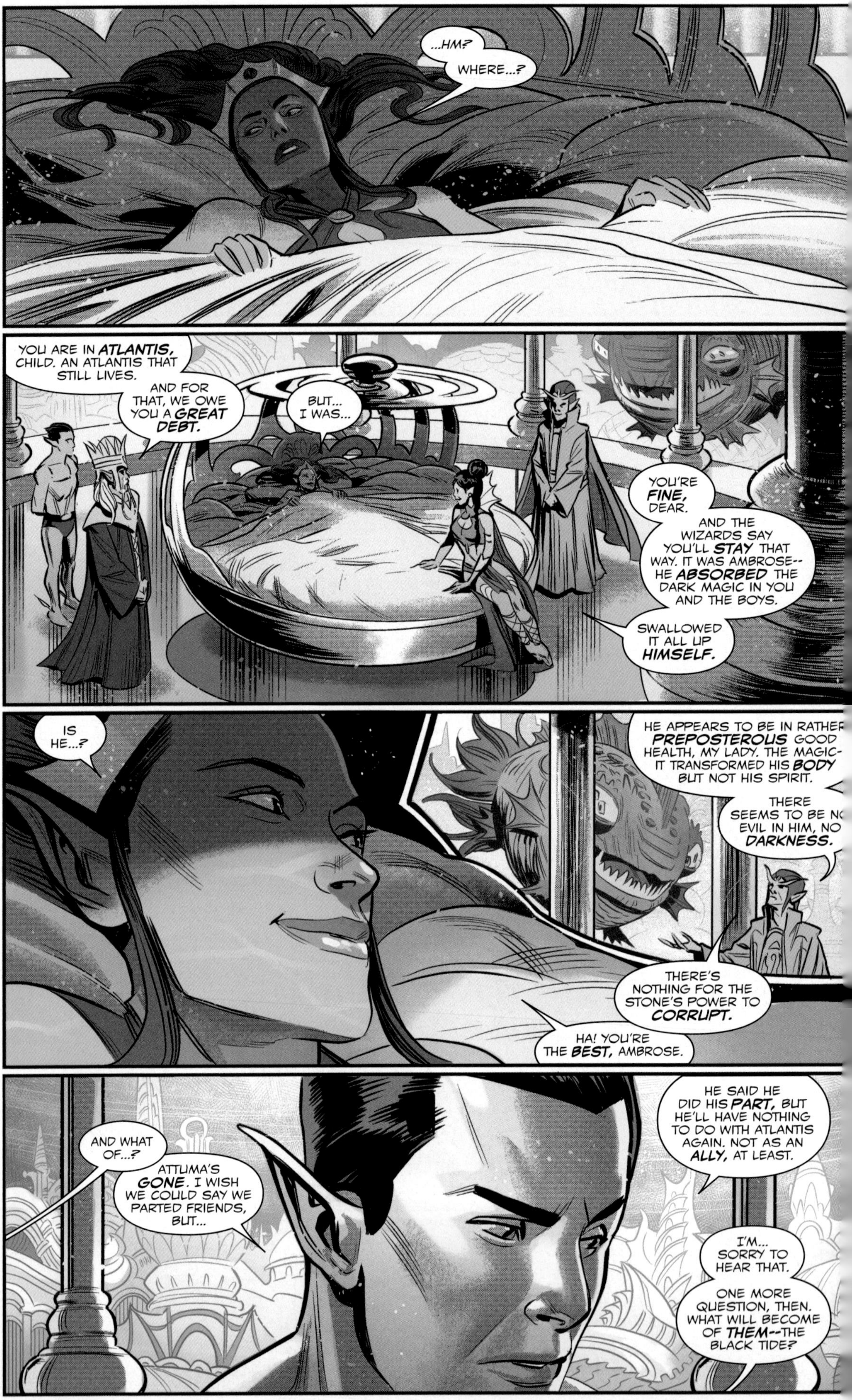
...HM?
WHERE...?
YOU ARE IN ATLANTIS, CHILD. AN ATLANTIS THAT STILL LIVES.
AND FOR THAT, WE OWE YOU A GREAT DEBT.
BUT... I WAS...
YOU'RE FINE, DEAR.
AND THE WIZARDS SAY YOU'LL STAY THAT WAY. IT WAS AMBROSE-- HE ABSORBED THE DARK MAGIC IN YOU AND THE BOYS.
SWALLOWED IT ALL UP HIMSELF.
IS HE...?
HE APPEARS TO BE IN RATHER PREPOSTEROUS GOOD HEALTH, MY LADY. THE MAGIC- IT TRANSFORMED HIS BODY BUT NOT HIS SPIRIT.
THERE SEEMS TO BE NO EVIL IN HIM, NO DARKNESS.
THERE'S NOTHING FOR THE STONE'S POWER TO CORRUPT.
HA! YOU'RE THE BEST, AMBROSE.
AND WHAT OF...?
ATTUMA'S GONE. I WISH WE COULD SAY WE PARTED FRIENDS, BUT...
HE SAID HE DID HIS PART, BUT HE'LL HAVE NOTHING TO DO WITH ATLANTIS AGAIN. NOT AS AN ALLY, AT LEAST.
I'M... SORRY TO HEAR THAT.
ONE MORE QUESTION, THEN. WHAT WILL BECOME OF THEM--THE BLACK TIDE?

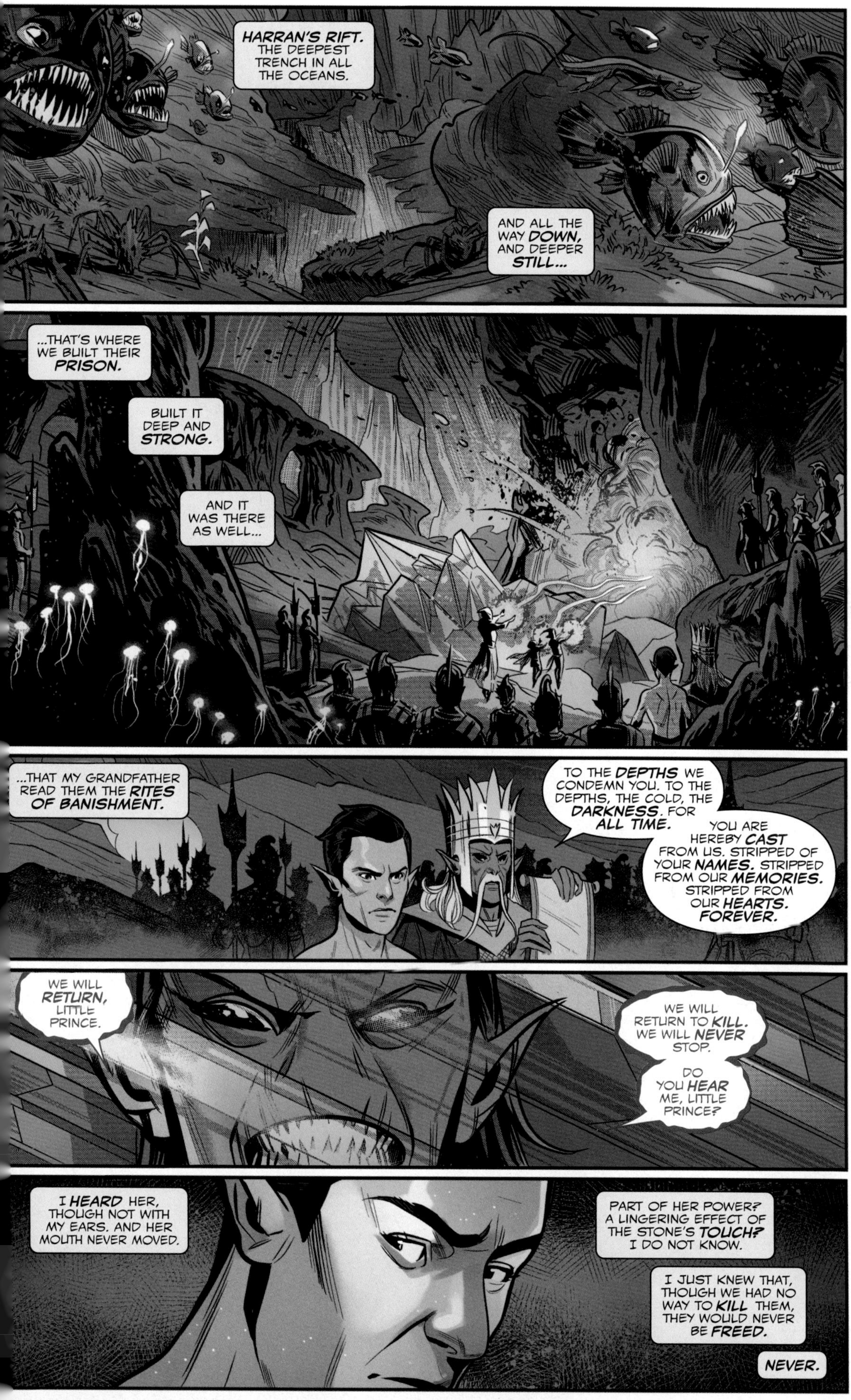
HARRAN'S RIFT. THE DEEPEST TRENCH IN ALL THE OCEANS.
AND ALL THE WAY DOWN, AND DEEPER STILL...
...THAT'S WHERE WE BUILT THEIR PRISON.
BUILT IT DEEP AND STRONG.
AND IT WAS THERE AS WELL...
...THAT MY GRANDFATHER READ THEM THE RITES OF BANISHMENT.
TO THE DEPTHS WE CONDEMN YOU. TO THE DEPTHS, THE COLD, THE DARKNESS. FOR ALL TIME.
YOU ARE HEREBY CAST FROM US. STRIPPED OF YOUR NAMES. STRIPPED FROM OUR MEMORIES. STRIPPED FROM OUR HEARTS. FOREVER.
WE WILL RETURN, LITTLE PRINCE.
WE WILL RETURN TO KILL. WE WILL NEVER STOP.
DO YOU HEAR ME, LITTLE PRINCE?
I HEARD HER, THOUGH NOT WITH MY EARS. AND HER MOUTH NEVER MOVED.
PART OF HER POWER? A LINGERING EFFECT OF THE STONE'S TOUCH? I DO NOT KNOW.
I JUST KNEW THAT, THOUGH WE HAD NO WAY TO KILL THEM, THEY WOULD NEVER BE FREED.
NEVER.

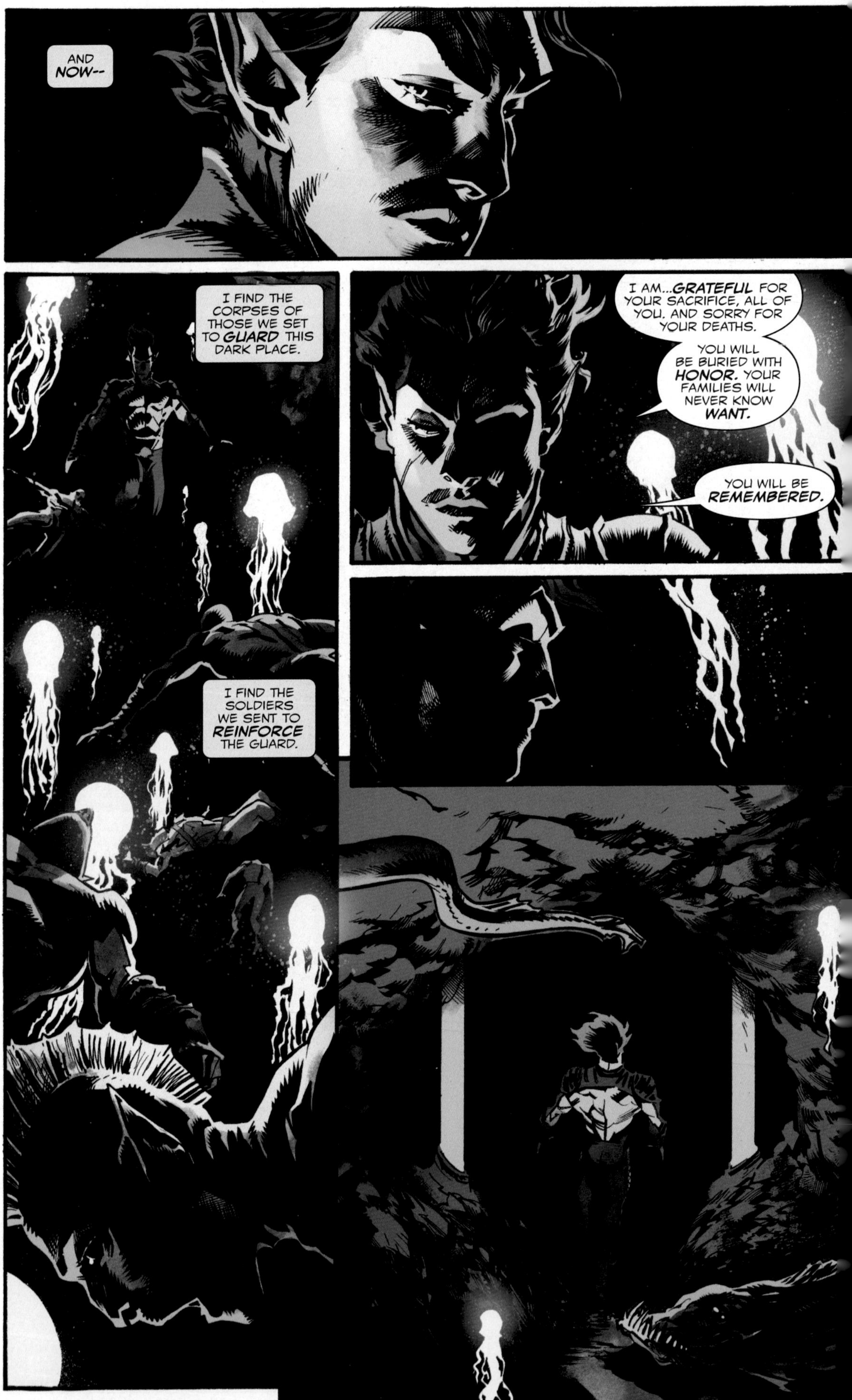
AND NOW--
I FIND THE CORPSES OF THOSE WE SET TO GUARD THIS DARK PLACE.
I FIND THE SOLDIERS WE SENT TO REINFORCE THE GUARD.
I AM...GRATEFUL FOR YOUR SACRIFICE, ALL OF YOU. AND SORRY FOR YOUR DEATHS.
YOU WILL BE BURIED WITH HONOR. YOUR FAMILIES WILL NEVER KNOW WANT.
YOU WILL BE REMEMBERED.

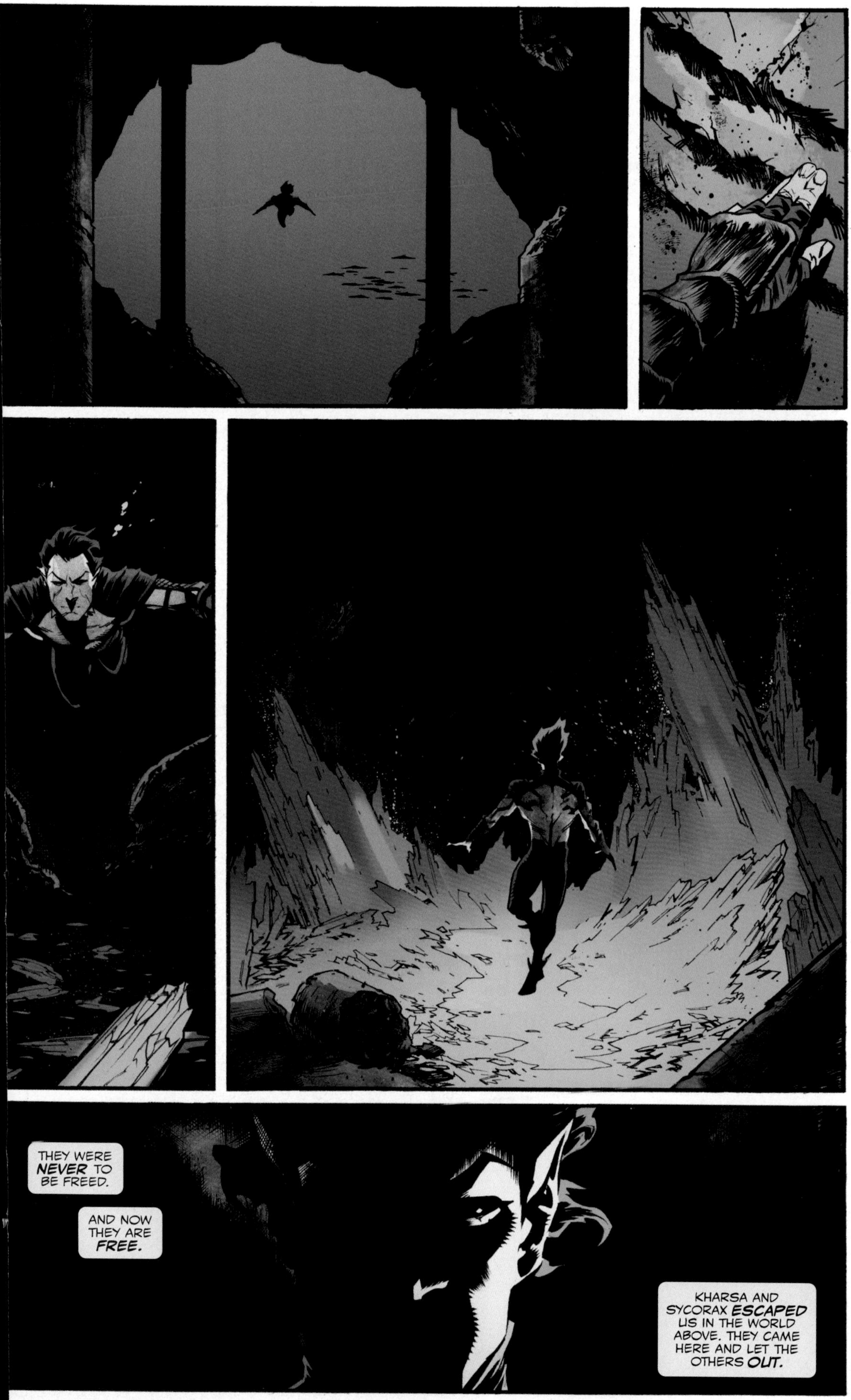
THEY WERE NEVER TO BE FREED.
AND NOW THEY ARE FREE.
KHARSA AND SYCORAX ESCAPED US IN THE WORLD ABOVE. THEY CAME HERE AND LET THE OTHERS OUT.

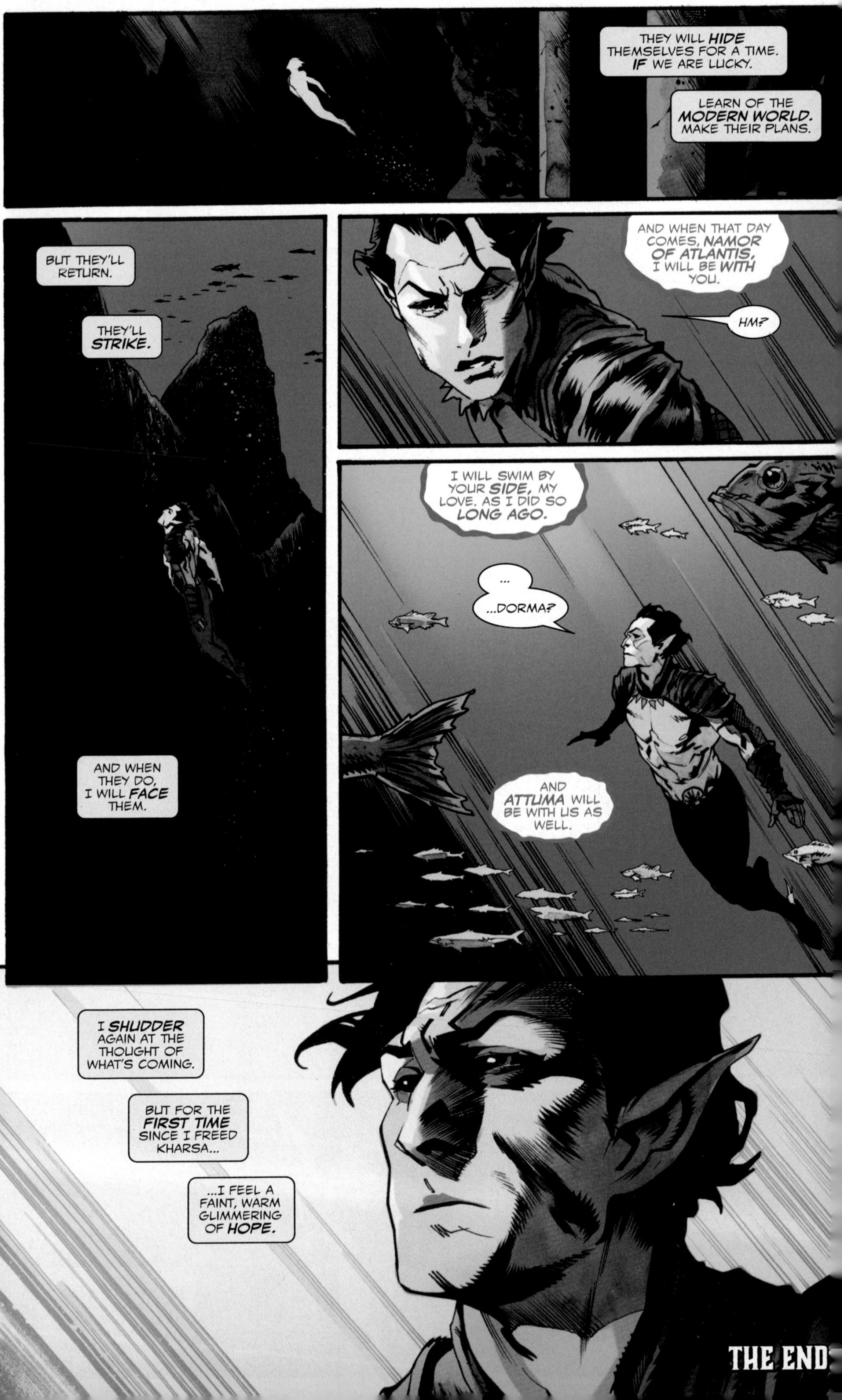
THEY WILL HIDE THEMSELVES FOR A TIME. IF WE ARE LUCKY.
LEARN OF THE MODERN WORLD. MAKE THEIR PLANS.
BUT THEY'LL RETURN.
THEY'LL STRIKE.
AND WHEN THEY DO, I WILL FACE THEM.
AND WHEN THAT DAY COMES, NAMOR OF ATLANTIS, I WILL BE WITH YOU.
HM?
I WILL SWIM BY YOUR SIDE, MY LOVE. AS I DID SO LONG AGO.
...
...DORMA?
AND ATTUMA WILL BE WITH US AS WELL.
I SHUDDER AGAIN AT THE THOUGHT OF WHAT'S COMING.
BUT FOR THE FIRST TIME SINCE I FREED KHARSA...
...I FEEL A FAINT, WARM GLIMMERING OF HOPE.
THE END

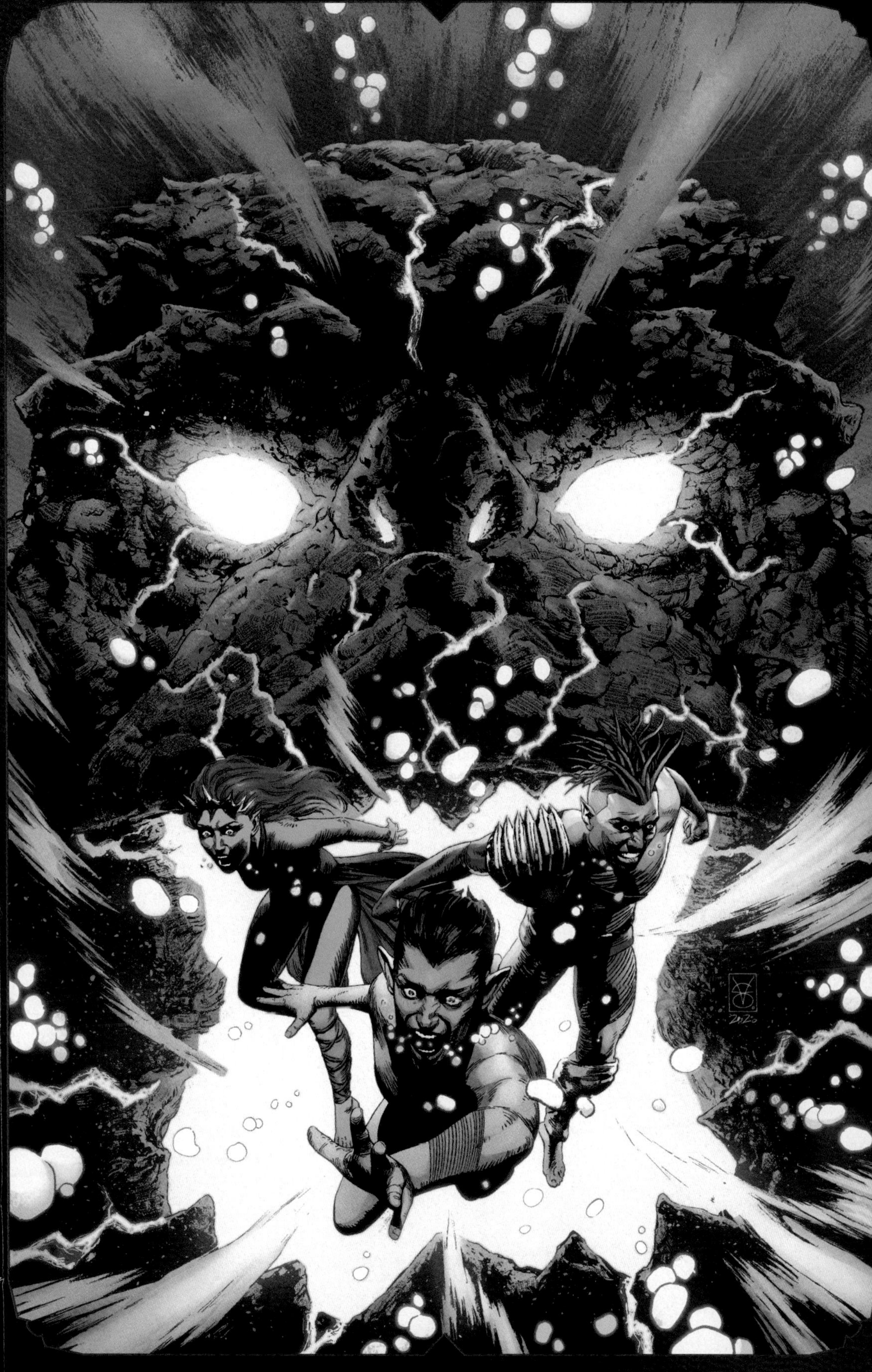

#4 VARIANT BY **VALERIO GIANGIORDANO & JASON KEITH**

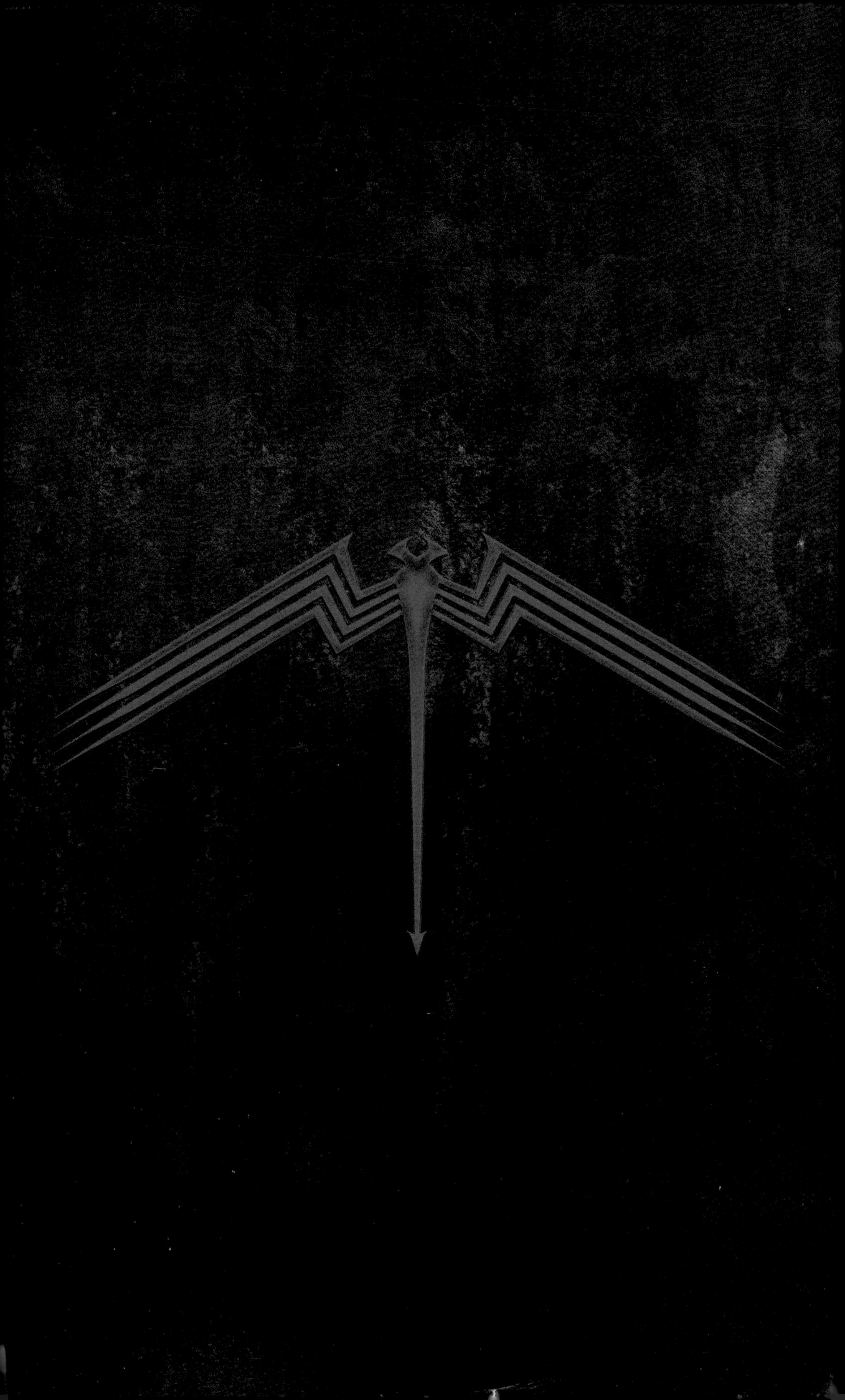